Behind the Veil

Some Other Titles from Falcon Press

Christopher S. Hyatt, Ph.D.
Undoing Yourself with Energized Meditation and Other Devices
Techniques for Undoing Yourself (audios)
Radical Undoing: Complete Course for Undoing Yourself (videos & audios)
Energized Hypnosis (book, videos & audios)
To Lie Is Human: Not Getting Caught Is Divine
Secrets of Western Tantra: The Sexuality of the Middle Path
Hard Zen, Soft Heart

Christopher S. Hyatt, Ph.D. with contributions by
Wm. S. Burroughs, Timothy Leary, Robert Anton Wilson et al.
Rebels & Devils: The Psychology of Liberation

Christopher S. Hyatt, Ph.D. & Antero Alli
A Modern Shaman's Guide to a Pregnant Universe

S. Jason Black and Christopher S. Hyatt, Ph.D.
Pacts With the Devil: A Chronicle of Sex, Blasphemy & Liberation
Urban Voodoo: A Beginner's Guide to Afro-Caribbean Magic

Antero Alli
Angel Tech: A Modern Shaman's Guide to Reality Selection
Angel Tech Talk (audio)

Peter J. Carroll
The Chaos Magick Audios
PsyberMagick

Phil Hine
Condensed Chaos: An Introduction to Chaos Magic
Prime Chaos: Adventures in Chaos Magic
The Pseudonomicon

Joseph Lisiewski, Ph.D.
Ceremonial Magic and the Power of Evocation
Kabbalistic Cycles and the Mastery of Life
Kabbalistic Handbook for the Practicing Magician

Israel Regardie
The Complete Golden Dawn System of Magic
New Wings for Daedalus
The Golden Dawn Audios
The World of Enochian Magic (audio)

Steven Heller
Monsters & Magical Sticks: There's No Such Thing As Hypnosis?

**For up-to-the-minute information on prices and
availability, please visit our website at
http://originalfalcon.com**

BEHIND THE VEIL

The Complete Guide to Conscious Sleep

by
Daniel Allen Kelley

Foreword by
Stewart Bell

THE *Original* FALCON PRESS
TEMPE, ARIZONA, U.S.A.

International Standard Book Number: 978-1-935150-62-6
ISBN: 978-1-61869-620-5 (mobi)
ISBN: 978-1-61869-621-2 (ePub)
Library of Congress Catalog Card Number: 2018943534

First Edition 2018
First eBook Edition 2018

Cover Image: *The Sleeping Beauty* by John Collier

The paper used in this publication meets the minimum requirements of the American National Standard for Permanence of Paper for Printed Library Materials Z39.48-1984

Address all inquiries to:
THE ORIGINAL FALCON PRESS
1753 East Broadway Road #101-277
Tempe, AZ 85282 U.S.A.
(or)
PO Box 3540
Silver Springs NV 89429 U.S.A.
website: http://www.originalfalcon.com
email: info@originalfalcon.com

DEDICATION

To Aima, for your guidance behind the Veil.
To my wife, Christina Sportiello, for being my dream come true.
And to the Collegium Cherubim: *Hoc Opus Hic Labor Est.*

Acknowledgements

I'd like to thank the following people, without whom this book would never have been written:

My daughter, Page Celeste Kelley, for enduring long creative absences. My wife, Christina Sportiello, for convincing me to share my story. My son and fellow Dreamer, Xavier Handfield, for long inspiring talks. My friend and student, Tom Kinney, for supporting my work and sharing it with others. My friend and coworker, Shane Mackey, for driving to and from work everyday while I worked on this book. Fellow oneironauts, Stewart Bell, Ivan Kos, and David Jay Brown, for your wonderful reviews and endorsements. A very special thanks to Nick Tharcher for his wise guidance and patience with this "green" author. Lastly, thank you, dear reader, for deciding to take this quest and choosing me to assist you on it.

TABLE OF CONTENTS

THE 120-DAYS CURRICULUM

FOREWORD
BY STEWART BELL

Whenever I find myself at the beginning of a new project I first must clear the way, so to speak, and often encounter similar hurdles each time. The main focus of my work is with music so for instance, when it comes to beginning the music writing part of a project, I'll often find myself unable to push past the initial stage of just sitting down and getting on with it. The perfectionist in me arises and often a reorganization of the work space is required—whether this be the physical rearrangement of my tools; desk, keyboard, sound modules, PC, etc. or; the virtual reshuffling of my digital workstation—only then can I proceed. In the case of this foreword, overcoming that first hurdle required that I obtain a physical copy of this book as opposed to scanning through lines of digital text on a flickering computer screen (I'm old school when it comes to reading!) Daniel quickly obliged and, with book in hand, I jumped that first obstacle. However, I quickly encountered another—I've never written a foreword before.

How does one start? What should it include? How long should it be? How should I proceed? Simple. I quickly resorted to seeking the help of that infinite database of knowledge—Google—but still, the hurdle remained. Upon finding numerous results on, "How to write a good foreword," the first and foremost piece of advice was, "Let the readers know how well you know the author." The problem here was that I didn't know Daniel that well—other than our conversations via e-mail and interactions in online groups related to the subject matter. Nevertheless, I wasn't going to let this get in my way, so I decided to side-step this hurdle and get started with the first task—reading the book.

The first thing that impressed me was Daniel's handling of the hurdles that many face when starting on the path to Conscious Sleep. It'll be no surprise to you to hear that people want a quick fix or some secret technique for sudden entry into the inner realms and, rightly so, Daniel doesn't promise to give either of these. From the start he points out that there is no quick way to achieve something as profound as the mastery of our own conscious experience, but he also quickly sets the reader on the right path for getting over those initial hurdles using techniques developed from his vast knowledge of old and new traditions alike. A type of mental and spiritual rearranging, if you like, that is necessary for laying the groundwork before one can proceed with such a profound project.

The second thing that became obvious to me is that Daniel has very much walked the walk and so he draws on his own extensive, lifelong experiences to teach others what he's learned. At an early age he was thrown behind the veil into the pit of his deep, dark unconscious mind where he ultimately learned to pacify the roaring beasts of that world, thus opening up the long, winding path through the subconscious realms that leads to the promised land beyond. (Ok, that's the Daniel in the lion's den analogy out of the way!)

Thirdly, as a lifelong Lucid Dreamer and Astral Explorer, I felt I knew all there was when it came to inner exploration, but I quickly realised in my reading of this book that I may have been overlooking some important aspects on the matter. Plus some techniques and practices that I'd discarded as archaic and deemed of no use in the modern world, were shown to me in a new light through Daniel's words. Having been brought up in a similar environment to Daniel, with strict religious parents, I found that later in life I dismissed many religious or spiritual philosophies and practices by passing them through the filters of my rebellious adolescence, and I was quick to resign them to the same fiery pit that I'd thrown the indoctrination of my childhood into. I see now, by revisiting these age-old ideas through the fresh and practical perspective given in this book, that I may well have thrown the baby out with the bath water.

An important factor that Daniel points out that is essential for proceeding on the path of conscious exploration is the practice of visualization, and, in particular, a method that is used to quiet down the mind and limit restlessness of the eyes sounded very familiar to me and brought back memories of childhood. My own inner journey started at 6 years old when my older brother taught me how to Lucid Dream to help me overcome a recurring nightmare I was having. Without realising, my brother, a natural Lucid Dreamer, had taught me an important lesson in how to recognise dream signs. I won't tell that particular story here—I've written extensively about it and my countless other experiences in my music projects, my video series and in my kid's storybook (shameless product plug—check!) What sprang to mind when reading Daniel's visualisation methods was another trick that my brother had introduced me to shortly after he had gifted me with the ability of dreaming awake. This trick involved staring at a particular point on the ceiling and holding your gaze until the room started to fade, forming a kind of tunnel vision (known as the Troxler effect). I would find this very relaxing, and, when practiced at bedtime, it would enhance another important method that my brother taught me. With the eyes closed and drifting off to sleep he guided me to focus on what ever it was I wanted to dream about. He advised me to try to bring into my mind's eye the scene I wished to encounter upon entering the dream world. On many occasions this had the desired effect and at other times it would lead to my drifting into a state of deep, Conscious Sleep. I'm not ashamed to admit that the first time I felt myself cross over in this way I thought I was dying and I came back to the waking world with a jolt!

Another childhood memory that was plucked from the deep sub-conscious recesses of my mind when reading the induction methods in this book was that of a little game my granddad used to play with me. It would start with me closing my eyes then my granddad would start with his finger on my lips and move upwards while saying, "mouth, nose, eyes a-blinky," then, while continuing up over my forehead, through my hair and down my neck to my lower back, he'd complete the game with the line, "over the hill to Johnny Stinky!" I, of course, found this highly amusing and enjoyed the tactile sensation involved. Usually, with my eyes still closed, I'd then follow the imaginary line started by my granddad's finger continuing down the hill to…well…down to Johnny Stinky! At that age I had an issue with incompleteness, with unfinished shapes and patterns—something that probably developed into that first hurdle I spoke about earlier—so I'd then be compelled to imagine the line continuing beyond Mr. Stinky and back up the front of my body closing the circle when it reached my lips again. I didn't see my granddad much so I'd often revisit the memory of that little game while lying in bed trying to get to sleep. The tracing of this imagi-nary circular line accompanied with my other early obsession of syncing my breathing with my heartbeat (4 beats to inhale, 4 beats to exhale) sounded very similar to one of the first methods Daniel covers in the book—*Embryonic Breathing* and the circulation of the breath through what's known as the *Microcosmic Orbit* (and particularly the aptly named "Wind Path"!) Reading this instantly struck a chord with me and that early imagination game that I'd play and I wondered, did this and the other early techniques I was unwittingly using as a child enhance my ability to have Vivid and Lucid Dreams which ultimately also led to Astral travel?

Is it just coincidence that, as a child, I was unknowingly utilising these methods which I now discover through this book are actually essential techniques for anyone serious about conscious exploration? The realisation that, all those years ago, I was quite possibly innocently tapping into some powerful inductions—trataka 'gazing' meditation, visualisation induction, Embryonic Breathing and the Microcosmic Orbit, Pellucid Sleep induction—was a rather profound moment for me and, was also just one of the affirmations for me that the path Daniel is proposing be taken here in this book is a powerful, unique and very comprehensive one. Borrowing from the best of the finest of the grandest old traditions—Shamanic, Kabbalah, Taoist, Vedantic, Tibetan and Tantric to name a few—and fitting them into an extensive *120-Days Curriculum* is certainly not the quick fix that many seek but, I'm extremely confident that it's a definitive path to the goals set forth in this book.

Needless to say, at this point I now felt confident in writing the foreword however, one thing was still niggling at the back of my mind—the hurdle set up by the fact that I didn't personally know the author. Side-stepping that second hurdle hadn't felt quite right but, by this point I had started to realise something. I did know Daniel. Our lives were so similar that, at times, it had felt like I was reading my own story. The sleep paralysis and night terrors starting at an early age; the strict religious parents; the vivid dream life; the rebellion against the indoctrination of our upbringing; the subsequent exploration of western traditions; returning to the path behind the veil initially revealed to us in childhood; our self taught piano playing and music-writing skills; our love of poem and lyric writing and; even our joint ventures into the construction trade! The parallels between the author and myself are uncanny and that second hurdle was now gone. (Incidentally, Daniel also happens to quote my favourite singer-songwriter in his writings. Just one of the many parts of the book that brought a smile to my face, and instantly brought to mind one of my own favourite and in this case, quite relevant, lines from the very same artist—"You've got to get in to get out.")

I then turned to the author's photo at the back of the book and looked into the eyes of the man who, through his words, had managed to teach some new tricks to this old dreaming dog and, even there, I saw similarities. I took a few moments to seek out some more photos of Daniel online and I quickly realised why that similarity was present. He bore a striking resemblance to, not one, but two important figures from my childhood and, specifically, figures from the period of my life where I was liberated from the confines of the religious organisation that my family was in. I saw an uncanny combination in Daniel's chiseled (and might I add handsome!) features—the face of my brother and the likeness of my best friend from adolescence. It was as if those two pivotal characters from that critical period in my life had been merged into one. As though my older sibling and my childhood buddy had gotten together and created a love child who…sorry, ok, I think I've made my point!

Joking aside, I find it very fitting that the author of this book more or less mirrors in appearance the two crucial figures involved in helping me escape from the limited perspectives of the childhood indoctrination that I grew up with. It seems like more than just a beautiful coincidence that in the face of this fellow oneironaut I saw the likeness of the duo of adolescent comrades that ushered in a new era of my life—an era of expansion, freedom, exploration, discovery and adventure. For that is exactly what Daniel's words are sure to do for those who wish to break free from the confines of the limited state of consciousness that most of us assume is all that we have access to. What follows here in this book is nothing short of a fully comprehensive manual on how to free oneself from the indoctrination of modern society with its limited perspectives on consciousness as Daniel ushers the reader into a new era of conscious expansion, inner exploration, adventures beyond imagination, deep personal discovery and, of course, the ultimate goal—liberation.

Stewart Bell is a composer, keys player, lucid dream teacher and author based in Scotland. He is the author of a wonderful children's story called *The Cupboard of Fear,* which teaches children how to overcome their fears via Lucid Dreaming. He's currently working on a project entitled *The Antechamber of Being* which includes a trilogy of concept albums, a video series, storybooks and art-books, all based on his long term experience as a lucid dreamer and astral traveller—a journey which started at 6 years old when a recurring nightmare prompted his older brother to teach him how to become aware in his dreams. He can be reached at:

http://www.learntoluciddream.co.uk

PART ONE

PROLOGUE

When I decided to write this book I didn't have a clear-cut idea as to how I wanted it to be written. I knew what I wanted to share, but how to present it in such a way that makes the information accessible to a larger audience didn't occur to me until I'd written well over two chapters. Happily, this book pretty much wrote itself. Like a dream trying hard to make itself come true the book you're about to read pretty much stands as its own creation. It's been written in a very conversational tone, using abbreviations and such, with minimal run-on sentences. Wanting to present the material in as comprehensive a manner as possible I've omitted any footnotes, opting instead to make each point as clear and descriptive as possible before moving on to the next one. Everything taught in this book is the result of over twenty years of my own personal experience as well as modern cutting-edge research on dreams and out of body experience (OOBE).

There are very few guesses here...

This book has been written to cover *all* aspects of Conscious Sleep, including the skills of *Dream Recall, Dream Interpretation, Auto-Hypnosis, Creative Inspiration, Vivid Dreaming, Lucid Dreaming, Pellucid Dreaming*, with forays into the more mystical and controversial aspects of *Premonition, Astral Projection, Dream Control,* and *Spiritual Epiphany*. The material is presented in two parts. The first section deals with *theory* and the second with *practice*. However, there are many practical tips and tidbits of information in the first part of the book so the best way to read it is from the first to the last page. I've provided a fairly robust peppering of books in the *Bibliography* should any particular topic provoke the desire for further study.

I'd like to say a few words about the information on Astral Projection presented in these pages. Anyone with experience with Astral Projection will likely have at least some experience with Lucid Dreaming, and anyone with dream Lucidity will oftentimes have some experience with Astral Projection. As you'll soon see, one of the primary goals of this book is to bring some clarity to the Lucid Dream/Astral Projection confusion. It's my sincere belief that anyone willing to devote their time and energy to the exercises in this book will eventually experience Astral Projection and see for themselves that it's not necessarily a synonym for Lucid Dreaming, similarities notwithstanding. I plan to write a companion piece to *Behind the Veil* specifically about Astral Projection sometime in the near future and flesh out the finer details of my system, *Subliminal Cognition Training*. For now, though, the introductory information presented here should be enough to get your Astral feet wet.

Before taking the plunge down the Rabbit Hole, I'd first like to voice a few admonitions. You'll find within these pages an assortment of practices, herbal prescriptions, and lifestyle suggestions that may or may not be suitable to the particulars of your situation. I'm not a doctor so please take the following seriously.

Always check with your doctor first before taking any nutritional supplements or making any drastic changes to your diet. That said, don't hesitate to get creative, and don't feel limited by any of my suggestions or personal experiences. Everyone has his or her own unique nature and I'm a firm believer that you can't cut the man to fit the coat.

Some of you reading this will experience success rather quickly while others may take some time. Or it happens often that someone will have "beginner's luck" but suddenly lose all behind the Veil access. Don't lose heart! This happens even to veterans of the art. Think about it this way:

How is it that we have handed down to us from antiquity countless documents, teachings, and methods in the various subtle arts filled with pointers and tips about when and where to best access their secrets?

The answer is:

Individuals just like you and I dared to explore and discovered that certain conditions promoted or precluded success. When enough adepts had the same experiences, and setbacks were discovered to have specific causes with specific solutions, then *experiences* became *rules* and those procedures were systematized. This information was then recorded and passed down to posterity. Of course, some rules are meant to be broken. All it takes is for someone to come along with a different degree of talent, perseverance, and a little bit of eccentricity, and voilà!

Who knows, maybe that person is you?

Individuals with the ability, natural or cultivated, to access worlds and mind-states apart, beneath, and above consensus reality, have always existed. I call such people "Veilers." This is a book for such persons and those wishing to become one.

In this book you'll learn:

- The 120-Days Curriculum of Vivid, Lucid, Pellucid, and Astral training.
- How to keep an accurate, organized, and comprehensive dream journal.
- The role that dreams and astral travel have played in Art, Science, and Religion.
- How to create the dreams you want to have before falling asleep.
- The role that herbs, diet, sexuality, and nutritional supplements play in Lucidity and Astral Projection training.
- Rudimentary skills in Subtle Body development, loosening of the Astral Body, and the storing and circulation of Etheric energy.
- The best times and conditions for Astral and Dream Work.
- Meditation methods to increase Lucidity in the dream state.
- The different dream Types and how to spot them, record them, and access their transformative power.
- The differences and similarities between Lucid Dreaming, Astral Projection, and other forms of Out of Body Experience.
- The role of Neuroplasticity in OOBE and Dream Control.
- Useful information about so-called Entity encounters.
- How to develop full-sensory Lucid experiences while in the dream state *and* while awake.

Within these pages you'll find everything needed to begin working creatively and safely with the art of Conscious Sleep. The main purpose of this book is to hand you the tools for successful Conscious Sleep and OOBE. In books two and three of this series, we'll explore some of the experiences you're most likely to have. In the meantime, I've tried my very best to be thorough and I trust you'll find this book indispensable in your quest, whether it be Lucid Dreaming, Astral Projection, or Spiritual transformation. It's my hope that the publication of this book will generate plenty of discussion, research, and debate in the future so that the art and science of Conscious Dreaming and Astral Travel will continue to evolve.

Your Fellow Traveller,

Daniel Kelley
12 December 2016, 5:46 pm

INTRODUCTION

LIVING THE DREAM: A PERSONAL STORY

For children of all times and places, the Veil that separates the conscious mind from the worlds which lie beneath and above has always been delightfully thin. For me, however, it was practically nonexistent and my earliest experiences behind it were anything but delightful.

My journey began as a lucid *Nightmare*, not a Lucid Dream.

It began when I was about nine years old. What at first seemed like the typical nocturnal disturbances experienced by most small children soon erupted like a volcano of psychic lava. First came the night-terrors. The cold-sweat producing visions usually reserved for the feverish, the psychedelic trip, or the clinically insane, were to my childhood self as common as a sneeze.

My mother was at a loss. My school teachers were concerned. I was terrified.

Imagine being nine years old. You share a bunk bed with your older brother, with you occupying the bottom bunk and he the top one. Every night, after your mother tucks you in, you lie in bed afraid to close your eyes. Your poor brother, a normal and healthy boy, is in the bunk above you wondering what type of theatrics will rob him of sleep this time. Your school work is suffering. Your social life is suffering. Your family life is suffering; and even at the tender age of nine you're beginning to wonder if you've lost your mind.

That was my early childhood...

My earliest memory of these psychic eruptions took place in that bunk bed. My brother and I had just been put to bed and the lights turned off. I can still remember the terror that seized me in those days as soon as the lights went out, and this night was no exception. I remember the air felt electrically charged, like a thunderstorm was brewing right there in my bedroom. Suddenly, as if in response to my fear of the dark, I saw as plainly as I see the words on this page a tin-hat light dangle down from my brother's bed and stop at about midpoint in the air. At first I thought my brother was playing a joke on me, but then I noticed something.

The light was on, *but the room was still dark*!

So I did the only logical thing a boy can do in such a situation and reached for the tin-hat light. I needed to know that what I was looking at was real and not some hallucination. As I reached out my left hand, by that time trembling and slightly pulling back, the light just hung there like a fish hook. It even swayed slightly as if moved by a gentle breeze that wasn't there. Then, with a burst of courage, I made a grab for the chain that held the phantom light aloft; and what happened next changed me forever.

It simply vanished like a soap bubble stabbed by a sharp pin. Poof! Gone. I remember pulling the sheets over my head and sweating under the hot blankets, barely breathing, for the rest of the night.

To expect a plunge behind the Veil to result in nothing but fun and fantasy is much like plunging into the ocean and expecting mermaids. Of course, there *is* lots of fun to be had, but I'd be remiss if I didn't warn you about how shocking these experiences can be.

After that experience with the phantom light, things became even more bizarre. From spontaneous out-of-body-experiences, to disembodied hands pulling at my hair, to a horrifying dissociative state with a peculiar species of amnesia rendering me unable to remember my name or recognize my own mother. Eventually I was sent to psychologists, M.D.'s, and even pastors, all in a desperate attempt to unearth the source of my "disorder." I've been through test after test, forced to stay awake all night so that I'd fall asleep during "testing" the following morning. I've been hooked up to electroencephalograph machines while lights were strobed in front of my eyes, probably to test for epilepsy. The psychologists blamed it on my parent's divorce, the doctors blamed it on my asthma medication, and the pastor blamed it on demons!

Yes, demons…

Finally, at age sixteen, there was one final "attack" and then it all suddenly stopped without rhyme or reason. I was left confused, traumatized, and curious.

Very curious...

I spent the next five years in single-minded pursuit of finding answers. In those days I'd spend entire days at the library, pouring over books and magazines. I read everything I could find on psychological disorders, religion, dreams, the occult, astral projection, night-terrors, and spirituality. I also began practicing some of the techniques that I'll be sharing in this book.

It took about five years of groping in the dark before the Veil opened again. I kept my practices very secret during this time. I'd already learned my lesson about what happens when one is too outspoken on these matters. Of course, I couldn't hide it for long. Soon I began meeting others of like mind, people with their own reasons for wrapping themselves up in shadows.

Then, in the year 1999, *It* happened!

Years of not knowing what had happened to me, of thinking that perhaps I was just crazy, and now things were starting to make sense! At the time, I began a strict regimen of meditation practice, Subtle Body exercises, and devotional practices, many of which I continue to this day. Through these practices I was able to tap into and awaken that part of my psyche which had experienced all those childhood horrors, only this time I did so from a lighter place. At first the terrors came back, but eventually they gave way to something altogether different and *definitely* the opposite of horrific.

I'm thirty-eight and have a family now. My world is more magical and meaningful than it ever was. In fact, it's far richer and more textured than ever! Why? Besides the blessing of a wonderful family, once I learned how to consciously tap into the raw, creative, and spiritual power behind the Veil, a whole new world opened before me. It's been largely a trial and error process. At times I thought that I might lose my mind! Sometimes it's terrifying. Sometimes it's breathtakingly beautiful. But if my years on this earth have shown me anything, it's that modern man has lost all sense of meaning and magic, and yet both are all around us awaiting our participation. Regardless how it reveals itself, an adventure is always waiting in these hidden worlds behind the Veil.

I invite you to join me in exploring!

CHAPTER ONE

THE ART, SCIENCE, AND RELIGION OF DREAMING

That dreams, visions, and Astral Travel have had a tremendous impact upon the arts, religions, and the sciences should come as no surprise. From the psychedelic paintings of Salvador Dali, to the groundbreaking discoveries of Albert Einstein, as well as the apocalyptic visions of St. John of Patmos, the subterranean realm of the human psyche has provided for some of the greatest minds a creative foundation composed largely of dream stuff.

As one begins to progress in these arts it helps to know they were shared by some of mankind's greatest heroes. This is especially true during the period when the training wheels haven't yet come off. Some of the personalities that are and were tapped into these realms are household names. Many of them are immediately recognizable by anyone who's ever read a physics book, followed trends in mainstream music, or pondered fine art.

Then again, many Veilers remain obscure. Some have never heard of terms like "Veiler" or "Subtle Body" or "Lucid Dreaming." In fact, there are a great many people with these skills who keep quiet for fear of being thought insane. Some of them *are* insane! Others seem to have been born with these abilities and think nothing of it. In fact, they usually grow up with the assumption that everyone can do it! Such people rarely seek further cultivation into the higher stages of skill because it's common to take the familiar for granted.

Still, others choose to advance.

In this chapter, we'll explore how dreams and visions have influenced humanity's development in the three great spheres of Art, Science, and Spirituality. We'll meet painters, dancers, sages, physicists, psychologists, musicians, medicine men and women, all of whom owe some of their best work to their adventures behind the Veil. Before we do that, though, let's learn a little bit about the system I use in this and forthcoming books.

Anatomy of a Veiler

"Our normal state of consciousness, waking consciousness as it's called, is but one special type of consciousness, whilst all about it, parted from it by the flimsiest of screens, lie other potential forms of consciousness."

— William James

Just a quick walk through the New Age or Religions section of a bookstore can give the first impression of a spiritual value-meal menu, and it can be daunting to approach the big picture with fresh eyes. You've got the *Christian* package, the *Buddhist* package, the *Shinto* package, the *Muslim* package, the *Pagan* package, and even the *Extraterrestrial* package! It's easy to assume that these are all discreet spiritual highways with very little in common, but that's just not true.

Over the course of my twenty years of involvement in the various Wisdom Traditions of the world, I've discovered their many commonalities despite their cultural differences. Whether we're talking about *Judaism, Hinduism, Taoism,* or any other *-ism* for that matter, we're still talking about people, and people have more similarities than differences. It should then come as no surprise that the myriad systems created by a given people or person to make sense of their rarified experiences should, at their core, have more in common than their surfaces might suggest.

What's the common core shared by the great spiritual traditions?

ANSWER: The Perennial Philosophy.

Put simply, the Perennial Philosophy is the oldest and most universal developmental model in the world. The belief that the universe, including human consciousness, is composed of an onion-like series of layers or nests leading from dirt to deity, from dust to divine, is found in virtually every known culture of the world. A common theme running through most versions of the Perennial Philosophy is that each level, world, plane, body, or realm is separated by "sheathes" or *veils*, much like the layers of an onion are separate and yet still comprise the whole onion itself.

The most stripped-down versions of the Perennial Philosophy tend to look something like this:

- **Earth=Man=Heaven**
- **Ecosphere=Biosphere=Noosphere**
- **Body=Mind=Spirit**

And so on...

I've worked with the Perennial Philosophy as it appears on the Kabbalah's *Tree of Life*, in the internal Alchemy of Taoism, the five *Koshas* of Vedanta, and, of course, the "five primary Veils" of my own system:

- **the Veil of Tears**
- **the Veil of Breath**
- **the Veil of Dreams**
- **the Veil of Ghosts**
- **the Veil of Bliss**

(These correspond to the *Physical, Etheric, Mental, Astral* and *Causal* realms, respectively. In this book we're working with the *Veil of Dreams* and the *Veil of Ghosts*. My system is called *Subliminal Cognition Training*. See the *Afterword* for more details.)

Another important principle of the Perennial Philosophy has to do with the energetic embodiment in which we travel through and behind these respective Veils. The most basic description of these "bodies" is found in the well-known format of *Body, Mind, Soul,* and *Spirit* and its many compact versions which typically look like this:

- **Physical Body/Etheric**
- **Mental Body/Ego Body**
- **Emotion Body/Astral Body**
- **Spirit Body/Causal Body**

Some systems go a step further and lump *Etheric, Mental, Astral,* and *Causal* under the general heading of "Subtle Body," with the Causal Body being, on the one hand, the very root of consciousness itself, and on the other hand, the subtlest aspect of the Subtle Body. Depending on how and why you choose to slice that pie, you could just as easily give a scheme of:

- **Gross** (not so subtle)
- **Subtle** (subtler)
- **Causal** (very subtle)

These correspond to the three basic states of *Awake, Dreaming,* and *Dreamless Sleep,* respectively. This is the basic scheme we'll be using throughout this book. As we'll soon see, our conscious participation in all three of these states holds the key to behind-the-Veil access. That said, how you categorize the levels of the Perennial Philosophy depends upon why you're navigating it in the first place. It all depends on which Veil you're stepping behind and the map you're using for this purpose. For example, in the tradition of Psychoanalysis, they use the triad of:

- **Id**
- **Ego**
- **Superego.**

In such a system, the Mental Body is obviously of primary importance, and the Veil which separates the *Biosphere* (physical life) from the *Noosphere* (the realm of Mind) is the one being stepped behind. Because most systems tend to favor one realm/body over the others, it's often left to another system to fill in the gaps. Take sports, for example. Most sports deal primarily with the Gross (physical) body. Of course, the mental aspect is there in the form of rules and strategy, but the bulk of athletic sports is a Gross Body endeavor. As a result, many progressive thinkers in the realm of athletic performance have begun to study "the zone," a flow-state experienced by many athletes that has non-dual characteristics. Today, it's not uncommon to find football players practicing Tai Chi, a Subtle Body exercise, or Mindfulness meditation, a Causal Body practice.

The bottom line?

If you're exercising Body, Mind, and Soul, you're a complete human being; and as long as you're capable of smoothly transitioning from your Gross to Subtle to Causal Bodies you're a Veiler!

One of the most significant points to bear in mind is that all of these "bodies" are just the limbs of one unified body. That *bodymind*, that organic unity, is the stuff you're made of. Being a "Veiler" is simply a snappy way of saying that you know how to lift the curtain to reveal the secret spaces within that mystery.

But being a Veiler is more than that...

If you wish to learn a skill, you first must possess the necessary equipment to perform it. You must have the right *anatomy* for the job, and I mean that literally. If I want to become a professional track runner I first need strong legs, a powerful core, and a strong heart and lungs. If I don't have these fundamental requirements I'm doomed to fail from the start. It's one thing to be able to walk. For that I only require the minimum in terms of physical functioning, but to be a track runner? Well, for that I'll need a strong body. Not only that, I'll need a specific type of body, too. The body of a runner is different from that of, say, a professional bodybuilder. A dancer's body differs in many obvious ways from that of a powerlifter's body.

My first encounter with this somewhat obvious fact came when I made the transition from bodybuilding to the Internal Martial Arts. I planned on keeping my bodybuilding practice as an adjunct to my Internal Martial Arts training, but it was clear from the start that this was an impossibility. The Tai Chi body is completely different from the bodybuilder's body! So different, in fact, that they're totally incompatible. So I had to make a choice: Tai Chi or Big Muscles?

I chose Tai Chi...

The same holds true in any serious endeavor. If I want to learn to play piano, it's not enough that I've got ten fingers and a piano. I need to have some degree of natural talent. I've got to have a good sense of pitch, good coordination, focus, and a good memory. All of these requirements demand a certain physiological and cognitive make-up. Without it, you may be able to play a few chords. You may even be able to learn to read some musical notation. But you'll never be a virtuoso if you're tone deaf or missing a few fingers. In much the same way, it's not enough that you have dreams every night. To learn how to have Lucid dreams you've got to be wired that way, either naturally or through sincere and long-term training. Lucid Dreamers and Astral Projectors have a unique neurology. Either they were born that way or they developed it over time.

A Veiler's body is different from other bodies...

Think about it.

What are advanced yogis, taoists, shamans, and monks doing when they meditate, eat consciously, practice Qigong, or go on vision quests? They're exercising, cultivating, and in a very real sense *creating* their Subtle Body and grounding it in their physical body! That's the whole process in a nutshell. Furthermore, two people can go to the gym and do the same amount of exercising and one of them will still burn fat and build muscle faster than the other.

Not all Veilers are the same. *Equality* isn't *sameness*.

Admittedly, this isn't the most popular aspect of my approach. In fact, it makes many people downright angry. After all, assuring people that you can teach anyone how to go Astral, or Lucid Dream, or contact their dead relatives, is a great selling point. I get it! Still, it doesn't change the fact that it's simply not true. To become a proficient Veiler you need to first possess and then cultivate a very specific anatomy (see *Chapter Four)*. There are many Subtle Body anatomy textbooks available. In this book we'll be working primarily with Taoist, Tibetan, and Tantric methodologies.

That's all fine and well, you say, but so what? What's the ultimate goal of being a Veiler?

The ultimate goal of a Veiler is to attain continuity of consciousness in the Physical, Dream, Astral, and Causal realms.

That sounds like a tall order, doesn't it? Well, yes it is, and no it isn't. Like any skill, being a Veiler is at least 40% talent. Like any talent, certain personality types tend to have more success with it than others. For example, look at most artists. Most of them tend to be introverted, reclusive, and dreamy. Now contrast that with the outgoing and extroverted personality of, say, a car salesman. So what's the best way to know whether you have a natural proclivity for being a Veiler? Well, first of all, you're reading this. Chances are you wouldn't be if not for the fact that you've got a natural interest in these topics.

In my experience, the natural Veiler tends to be a little introverted, right-hemisphere of the brain dominant, emotionally dynamic, and a sensualist. This doesn't necessarily mean that other Personality Types can't learn how to go Astral or Lucid Dream, only that they'll probably have to take an unorthodox route to get there. We'll discuss some of these unorthodox methods in *Part Two* of this book. For now, though, let's look at this thing called dreaming. We must start there. Why? Because, as we'll soon see, dreams represent a bridge between the Etheric and Astral Realms.

The Stuff That Dreams Are Made Of

Sigmund Freud referred to dreams as "the royal road to the unconscious." He believed that dreams, properly interpreted and placed in the correct context, served as a sort of lighthouse that guides the therapist and client to the source of mental illness. Detractors of this view have argued that dreams are nothing but the brain's way of throwing off emotional stress and are little more than psychic garbage. Indeed, some researchers have discarded the *psychological* aspect of dreams altogether and consider the issue in a strictly *physiological* context. One name that immediately comes to mind is Dr. David Maurice, Ph.D. He proposed that **REM** (**R**apid **E**ye **M**ovement) sleep is merely an exercise of the eye! His theory states that the aqueous humor (the fluid behind the eye) is churned or "mixed" by the rapid eye movements associated with dreaming. This nocturnal movement of the eyes oxygenates the cornea, which would otherwise starve during sleep without it.

So, you can add that to your workout routine!

Another contemporary researcher of dreams, Cristina Marzano, demonstrated that dream recall is enhanced by waking up during or shortly after the **REM** phase of sleep. Marzano proved that the same low **THETA** brainwave activity observed in the frontal cortex during REM sleep is the same frequency observed in the frontal cortex while we're awake and engaged in memory recall. The point being made is that dreams appear to be the brain's way of digesting autobiographical material and nothing more. Because the bioelectrical and neurological processes we use to process, envision, and recall the events of our daily lives are the same ones used to dream and recall our dreams, the logical conclusion is that they're merely two expressions of the same cognitive function.

In the Taoist Tradition, dreams are believed to be the result of the rebalancing of life force (***Qi***) along special pathways (meridians) in the Etheric energy. The sights, sounds, smells, tastes, sensations, and emotions we experience in our dreams are, in this system of thought, simply the reorganization of ***Qi*** reflected in the sensorimotor centers of the brain (more on this later). It's interesting to note in this regard that the aim of Taoist Alchemy bears a striking resemblance to Astral Projection. In the higher stages of training, the adept unites his intent and his refined life-force to create a "spiritual embryo." He then raises this spiritual energy up to his brain to re-open the third eye, at which point he begins to train his consciousness to leave his body for longer and longer periods of time until the day of his death when it's believed he has attained eternal life in his new spirit body.

Do you want to know what I think? I think that all of these perspectives have something to offer.

One of the problems with the current scientific paradigm is that researchers tend to specialize. Not that there's anything wrong with specialization. It's just that it often results in a bad case of tunnel-vision. If one has a biological bias, for example, then all experiences are interpreted biologically. Or if one has a strictly psychological education, then all experiences are interpreted psychologically. This is nothing new. Consider the fact that in Medieval times, were one to suffer from epilepsy, then it simply *must* be demonic possession. Because the predominant worldview at the time was drenched in Church theology, any physical or psychological illness for which a natural cause couldn't be found was instantly dubbed the work of God or the Devil. Now, when it comes to so diaphanous a thing as dreams, it's hard to pin down just exactly what they are. So, in walk the specialists! One says that dreams are nothing but the brain going to the bathroom, another says that dreams are divine, and another says that dreams are just eye aerobics.

Yes! Yes! And Yes! So, here's my two cents:

The phenomenon called *dreaming* is a natural psychedelic experience. The word *psychedelic* means "mind enhancing" in the sense of enlarging the contents of the psyche, both conscious and subconscious, so they become available to conscious awareness. Dreaming is one of many natural and healthy altered states of consciousness available to us and *conscious* dreaming is a rarified version of it. In my opinion, consciousness is itself a psychedelic experience that most of us become accustomed to by the time we hit puberty. At that point we typically begin to take this miracle for granted.

What to say of dreams?

Imagine for a moment that you're in the middle of the ocean surrounded by chaotic waves. You're so preoccupied with the task of staying afloat and fending off the waves that you have little time to notice all the fish swimming around and beneath you. This can be likened to the wakeful state of consciousness **(Beta).** Now imagine that I come along and give you a scuba diving suit equipped with oxygen and goggles with night-vision. Exhausted from the struggle, you put on the scuba gear and allow yourself to rest and slowly sink to the ocean floor. On your way down, you look up and see the tossing waves from a quieter place. This is like the lighter stage of sleep **(Alpha).**

You rest in this calmness for a little while and then decide to look around you. All at once you're transported to another world inhabited by strange creatures. Whales, fish, sharks, glowing jellyfish, and an entire panoply of strange and exotic creatures surround you. This is much like the deeper stage of sleep, called REM **(Theta)** sleep.

Finally, you sink to the ocean floor where it's absolutely dark. You're still aware of yourself and the life forms around you. You're even aware of the waves tossing around on the ocean surface. But you're not concerned at all. Or maybe you are. It's up to you, and you know it! This can be likened to the deepest phase of sleep where dreaming, and usually awareness itself, is obliterated **(Delta)**. However, it's possible, and even easy after a while, to remain alert even in this state of deep dreamless sleep. The Vedantists refer to this state as *Turiya*.

We'll be revisiting and elaborating these topics throughout this book. For now, simply take note of the fact that dreaming is a very complex phenomenon. It's an error to approach the subject of dreaming from only one perspective and then call it the final word. Each new discovery, collection of new data, context, and theory, have an equally valuable role to play in our understanding of dreams and related phenomena.

It's understandable that there's some confusion as to the details— how to qualify and tease apart experiences that look similar but aren't the same, and so on—but if you lay all perspectives and discoveries on the table you'll start to see patterns emerge. Take, for example, the discovery that dreams and the brain-centers used for processing emotions are closely linked. Many systems of thought link the *Astral Body* to the *Emotional Body*. The Theosophists, to give one prominent example, made this connection. If you experience Astral Projection and Lucid Dreaming and then examine those two experiences, you'll understand the association.

Still, they're not the same thing.

However, because both experiences involve many of the same experiential elements, and because they involve many of the same neurological structures and psychological responses, it's easy to just assume that they're identical. Strangely, we don't apply the same reasoning to other experiences. To give but one example, when we watch a stimulating movie we register many of the same biological reactions we'd have were the experience actually happening to us.

We don't therefore conclude that what happens on the Silver Screen is the same as what happens to us in real life.

So, what are dreams? I'd have to say that it depends on who you ask. After all, there are many people who swear that they never dream! If you were to ask me what dreams are, I'd tell you that they're not *the* royal road to the unconscious. Rather, *they're one of many roads to the unconscious,* by whatever name. They're more than that, though. They're fun! They're creative, inspiring, exhilarating, terrifying, sexy, mind-blowing, psychedelic, and spiritually potent expressions of a highly complex bodymind.

And that's good medicine.

Shamanism (The Physician-Priest)

The earliest record we have of Conscious Sleep playing a pivotal role in society is arguably that most universal of religions called Shamanism. Shamanism has existed in virtually every part of the globe from the Foraging age to our current Digital age. Anthropologists can't seem to agree upon an absolute definition of shamanism, but the basic consensus is that a shaman:

• Serves as priest and healer of a community.
• Is a medium between the Seen and Unseen worlds.
• Accesses these worlds and the inhabitants of these worlds by way of trance, lucid dreams, psychoactive plants, meditation, ecstatic dance, astral travel, fasting, contemplative prayer, and so on.

The role of shaman is typically inherited *patrilineally* or *matrilineally*—through the father or mother who serves as the Medicine Man or Woman of the community. But this isn't always so. Anthropologists have noted that oftentimes the role of shaman is foisted upon an individual by a spontaneous initiatic ordeal called "shamanic crisis" in which the shaman-to-be undergoes a powerful death and rebirth experience. The visions and psychodrama of the shamanic crisis is a spiritual crossroads with one path leading to enlightenment and the other to insanity. Which path prevails depends largely upon cultural support and the psychological fortitude of the sufferer. Assuming the candidate is successful, he or she assumes the post of Seer, Sage, and Physician of the tribe.

The role of shaman is unique in that it combines artist, doctor, and priest under the same heading. Most medicine men and women are a colorful synthesis of musician, dancer, painter, singer, sage, doctor, and priest. In other words, a true shaman embodies Art, Science, and Religion simultaneously.

Core to most forms of shamanism is the belief that dreams and visions are produced by spirits (or the Great Spirit, by any name) and can be suppressed by them as well. Totem animals, power objects, and sacred symbols are often used by shamans to induce a vision or to terminate one. In the mind-bending film, *Inception,* Leonardo DiCaprio uses a spinning top to determine whether he's awake or having a Lucid Dream. In the classic film and children's book, *The Wizard of Oz,* Dorothy Gale wields the protective power of ruby slippers to ward off the evil intentions of the Wicked Witch of the West. We see totems whenever we enter a Catholic Church. Rosary beads, icons, and even the Sacraments of the Holy Mass, are all examples of these shamanic power-objects, the objections of clergy notwithstanding. Millions of people all over the world hang religious symbols and icons over their beds and the beds and cribs of children to ensure the production of good dreams and the banishing of nightmares. And many place a Dream Catcher over their bed to trap vagabond dreams and visions drifting through the aether.

All of these practices, it can be said, are vestiges of our shamanic roots.

But what do present-day shamans have to say about stepping behind the Veil? Are they for or against it? After all, if most of the vision quests conducted by shamans are revelatory in nature, might dream manipulation and other willful forms of Conscious Sleep be a form of interference? While taking notes and gathering data for this book, I attempted to contact several institutions claiming authentic shamanic roots. Most of them refused to be interviewed, and those willing to discuss these topics at all took an almost nonchalant stance towards them. However, I believe these practitioners to be in the minority. For most shamanic practitioners in today's world it's the premonitory, visionary, and psychospiritual (soul-quest) dream types that seem to matter most.

Debunkers of shamanism believe it to be no more than a vestige of our infantile past as a species. They point to such primitive notions as the Law of Signatures, or Pantheism, and the almost mandatory use of psychoactive plants as just some of the reasons for justifying their contempt. Indeed, many of these practices *are* infantile. They're supposed to be! After all, forming a bridge between the innocence of childhood and the pragmatism of the adult is just one of the functions of a Seer. As I said in the *Introduction* to this book, the Veil that divides the seen and unseen worlds is delightfully thin in early childhood. Shamanism continues to be just one among many ways to re-enter that stage of development, not just one's own inner child, but the inner child of an entire culture and possibly our entire species.

Yes, one of the many ways this is done is through the creative use of psychoactive plants. In many (but not all) shamanic traditions, psychedelics such as psilocybin, ergot, salvia, LSD, ayahuasca, mescaline, Hawaiian baby woodrose seeds, and so on, are ingested as a sacrament to loosen the self-contraction and attune one's psyche to the subtle-realms. In fact, much of what occurs while under the influence of that infamous psychoactive tea, *ayahuasca*, bears a striking resemblance to many types of Lucid Dreams. Readers interested in the connection between Lucid Dreaming, Astral Projection, and Psychedelics are encouraged to consult the book, *Dreaming Wide Awake,* by David Jay Brown.

An important component of the shamanic voyage has to do with grounding the forces encountered behind the Veil by actively participating in the community. Far from being neurotic self-preoccupation, the powerful experiences evoked by these "primitive" methods are anchored in a deep respect for productive work, altruistic self-sacrifice, and overall holistic functioning. Contrasted with the often one-sided emphasis of modern science on the behavioristic, chemical, and biological facets of human life, these so-called infantile methodologies are the cooler side of the pillow. In fact, one culture's shamanic tradition even specializes in Dream Yoga. What culture, you ask?

Ladies and Gentlemen, let's take a journey to Tibet!

The Tibetan Book of the Dead

The *Bardo Thodol,* erroneously called *The Tibetan Book of the Dead,* is truly a classic text for anyone interested in life behind the Veil. In fact, the so-called "Bardo Realms" described in this text include the dream state among the myriad "in-between" states experienced by consciousness on its journey from womb to tomb (and reincarnation into a new womb). The psychedelic high priest, Timothy Leary, even used the *Bardo Thodol* as a template in his mapping out of the anatomy of an LSD trip! Written in the eighth century A.D. by Padma Sambhava, the text literally describes the skillful use of Conscious Dreaming at the moment of death.

I find it interesting that the full title of the text is *The Liberation Through Hearing During the Intermediate State.* Something that's always struck me as too odd to be coincidence is that the parietal lobe, that part of the brain associated with proprioception and balance, is clearly involved in Lucid Dreaming as well as the Astral experience. Indeed, one of the most potent techniques for inducing Lucidity is to imagine yourself at a point in space opposite that of your sleeping body ("Phasing"). The inner part of the ear, also heavily involved in balance and one's sense of spatial orientation, is the window through which the officiating Tibetan priest communicates with the soul of the dying person. By way of chanting, ritual, verbal description and reassurance, the soul of the dying man is guided through the Bardo realms to its new or final destination.

Is it possible that the tether which links consciousness to the physical brain remains in residual form for a limited time after the death of the body? Do the facts of Astral Projection, Conscious Dreaming, and Near-Death Experience (NDE) prove the existence of a "Jacob's Ladder" of consciousness? Does the brain or some Etheric part of it still briefly register sound and assist in proprioception after the heart stops beating? To what extent is the oxygen-deprived brain capable of interpreting sound, imagery, and spatial location immediately after death?

When my grandfather was dying, I was present at his bedside. After the ordeal had passed, I had everyone leave the room so that I could say my goodbyes. His eyes were partially closed but still looking directly at me. I told him that I believe he can still hear me, that I love him, and that it's okay to move on. That was eleven years ago today and, out of all those I've lost to death, my grandfather is the only one of them who still visits me in my dreams.

I wonder…

One thing that's always puzzled me is how hearing, and even the sensation of touch, can be experienced on the Astral plane. That the five senses can be experienced in the dream state is clear enough, but how to explain someone leaving their physical body and eavesdropping on a conversation happening some two-hundred or so miles away and accurately reporting what the conversation was about? I personally feel that it has something to do with electrical signals coming to and from the brains of those involved. In much the same way that sound is but a vibration interpreted by the brain, it could be that all sensory phenomena experienced in the Astral is the result of a direct feedback loop running from the Astral body to the brain. Have you ever had the experience of knowing immediately beforehand who was going to knock at your door or call/text you on your phone? Or have you heard a song playing in your head only to have it come on the radio seconds later?

Could it be possible that these phenomena are somehow related?

The *Bardo Thodol* also vividly describes the "exit-symptoms" of OOBE experienced by most Veilers. The powerful "thunderings," "vibrations," and "rays of intense light" are among the most common symptoms reported by most projectors and survivors of Near Death Experience. I personally believe that the fifth Bardo, called the *Chonyi Bardo,* is synonymous with the Astral plane. The difference between them is that in the fifth Bardo, the "Silver Cord" (astral link to psychosexual energy) has been severed whereas Astral Projection occurs with one's vital force still intact and circulating.

In the *Bardo Thodol,* the dream state is considered the second Bardo realm, called the *Milam Bardo.* This is considered by some Buddhists to be a crucial component in any truly complete Sadhana ("spiritual practice"). Although originally a Tantric transmission, this so-called "Dream Yoga" has become an advanced level of practice in the Hindu, Yogic, and Buddhist traditions of India.

The gist of Dream Yoga, like that of the *Bardo Thodol* itself, lies in the attainment of the *continuity of consciousness.* To get an idea of what this means we need to imagine that the mind and its objects are like the weather, whereas our overall consciousness is like the sky in which the changing weather occurs. The problem is that we tend to identify with the changing weather and forget that we're the unchanged sky. This is necessarily a very crude description of the facts, but it's all you truly need to know to put it into practice. After some time, this continuity of consciousness evolves from being a mere passing *state* and becomes a stable *trait* of consciousness. In other words, it ceases to be something that you *do* and becomes something that you *are*. This eventually grows into the experience of non-dual enlightenment, or the realization that all things are arising and passing away as unified parts of the same dance of life and death, and *you are that dance!*

Remember that the mind, of which the brain is the physical embodiment, cycles through three broad states (or weather) on a regular basis:

- **Wakefulness**
- **Dreaming**
- **Deep Dreamless Sleep**

For most people, these three states of consciousness are mutually exclusive. The goal of Subliminal Cognition Training is to maintain conscious awareness throughout these three states, giving rise to a fourth state (or stage?) of consciousness that never blinks and embraces them all in one glance.

Next, we'll look at what these states of awareness look like when put on paper.

The Electric Brain

That tribal priests, some Tibetan monks, and psychics have access to worlds behind the Veil is all good and well; but what's happening inside the brains of such individuals? Is there a way to measure and record such phenomena?

In fact, yes, there is…

In the year 1924, a scientist by the name of Hans Berger created a revolutionary device called the Electroencephalogram (EEG). This device works by registering electrical activity in the brain via electrodes attached to the scalp. These electrodes are attached to wires leading to the EEG machine whereupon the electrical activity of the brain is recorded on paper by sensitive needles that scribble out the peaks and valleys of brainwave activity flowing along the scalp.

Arguably the greatest discovery made using this device was that of the Five Basic Brain Waves:

- **GAMMA**
- **BETA**
- **ALPHA**
- **THETA**
- **DELTA**

An important fact to know about these brainwaves is that even though they represent discrete states of awareness they can and do overlap. For example, infants almost always register **DELTA** waves regardless what they're doing. Similarly, an adult can register high **BETA** while involved in some task, but **ALPHA** may be present also.

Although I can't prove it, I believe that future research will show that Lucid Dreaming, Astral Projection, and various other psychic talents are largely a product of Neuroplasticity, in which the adept creates new neural connections in the brain and learns to combine, receive, and emit bioelectrical frequencies in creative and novel ways (see *Chapter Four)*. Since dreams are largely the brain's attempt at memory consolidation and the neural hardwiring of new skills, the skills associated with Conscious Sleep are a peculiar case of a brain-function rewiring itself to enjoy itself. That said, there are certain situations in which one brainwave will predominate over the others. Take meditation, to give just one example. Although all five brainwaves may register on a graph during a meditation session, the dominant one might be **GAMMA.** Or, let's imagine that you're fast asleep and hooked up to an EEG machine. Although **THETA** may be present to a degree, **DELTA** might be the dominant brainwave. It's helpful to understand that the process of sleeping and dreaming is a cycle that repeats about four to five times in a full and healthy night's rest. This cycle is not merely a straight line moving from awake to asleep to awake again, but rather one which *cycles and spirals* in 90–120 minute intervals.

For our purposes, delving into what's experienced during the sleep cycle is at the heart of our inquiry. In the meantime, I'd like you to take note of the timing of the sleep cycle. Why? Because what we're calling "the Veil" is more like a series of small windows of opportunity, and those windows contain windows, too. In other words, there are *veils within veils*. In my own system, I refer to these as *Primary* veils, *Secondary* veils, *Tertiary* veils, and so on. These veils are just variations and hybrids of the Primary veils. We encounter them during psychedelic trips, ecstatic trance, and visionary experiences. Our primary area of interest in this volume is the *Veil of Dreams* and its sub-veils. I'll delve into the others in subsequent publications.

The thresholds which separate the different phases of the sleep cycle represent a series of veils that only open for a small fraction of time before they close again behind you. If you don't enter these thresholds consciously your chances of achieving Lucidity or Pellucidity are greatly reduced. This is especially true during sleep transitions when Sleep Spindles, K-Complexes, and PGO-Waves are present (more on this later). In my experience, Lucid Dreamers can learn to prolong these brainwaves; surfing them, so to speak. In *Part Two* of this book, we'll explore a popular technique of Lucidity entrainment with which you'll teach your subconscious mind to invite Lucidity while asleep *and* awake. We'll also go a bit more into detail about the technicalities of the sleep cycle.

For now, though, just take note of the fact that the sleep and dream cycle repeats many times throughout the night. Let's assume that you fall asleep at 9:00 pm every night. The most potent times for behind the Veil access would be shortly after you begin to feel drowsy, say, at around 9:30 pm. From there, every ninety minutes marks an entry point for Lucidity, especially between 4:00 and 5:00 am. In between these ninety-minute intervals marks an entry point for Pellucidity.

If Lucidity is the peak, then Pellucidity is the valley. In *Part Two* I'll discuss at length the differences between Lucidity and Pellucidity. For now, just note that Lucidity refers to conscious dreaming in which the sleeper takes an active role in the dream narrative, whereas Pellucidity finds the sleeper more concerned with and absorbed in the essence of the dream. Lucidity is primarily concerned with the forms and scenarios which arise in the dreamscape. Pellucidity, on the other hand, is concerned with the very fabric behind those forms. You might think of it as meditation carried into the sleep cycle.

Another time-zone to bear in mind is 4:00 am when the sleep hormone *melatonin* is beginning to diminish, and the brain is beginning to flood the body with chemicals to wake you up. Melatonin delays the **REM** (Rapid Eye Movement) phase of sleep, but it seems to create a sort of slingshot effect in which **REM** bounces back with full intensity. Melatonin, while not necessarily a dream *inducer*, certainly is a dream *lubricator*. That is, it assists in loosening the rigid grip of **BETA,** allowing the Veil to open more tangibly into **ALPHA, THETA, DELTA**, and possibly even **GAMMA.** For this to work in a way that enables you to remain physically asleep and yet remain mentally aware that you're sleeping requires techniques which specifically target this skill.

The Five Brainwaves, along with their respective states of awareness, are listed below. Please note that these are generalizations. Readers interested in a deeper discussion of this topic are encouraged to consult the *Bibliography*:

GAMMA: Meditation. Learning. Paradoxical thinking. Microcosmic Orbit (the gamma wave literally follows this meridian. See *Chapter Nine* for more details). Compassion. Feeling blessed. In the "zone." Peak performance. Dream Mastery (as opposed to mere Lucidity, which is only a state of alert dreaming, but not necessarily a state used skillfully)

BETA: Awake. Task oriented. Problem solving. Activity. Test taking and exams. Socializing. Goal oriented.

ALPHA: Relaxed awareness. "Auto Pilot." Resting. Reading. Musing. Global attention. Zen meditation.

THETA: Dreaming. REM sleep. Creativity. "Aha!" Moments. Lucid dreaming. Astral projection.

DELTA: Deep dreamless sleep. Pellucid Sleep. Coma. Hibernation. Fertile ground for Premonitory dreams.

Some believe that the art of Dream Control lies somewhere between **THETA** and **DELTA**. There's some truth to this claim, but recent research out of Frankfurt University suggests that **GAMMA** is the dominant brainwave for consciously stepping behind the Veil and taking action. It truly is a significant find, for as we'll see in our discussion of various forms of meditation, Conscious Dreaming isn't so much a matter of dreaming *colorfully,* but rather, dreaming colorfully and *skillfully.*

The interesting thing about this electrical cerebral activity is that it's but one part of a rather complex electrical/Etheric anatomy. Let's take a closer look at this network of subtle energy with an eye to how it might relate to our topic.

The Tao of Dreaming

In Taoist Internal Alchemy and Traditional Chinese Medicine, it's known that bioelectricity (*Chi* or *Qi*) moves in specific patterns and pathways throughout the body. These "meridians" are intimately related to the seasons and tides of Nature. In these systems, it's believed that the nightly cycling and rebalancing of bioenergy plays a part in the types of dreams you have. For our purposes, the three most important of these *Qi* cycles are found in the *Du* and *Ren* channels of the Microcosmic Orbit ("Small Circulation"), the energy flowing in the Central Channel of the spine (*Chong channel*), and the pattern of *Qi* distribution throughout the Twelve Internal organs/Meridians ("Grand Circulation").

Bioelectricity flows strongest in the *Ren* channel during the daytime hours and strongest in the *Du* and *Chong* channels at night. The *Ren* channel, also called the Conception Vessel, runs from the nose-tip down the front of the torso and ends at the perineum. The *Du* channel, also called the Governing Vessel, runs from the perineum up the back of the spine, around the head, and ends at the nose-tip. The *Chong* channel, also called the Thrusting Vessel, flows down the central channel of the body along the interior of the spine, starting at the *Baihui* point on the top of the head and ending at the *Huiyin* point at the perineum.

The Microcosmic Orbit looks something like this:

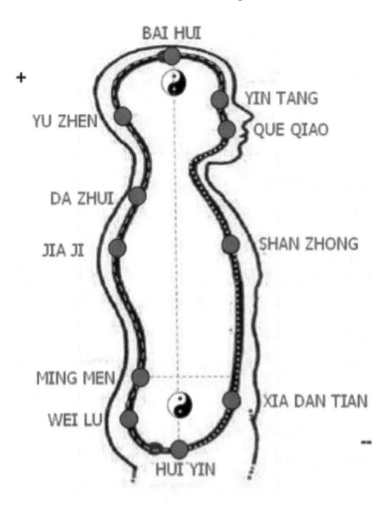

I'm introducing this to you now because we're going to be learning Microcosmic Orbit meditation in *Part Two* of this book along
with a practice called "Embryonic Breathing." The latter works
primarily with the ***Chong*** channel and the former with the ***Du*** and
Ren channels. The main reason I'm teaching them to you is because
Microcosmic Orbit and Embryonic Breathing practices are literally

Etheric System workouts. Etheric muscles support Astral muscles. Furthermore, a clean and healthy Etheric System supports and fuels Lucidity and makes it noticeably more *mobile* (more on this later).

It took me roughly four years of consistent practice to open the cavities running along the Microcosmic Orbit enough to sense the circulation of energy flowing along the **Ren** and **Du** meridians. Knowing how to cleanse and balance your *Qi* after Vivid or Lucid Dreaming and Astral Projection is an indispensable skill, and the Microcosmic Orbit practice is a powerful way to accomplish just that. Furthermore, Embryonic Breathing specifically targets the **Chong** meridian, and is the fastest method I know of for balancing and neutralizing the intense, and sometimes exhausting, energies of Subtle Body work.

In Traditional Chinese Medicine, they've discovered that the internal organs of the physical body are inextricably linked to the Twelve Primary meridians of the Etheric force. They also discovered, through centuries of trial and error, that the twelve organs and their corresponding meridians can be divided into six **Yang** organs (positively charged) and five **Yin** organs (negatively charged), like the two poles of a magnet (Some Taoists consider the Pericardium to be the 12th *Yin* organ.) Just as the Microcosmic Orbit is considered a "small circulation" of *Qi* (called *Small Cyclic Heaven*), the circulation of *Qi* through the Twelve Primary meridians is considered a type of "grand circulation" (called *Large Cyclic Heaven*). Whether this energy is circulating naturally without conscious assistance, or one is consciously circulating it with a technique, both *small* and *grand* circulations are inseparable and form a continuous energetic feedback loop within and around the body.

These organs/meridians are also associated with specific emotions and are most affected by them, for better or worse. They each have their own cycles and times of night and day when energy circulates most powerfully in them. It's important to know how to cleanse and balance these meridians to some degree because your "dream body" is also your *emotional* body, and intense dreams dramatically affect the way *Qi* circulates through your Meridians and internal organs. This is especially true for the five **Yin** Organs, which I'll list in a moment.

How far one chooses to go with these Taoist practices is entirely arbitrary, but this alignment with the Tao helps dream and Astral development considerably. You might call it the *Feng Shui* of the subtle-realms. To be clear, though, this is NOT a requirement. Most people with skills in Lucid Dreaming and Astral Projection know nothing about these Taoist concepts, although they often employ them without knowing it. I only include it as part of my system because I know it helps tremendously. These practices open doors not typically available to the average Veiler.

Please don't be intimidated by any of these concepts. It's going to be easier than you think. Believe me, one doesn't have to be an advanced Yogi/Yogini or Taoist Immortal to successfully employ these concepts. I'm certainly no master of them! Neither does one have to work with all the Meridians to reap benefits.

The Twelve Organs/Meridians and their corresponding emotions are as follows:

Gallbladder: Kindness. Cruelty. Joy. Cowardice.

Liver: Protectiveness. Cleanliness and Purity. Feeling Unclean or shy.

Lung: Sorrow. Fear. Openness. Clarity. Certainty. Anxiety. Vitality. Forthrightness.

Large Intestine: Irritable. Grounded. Bored. Bodily Awareness.

Stomach: Anger. Endurance. Tolerance. Rootedness. Instinctiveness. Excitement.

Spleen: Nostalgia. Fairness and Justice. Feeling Open or emotionally sluggish.

Heart: Protectiveness. Love. Courage. Passion. Morale. Devotion. Hatred. Anxiety.

Small Intestine: Anxiety. Over-emotional. Moodiness. Enthusiasm.

Urinary Bladder: Lack of confidence. Peacefulness. Fear. Embarrassment. Relaxation.

Kidneys: Sexuality. *Élan Vital.* Determination.

Pericardium: Protectiveness. Altruism. Devotion.

Triple Burner: Bodily Awareness. Sexuality. Appetites. Surrender. Mortality. Survival.

(NOTE: The pericardium is the sack which surrounds the heart and serves, among other things, as a lubricant and buffer for the heart. The emotions associated with the chest area in general share the same energetic and hormonal structure, so what affects the lungs will also affect the heart, and *vice versa.* More on this below.)

It's important to understand that the circulation of *Qi* follows an "entry" and "exit" phase through each of the twelve Meridians. When *Qi* is entering a meridian, its corresponding internal organ is becoming **Yang**. When *Qi* is exiting a meridian, its corresponding internal organ is becoming **Yin**. This is much like high and low tides in the sea, only the sea here is your Etheric System. This energetic dance between **Yin** and **Yang** is the generator which powers your behind the Veil travels. Without it, you'd have no fuel with which to think, move, feel, dream, or go Astral. The Etheric/*Qi* network becomes especially important when developing Astral Projection, and though it doesn't seem to play a dominant role in how *Vivid* your dreams are, it influences how *Lucid* you can become and especially how long you can sustain Lucidity. Your *Qi* status also affects the *type* of dreams you have. This is due to the powerful link between your Etheric System, your emotions, and the vitality of your will/desire.

For our purposes, it's not necessary to discuss the finer points of the *Qi* network. All we need to know are the basic energetic rhythms of this network, the corresponding emotions associated with the internal organs, and how we can balance them after an intense dream or other Subtle Body practice. Emotions behind the Veil can get intense, and it helps to know how to balance and circulate the energies associated with them to avoid *Qi* stagnation or potential illness. Remember, dreams are the cognitive reflection of the Etheric process of rebalancing *Qi* (Etheric energy). You're interfering with that process whenever you have a Lucid Dream and manipulate the dream content. The same holds true for Astral Projection. It's an often ignored, but very important, skill for a Veiler to learn how to balance these energies after stepping behind the Veil.

One of the reasons why the various Yogas of India and Tibet use the Chakra system is to show that all the emotions, along with their virtues and diseases, can be grouped together under one central theme. For example, the negative emotion associated with the heart is *hatred*. However, the lungs are in the same vicinity as the heart (*Upper Burner*). The negative emotion associated with the lungs is *depression*. It goes without saying that too much hatred will exhaust you and eventually lead to a depressed state. Conversely, people often hide their sadness behind a facade of anger. This leads to more depression and eventually to heart and lung diseases. This shows the reciprocal nature of the energies within a given Chakra area. We're not using the Chakra system here because the timings of the Meridians are often separated by many hours, the heart and lungs being just one example. The Chakras become more central when cultivating meditative skill and Pellucid Dreaming, which is more *stationary* than, say, Lucid Dreaming or Astral Projection (more on this later).

Lastly, the *Triple Burner* has no emotion *per se* associated with it. The Triple Burner's *feeling* is centered more on issues of mortality and survival and is more fundamental and consistent than the other "organs." You may be wondering why something like the Triple Burner, which vertically encompasses many other internal organs, is considered an internal organ. The reason is that the Chinese consider the biological internal organs and their corresponding Meridians to be inseparable, much like the ocean isn't separate from its waves and the sun isn't separate from its rays. The Triple Burner is best thought of as the *metabolic* function of the *second*, *third*, and *fourth* Chakras (ascending), with their respective cluster of internal organs sharing an energetic sympathy, as described in the above example of the heart/lungs/pericardium matrix.

The Triple Burner's *Qi* becomes most active at night. This is because the energies typically burned up in the activities of the day, particularly the energies employed in the digestive process, are now freed up to focus on the rebalancing of *Qi* in the body. At night, in the cold months, when ill or depressed, or when fasting, the guardian *Qi* (aura energy) and body heat shrink inward toward the bone marrow and internal organs to protect and nourish them. This assists in the burning away of toxins and the replenishing of hormones. I believe that this is one reason why it's called the Triple *Burner*.

In conclusion, our concern is primarily the Five **Yin** Organs of the Meridian system as they appear to be the ones most affected by intense dreaming and OOBE. I only include the Six **Yang** Organs for introductory purposes. That way, those wishing to advance their training further will have a handy reference.

The Five *Yin* Organs are:

- **Heart**
- **Lungs**
- **Liver**
- **Kidneys**
- **Spleen**

Now that we've been introduced to some of the rudimentary concepts with which we'll be working, let's look at some of the dream types and how we can spot, qualify, and ultimately use them to our advantage.

CHAPTER TWO
THE SEVEN CATEGORIES OF DREAM

Below you'll find a list of some of the myriad types of dream. This is by no means an exhaustive list and the order is totally unimportant. I've only listed the dream types most related to our topic.

- The Hedonistic Dream.
- The Physio-Etheric Dream.
- The Premonitory Dream.
- The Biographical Dream.
- The Archetypal Dream.
- The Educational Dream.
- The Astral Dream.

These categories are not rigid compartments, and they do shade into each other more often than not, but for the sake of convenience let's take them one at a time. I can't stress enough how important this section of the book is to your navigation of the world of dreams and Astral realms. You may even be able to add to this list sometime in the future, and I hope that you do! In *Part Two* of this book, I'll show you how you can use these categories to get the most out of your dream journaling. Life behind the Veil can get confusing and it helps to be able to make sense out of the kaleidoscope of phenomena encountered there.

The Hedonistic Dream

To understand this type of dream we could do worse than to consult that most notorious doctor of dreams, Sigmund Freud. Most of us are familiar with Dr. Freud's apparent obsession with sexuality and its expression in the dreams, slips of the tongue, and body language of those who repress it, confuse it, or fail to fully express it. In *Dream Psychology: Psychoanalysis for Beginners* (1921), Freud wrote:

> "The more one is occupied with the solution of dreams, the more willing one must become to acknowledge that the majority of the dreams of adults treat of sexual material and give expression to erotic wishes."

Unfortunately, Freud seemed to completely ignore, or didn't deem worthy of attention, the subtler psychological, physical, and spiritual aspects of human life as seen from outside his sexual theory. Consequently, he saw their expression in dreams as just another example of the sex drive gone mad. Should one's dream be of a spiritual nature, for example, Freud would say that this was no more than "sublimated" sexuality: the dreamer is unconsciously attempting to merge with a divine personage due to unfulfilled sexual desires with a mortal man or woman (oftentimes one's own mom or dad!)

It would take a petulant child of Freud's own Secret Committee, Dr. Carl Gustav Jung, to break with Freud and reaffirm what he called the "the essentially religious nature of the human psyche." We'll return to a fuller discussion of Dr. Jung later. For now, though, we must give the Father of Psychoanalysis his due praise, for despite his short-sighted castigation of all things outside the confines of his sexual theory (he called other theories "the black tide of occultism"), Dr. Freud was obviously highlighting a very common form of dream.

Up-to-date research on dreams reveals that Freud was, at the very least, onto something. Researcher Daniel M. Wegner, Ph.D. demonstrated how the suppression of thoughts and urges reappeared in the dreams and thoughts of research subjects in his Thought Rebound Experiment. Basically, Dr. Wegner and his colleagues discovered that whenever someone suppresses or otherwise ignores a thought, urge, or intuition, the rejected impulse resurfaces in the form of dreams or incessant thoughts. For many people reading this, this will seem like common sense. However, many people are unaware of these clandestine psychic processes. Add to this the fact that a great deal of our subtler energies often gets tangled up in largely unconscious complexes: it's possible to misread and misplace our energies and their related drives, causing otherwise discreet urges to tangle and intertwine. These "complexes" become what are known as "neuroses", "fixations", "fetishes", and so on.

Many hedonistic dreams, particularly the sexual variety, are influenced by the increase in sex hormones during deep sleep. It's important to understand that not all hedonistic dreams are sexual in nature, though they're almost always linked to sexual energy. The so-called pleasure-principle is a complex phenomenon. Many things which seem sexual have a non-sexual root, and *vice versa*. Many hedonistic dreams involve flying, not the other "F" word. Indeed, flying is by far one of the most coveted Lucid Dream of which I'm aware! Other dreams which fall under the heading of "Hedonistic" are dreams about eating fantastic feasts, breathing underwater, commanding the elements of nature, and interacting with celebrities. The true significance of willful pleasure dreams is what they say about the dreamer, namely what he or she feels is lacking in daily life, addictions, and unexpressed energy. For our purposes, the take-home message is found in the adage:

"All that is hidden in you shall be revealed."

Taoists believe that our *Third Eye* became closed because we began to hide things from ourselves and others. You can choose to take this with a grain of salt or experiment with it and see where it leads. Properly understood, Conscious Dreaming is a powerful form of Psychoanalysis.

Lastly, one of the rewards of learning how to manipulate the dream world is that there truly is no limit to what you can experience. It's just downright fun! Having any adventure you desire at your fingertips and getting all of your senses involved in the process can be exhilarating, even addicting, which is where balance becomes a top priority. As one Veiler I know once put it:

> "I'm not totally for it. In fact, creating dreams became something of a guilty pleasure for me and I got a little carried away with it. I think there's value in both playing with dreams and letting them just play by themselves. The subconscious mind needs to be allowed to do its own thing sometimes."

How far down the Rabbit Hole are *you* willing to go?

The Physio-Etheric Dream

To understand how physiological processes affect the way we dream we need to know a bit about the changes our bodies undergo while sleeping. In *Chapter One*, we learned about the Five Brainwaves and their measurement on an electroencephalogram (EEG). We saw how these brainwaves and their related states of consciousness can be self-induced by artists, monks, and anyone with a little natural talent who takes the time to cultivate this skill. It serves our purposes to understand that the body, like everything else in Nature, has its own tides, rhythms, and seasons; and these biological seasons are intricately bound to the tides and timings of Great Nature. For our purposes, one of the most important of these bodily rhythms is called the Circadian Rhythm.

The Circadian Rhythm has aptly been dubbed the "internal clock" of the physical organism. Without getting too technical, the function of this internal clock is to enable the body's chemistry to conform to the patterns of light and dark one regularly experiences. A tiny pinecone shaped gland located deep within the brain, the Pineal Gland, responds to the approaching night (or darkness) by secreting a hormone called Melatonin which, as we've seen, induces sleep. I'd like you to take note of the importance of establishing a regular Circadian

Rhythm. I realize that this is impossible for some people in today's jet-lagged world, but it really is worth serious consideration if you wish to gain conscious control of your dreams in a healthy manner.

So how does one establish a Circadian Rhythm? Well, it depends upon a few factors. For starters, working the Night Shift is the absolute worst thing you can do. Also, going to bed at different times every night is a no-no. The best way to honor your own internal clock is to follow the Sun. That's all there is to it! The bodymind is a creature of habit and will get used to performing certain tasks at specific times once a regular pattern is established, so it helps to align yourself to the tides and timings of Nature to see the best and most balanced results.

Perhaps the most well-known physiological process believed to affect dreaming is the digestion of food, especially the food we eat just prior to going to bed. Although studies indicate little to support this claim, they do however show that eating does affect the way we recall our dreams. Dr. Gary Wenk, in his informative book, *Your Brain On Food,* even suggests eating a peanut butter and jelly sandwich before going to bed to provide the brain with the right amount of sugar it needs to fuel the dream state!

Also, pay attention to the seasons and how they affect you. Anniversaries, birthdays, and so on, also stimulate certain types of dream. Of course you may have to compromise with the demands of work, family, and so on, but try to go to sleep when the Sun goes down or shortly thereafter. Arrange your sleeping space in such a way that you can ensure a good night's sleep without interruption, and align your body with the Earth's magnetic field (more on this later) as the pineal gland has tiny magnetic crystals within it that resonate with the magnetic fields of the Earth, Sun, Moon, and other sources (called *Pulsed Electromagnetic Fields* [PEMF]).

Lastly, make sure your sleeping environment is pitch black, well ventilated, not too cold or hot, and try to wake up at Sunrise or shortly thereafter. Once you've established a rhythm, I'll introduce you to a technique called "the 4:00 am method," which has helped countless people in their quests for Dream Control, Astral Projection, and Spiritual Enlightenment *(Chapter Three).* With this in mind, let's examine two physiological processes you can utilize to your advantage while practicing Conscious Sleep.

Breathing

While we're awake the average breathing pattern is erratic with alternating patterns of shallowness and depth. This is due to factors such as emotional response, exercise and work, the neurotransmitter Serotonin, daytime fluctuations in the Endocrine System, and ingrained breathing habits. During sleep, however, breathing rhythms become a bit more predictable, alternating between deep and slow during dreamless sleep (Delta) and becoming more erratic during **REM** phases of dreaming (Theta). Unless sleep disorders are present—such as apnea, asthma, insomnia, restless leg syndrome, and so forth—this tends to be the norm for most sleeping humans.

One of the worst postures for breathing during sleep is the "supine" posture. This is the posture in which one lays on one's back. While great for Astral Projection and various yoga practices, the supine posture is terrible for sleep, promotes mouth-breathing, and puts unnecessary strain on the lungs. A wonderful posture for healthy breathing during sleep is the so-called Fetal Posture. Although we won't be employing it in any of our practices, once you gain some skill in Lucid and Pellucid Dreaming, give it a try and you'll no doubt see what I mean.

That's not to say that any other posture precludes Conscious Sleep, only that certain postures can adversely affect breathing and how much oxygen the Lucid brain receives during sleep. Personally, I've found that the ideal posture can be achieved by elevating the upper body on roughly a forty-five-degree angle. Hospital beds, for example, have this feature. There are also Memory Foam Wedges that serve the same purpose. In this way one can still utilize the benefits of sleeping on one's back without having to worry about the negative consequences of doing so. This elevated posture is midway between lying down and sitting up, signaling the subconscious to remain slightly alert but relaxed enough to fall asleep.

Certain supplemental practices such as the yogic practice called Savasana, Sung Breathing, Massage and Stretching, even increasing Magnesium in your diet, can promote better Basal Breathing habits and the amount of oxygen which the brain receives. In *Chapters Six* through *Nine,* we'll give these practices a closer look. None of them are necessary to begin working behind the Veil, but I assure you that they do help significantly.

Digestion

We've already seen how digestion may affect how we dream. But what about Lucid Dreams in which the dreamer experiences digestion in a dreamlike context? A rather interesting type of Lucid Dream, but one not often discussed, involves a synesthesia in which digestive and other metabolic processes are experienced as color, music, smells (very rarely), changes in body size, shape and location, as well as all manner of psychedelic hallucinations. This is admittedly very rare, as most of our dreaming involves a sort of numbing of the physical senses as we enter the "dream-body." In my experience, this type of dream has less to do with the act of digestion and more to do with the readjustment of bioelectricity in the body.

Anyone with an intermediate to advanced level of cultivation in any Subtle Body practice is acquainted with the peculiar sensations which often accompany the movement of lifeforce in and around the body. Whether one practices Tai Chi, Yoga, Feldenkrais, Taoist Alchemy, or what have you, one eventually becomes intimately familiar with these energetic/neuronal sensations. This is especially true during sleep as the Gross Body relaxes and the Subtle Body expands. A major storage center of bioelectricity is located about three inches below the navel and three finger-widths inward toward the spine (more on this later). From this perspective, one can see how the digestive process might interfere with, or at least influence the movement of this energy.

Most Subtle Body arts share the advice never to eat a heavy meal before or after Subtle Body practice. When we consider the fact that dreaming and OOBE are subtle-realm phenomena it becomes clear that digestion plays a role in how successful we are in consciously tapping into those skills. Indeed, the practice known as *fasting* works to purify the bodymind since digestion "grounds" one's energies and slows down the circulation of bioelectricity. In other words, so much energy is used up in the digestive process that there isn't enough left over for detoxification, Subtle Body exercise (such as dream work), or spiritual practice.

One of the reasons why many sages advocate a vegetarian diet is due to the muddying of one's Subtle Body energies with the fear, karma, and "fight-or-flight" hormones said to be trapped inside the muscle (meat) of the slaughtered animal. At some point in the cultivation of sensitivity to the Subtle Body and its needs, one becomes immediately aware when something negative has entered into one's bodymind. Whether it's a virus, a negative environment, a malicious person close by, or even the approach of one's own death, a skilled Veiler can sense it immediately. Digestion, being so close to that Second Brain called "the gut," occurs primarily at a center where this sensitivity tends to be strongest.

***

Before moving on, I'd like to stress one more important facet of the Physio-Etheric dream type.

One of the functions of dreaming is to inform the conscious mind of important issues happening below the threshold of awareness. You don't have to take my word for it; you'll find this out for yourself soon enough. A great practice involves learning how to spot these messages as they appear in recurring dreams and your Dream Journal. Bear in mind that a dream symbol often represents more than one thing at the same time. Thus, to give one example, a recurring dream about losing your teeth can simultaneously mean that you feel powerless *and* that you need to see your dentist. Or a trend in your Dream Journal of, say, being unable to breathe can mean both a suffocating relationship *and* an approaching illness affecting your lungs.

I remember having one Vivid Dream that foretold a terrible spinal injury I sustained. I dreamt of a powerful brown horse that was being ripped apart along the axis of its spine. Three days later I injured the thoracic region of my spine so severely that I was forced to miss a great deal of work. The horse, a universal symbol of labor, is also a symbol of virility and confidence in one's physical abilities. That the horse in my dream was being ripped apart along its spine symbolized an approaching spinal injury that would not only affect my job, but also my joy and confidence as a man of intense physicality.

I highly recommend the Subtle Body practices listed above. The books I've listed in the *Bibliography* should be enough to get you started. Especially recommended are any Subtle and Causal Body arts which train how to raise, store, and circulate lifeforce within and around the body. I've been deeply involved in these practices for over seventeen years now and can attest to their ability to assist in Conscious Sleep. To be clear, they aren't mandatory requirements for a Veiler, but I'd be lying if I said they weren't important. In *Chapter Six* I'll introduce you to two powerful practices for Subtle Causal Body development.

Now let's move on to the next category of dream. This type of dream is a bit controversial. It's called the Premonitory Dream.

The Premonitory Dream

It was the summer of 2012. I awoke from a terrible dream in which my wife was lying on the side of the road in front of a building. There was a sign in front with the word "Moe's" written on it. She was trying to tell me something, but appeared groggy or drunk and unable to form words properly. The dream had an aura of foreboding to it, and it really bothered me, so I told her about it the following morning. Two weeks later I received a frantic phone call in the middle of the night.

It was my wife…

She'd been in a terrible car accident. The car was a total loss but she, miraculously, walked away completely unscathed. Grateful that she was unharmed, I asked her where she was and if the police had been notified. She told me that she was somewhere in New Jersey in front of a restaurant called "Moe's Bar and Grille." I suddenly recalled the dream I'd had two weeks prior and reminded her of it.

She was just as shocked as I was…

The strange thing is that I'd come to live in New York only recently. I grew up in Western Massachusetts where the Moe's franchise doesn't exist. I'd never even heard of Moe's Bar and Grille before! My wife and I marvel to this day about how accurate that dream was in predicting her car accident. Granted, there were no automobiles in the dream but there was a road, a Moe's, my wife, and an ominous atmosphere.

That's four out of five!

When a dream predicts a future event, its technical name is Premonition. These prognostic visions are more common than you might think. In fact, even hugely successful persons the likes of Bill Gates and President Donald Trump have cited premonitions as a major source of their success. For a truly captivating discussion about premonitions, I highly recommend the book, *The Power of Premonitions: How Knowing the Future Can Shape Our Lives,* by Larry Dossey, M.D.

One rather interesting theory on premonitions proposes that they may be a biological function that evolved over time. This puts prognostic dreams in the same category as "hunches," "gut-feeling," "intuition" and "déjà vu."

Most of us can remember at least one time in our lives when our intuition told us something that turned out to be true, whether it was a person who gave us a bad vibe, or a vacation plan that created in us a sense of dread, or just a general feeling of something bad about to happen. Perhaps premonitions tend to be primarily of negative events because the ability evolved to ensure our survival. Like my wife's car accident, there tends to be in premonitions a psychic attempt to prevent emotional pain, loss, injury, and especially death.

I've been a Tarot card reader for over a decade now and I'm repeatedly impressed with how accurate the cards can be in stimulating the premonitory process, particularly in dreams. When I first set out to learn to read Tarot cards my interest was mainly in their usefulness as a psychoanalytical tool. I noticed that they were a great way to explore different issues in the life of the querent, as well as my own, in that they provide a creative and fun medium upon which to project the various issues with which we all grapple. Instead, I noticed the cards were doing more than that. I've seen them predict pregnancies, job promotions, infidelities, and much more. My opinion is that what we're calling "predicting the future" is just an expanded view of the present moment.

Besides the premonition about my wife's car accident, one of the most shocking premonitory dreams I've ever had involved someone whom I've never met! The dream took place in the studio apartment of a good friend of mine. He was sitting at his computer while a beautiful woman, a brunette of perhaps twenty years, was lying down on his bed behind him. She was wearing a short white skirt and had a tattoo covering almost the full length of her outer thigh. I introduced myself to her and she told me, in a hippie-chick sort of tone, that her name was *Breeze*. A few days later, I told my friend about my dream. He looked at me with astonishment. As it turns out, he did in fact recently meet and start dating a woman named *Bree*. The name was only two letters short of the name she gave me in my dream, but it gets even more strange. Not only was she in her early twenties, she was also a brunette, was a hippie-chick, and indeed did have a full-length tattoo on her outer thigh! I met her about a week later and confirmed it for myself.

Premonitions are just one example of how interesting things can get once you step behind the Veil. After all, people aren't supposed to be able to foretell the future or meet strangers in their dreams before they meet them in real life. To be sure, most people to whom I've told these stories think I'm either crazy or just plain lying. Perhaps you've already had a few of these experiences yourself? Well, if not, you will!

The Biographical Dream

Without doubt the most common type of dream involves events and personalities from the life of the dreamer. Indeed, the dream type which hardly needs an elaborate explanation is the biographical variety. Be that as it may, there are a few key points I'd like to highlight regarding this category of dream. After all, if dreams about one's personal history-in-the-making occur on a regular basis then these are precisely the dream scenarios we can readily tap into.

One of my most memorable Lucid Dreams involved a heavy metal band I'd never heard of, my wife (she shows up a lot!), and an ex-girlfriend. We were all hanging out in an apartment I lived in seventeen years ago. There was a song playing on the stereo by a band which the radio DJ called *Ichabod Krane*. My ex-girlfriend was in the living room drawing small cartoons on white paper (she was an artist) while chatting with my wife. The scene was so utterly improbable that I suddenly became aware that I was dreaming! I looked at my ex-girlfriend and said, "Wait! None of this is real. I'm dreaming right now."

To which she responded, "What are you talking about? Of course, this is real."

So, I took her hand in mine, lifted her to her feet, and then walked with her into the kitchen where my wife was preparing an elaborate feast. I looked at my ex-girlfriend and said, "Are you ready?"

I then rose with her through the air, through the kitchen ceiling, and onto the roof of the apartment building. She looked at me with a look of utter shock and exclaimed, "Holy shit!"

And the dream faded out like a movie as I woke up.

The above is just one example of how biographical elements can be used as triggers for Lucidity. I must point out that in the above dream I was *very* deeply asleep and *very* Lucid. I experienced my dream environment and the people in it as vividly as I experience them while awake. This was no mere reverie or fantasy. More importantly, though, is that three elements of my personal life—my wife, ex-girlfriend, and my old apartment—were present in the dream, and the very thought of these three figures casually occupying the same moment was so outrageous to *both* my conscious *and* subconscious mind that it assured that part of the brain I call "me" that I was in fact dreaming! This sort of thing happens to most of us in daily life. Whenever we find ourselves in a situation so absurd or improbable that it defies all reason we often exclaim, "I must be dreaming!"

Many Lucid dreamers consider Biographical dreams to be quite therapeutic. I agree with this evaluation. Just think about that recital you messed up back in the second grade. Or that embarrassing first date you went on with Mr. Right and spilled hot coffee all over him. Or that creative project you worked so hard on that never saw completion. Well, you can fall asleep and consciously ace that recital. You can move Mr. Right's coffee slightly to the left. You may even dream a solution to that creative project gone awry. Personally, I've experienced all kinds of closure and experienced a great deal of healing as a direct result of lucid Biographical dreaming. There truly is no limit to how far you can go once you learn the trick.

Oh! By the way. That heavy metal band, "Ichabod Krane," that was playing on the radio in my dream? I did an internet search on them the following morning. As it turns out, they do exist. Sure, that could be a coincidence.

But what if?

So now that we know that Biographical dreams are a wonderful place to begin utilizing the psychotherapeutic aspects of Lucid Dreaming, how do we begin doing so? Well, for starters, instead of manipulating the dream to do as you *want*, you can ask the dream to reveal what you *need* to learn from the central issue in the dream. For example, I've had many dreams about my deceased grandfather in which I became Lucid and asked him what it is he wishes to communicate to me. I'm not necessarily saying that these were visits from beyond the grave. Maybe they were, maybe they weren't. In either case, the responses were always helpful, and it was nice to interact with the man who served as the only real father figure I had as a child. In one dream I even hugged him, and he was as real as he was while living!

It often happens that a key figure from the dreamer's past or present manifests, not as a person, but as a voice. This is especially common during the hypnagogic (falling asleep) and hypnopompic (waking up) stages of sleep. In my experience, these are the most common times at which voices of people known by the dreamer tend to manifest. Oftentimes these are nothing more than audible psychological loops from the past replaying like a broken gramophone record. These are also common "exit symptoms" of an impending OOBE.

If you're attempting an Astral Projection, it's best to ignore these voices and sounds and focus instead on getting up and out. However, if you're interested in opening a dialogue for psychotherapeutic purposes, be sure to ask targeted questions that are meaningful to you. The first question should almost always be, "What do you wish to communicate with me?" It's very important that you stay in charge of the conversation and banish all fear or temptation to ascribe any authority to the voices you hear. Simply listen to what's said and then record it immediately in your Dream Journal.

The Archetypal Dream

By far one of the most spiritually pregnant types of dream, the Archetypal dream, usually points to where the dreamer's psyche (the Self) is centered at the time. Soul-lessons that need to be learned are represented by one or more of the panoply of characters familiar to human beings regardless of race, culture, or creed. The figures of *the Teacher, the Guide, the Clown, the Hero, the Lover, the Mother, the Father, the God and Goddess*, and so forth, are among some of the central themes we encounter in this dream type.

The famous Depth psychologist, Carl Gustav Jung, made the study of archetypes part of the core of his life's work. Who could blame him? I'd be lying if I said that this wasn't also my favorite category of dream. You see, what Dr. Jung called Archetypes function as a sort of dream-like bridge between the human ego and the far greater energy (I'm tempted to say "power") of which the archetype is but a reflection. I say "reflection" because the archetypes truly do appear to use (or pass through) the medium of the collective human psyche and its common symbols in order to make themselves known (or comprehensible) to the recipient. In fact, the archetypes are unknowable. We only see the archetypal images and their innumerable combinations.

The appearance of an archetype in the life of an individual or group of individuals often contains trans-personal as well as trans-group elements. This should come as no surprise, really, because archetypes are part of the collective unconscious of mankind. For example, let's imagine that the archetype known as "The Lover" appears in the recurring dreams of some young woman. The archetype will typically appear not only in that woman's daily life, but often in the lives of those closest to her as well. This will often take the form of an actual man possessing all the qualities of the archetype as he appears in the dream (or they will be "projected" upon him). The woman will be haunted by a nagging feeling which goes on in the background of her psyche regardless of what task she's engaged in. Songs on the radio will seem to be playing with a message specifically for her. The birds, the clouds, the streams, the waves in the ocean, will all seem to whisper to her, "I love you!"

This emergence into the conscious sphere of a primordial force such as love can sometimes become so powerful that others can sense it without being given so much as a hint! Imagine that you're a single young woman. You're career driven, logical, sane, and practical, when you're suddenly invaded by this presence, not just in your nightly dreams, but also in your daily life. To make matters worse, you're head over heels in love with...

Well, with what exactly?

In India, there once lived a woman by the name of Meera Bai who had such a powerful archetypal encounter with the god Krishna that she came to believe she was his wife. Dr. Jung himself credited an archetypal manifestation of "The Teacher" whom he called Philemon for some of his greatest insights, and claimed to walk with him through his garden having many fruitful discussions. Jung also made it clear that he could often see Philemon as clearly as he could see a physical being. Readers who are interested in the byproduct of this archetypal relationship should consult *The Red Book,* by Carl Gustav Jung.

My opinion is that archetypes are entry points into the recipient's soul, driven by intelligences beyond our current understanding. That they contain what seem to be universal human principles is confirmed by their oftentimes contagious nature. For example, the "Loving Father God" of Jesus of Nazareth was so contagious that it often effected cures, transformed entire personalities, and even scared the wits out of (and eventually became the sole religion of) the Roman Empire! The Islamic prophet, Muhammad, apparently had an encounter with the archangel Gabriel so earth-shattering that it almost sufficed to usurp the tyranny of the Catholic Church six-hundred or so years ago. Saul of Tarsus, at one time one of the most virulent opponents of the early Christian cult, was temporarily physically blinded after an otherworldly encounter with the disembodied voice of Christ, an archetype in his own right (i.e., the Martyr). He then changed his name to Paul (St. Paul of the New Testament) and became one of the most passionate Christians known to history.

Many times it happens that to be in the grip of an archetype is to have psychic access to that which the archetype represents. Taken far enough, this can border on the prophetic and paranormal, as the above examples illustrate. However, the true importance of the emergence of an archetypal image in dreams has more to do with the lesson it carries with it for the dreamer. Next, we'll examine Educational Dreams and see how archetypes might be used to enhance the transformative power of dreams.

The Educational Dream

Of all the things for which journaling is useful, the first that comes to mind is the recognition of patterns over time. Symbols, characters, and recurring themes are an extremely common facet of a vivid dream life and learning to spot and decipher what they mean is an invaluable tool for personal growth. Therefore, keeping a descriptive and regular Dream Journal is extremely important. Not only that but cultivating the ability to become Lucid and communicate with these dream figures, navigate the dreamscapes, and consciously scan the environment of the dream for lessons, messages, and the solution to various problems, represents a real milestone in one's psychic development.

The Educational dream type takes on many different forms, some not so obvious at first blush. However, one needn't become an expert at interpreting dreams to spot them and work with them in a constructive way. For our purposes, there are three key points to learning from dreams. First, mostly all creative problem-solving in dreams occurs when **THETA** brainwaves predominate. Granted, one isn't necessarily Lucid when these dreams occur, but by way of dream-recall and journaling many patterns can be detected and messages decoded. Second, when one *is* having a Lucid Dream, then **GAMMA** brainwaves predominate. As we've already seen, **GAMMA** waves are associated with vision-logic and intuitive problem solving due to greater hemispheric synchronization in the brain. What that means is that *you* are present in the dream to learn and respond directly to challenges and insights. Lucid Dreams are also easier to recall upon waking. Third, once you begin tapping into the Astral type of dream you'll start learning on an entirely different level…literally.

In my own system, I've identified four subcategories of the Educational dream type. They are:

- **Creative/Intellectual**
- **Spiritual/Moral**
- **Psychological**
- **Psychosocial**

Let's discuss them one at a time and in the order listed above.

Creative/Intellectual

Have you ever grappled with a problem the solution of which was so elusive that you eventually gave up only to have the answer suddenly dawn on you in a sudden flash of illumination? Or have you ever forgotten someone's name and remembered it only after you've given up trying? These *Aha!* moments almost always occur in the shower, in the car or plane, on the toilet, or while lying down to rest. That is, they happen while **ALPHA** brainwaves predominate. Why? Well, when it comes to **ALPHA**, it's your worst enemy when trying to learn something new, but your best friend when trying to remember something you already know. Therefore, *trying* to remember a dream is an exercise in futility. You become like the fabled centipede who forgot how to walk because a mischievous toad asked him how it's possible to walk with so many legs. Because the centipede had never considered such a thing he became self-conscious and began to stumble.

When it comes to creative breakthroughs in dreams, the dreamer usually forgets immediately upon waking because he brings **BETA** where **ALPHA** should be. The best way to avoid this is, of course, to learn how to become Lucid while dreaming. However, there are two more methods that can be used to keep these breakthroughs from slipping away forever. First, don't just hop out of bed upon waking. Relax and lie there for a while and just watch the free flow of thoughts floating through your mind. Second, get out of bed slowly and leisurely. Third, open your Dream Journal and start writing everything you remember about your prior night's dreams. Do this as passively as possible, avoiding any unnecessary cerebration or intellectualizing. This isn't unlike the mindset adopted by psychics for automatic-writing.

Many famous films, musical compositions, and works of literature owe their creation to this dream mechanism. John Lennon's *#9 Dream* is just one example. Christopher Nolan, creator of the film *Inception,* wrote the film based on his own experience as a Lucid Dreamer. The Surrealist painter Salvador Dali's famous *Persistence of Memory* painting came from his dreams. The poet Edgar Allen Poe wrote many of his poems based on his Vivid and Lucid dream life. The poems *Dream Land* and *A Dream Within a Dream* are the most notable examples. As a musician and poet, I've composed music, poetry, and even came up with the titles to two of my books, all from the creative power of Lucid Dreaming.

Spiritual/Moral

These are the dreams which reflect back to us our system of values, priorities, philosophy, and cultural ethics. Sometimes these manifest as one or more of the archetypes, at other times as people we know, or simply as a moralistic theme. Political dreams also fall into this category insofar as they embody one's political philosophy or cultural background. How *self-centric*, *ethno-centric*, or *world-centric* this variety of educational dream is will depend upon the dreamer's level of spiritual growth. After all, what we value is based largely upon our capacity to see perspectives other than our own or those which we borrow from our cultural environment.

Pay close attention to who the primary focus is in these dreams. If the focus is you, take note of what you *feel* more than what you *think* about what you feel. Do you feel guilty? Elated? Superior? Inferior? More importantly, how (if at all) does the theme apply to your everyday life? Also, don't take this sort of dream as gospel. It isn't. It's simply a mirror of your own values. The important thing is to ask yourself whether your values are evolving or arrested in their development.

The value of spotting this kind of dream lies in how honestly our subconscious mirrors back to us how we really feel as opposed to how we think we should feel and behave. The lessons of these dreams are found in the recognition of disparity or accord between our moral code and our true level of growth. What you're driven to do versus how you believe you should conduct yourself is a source of tremendous waste of psychic energy. There's a lot of truth in that old saying of Jesus:

"If thine eye be single then thy whole body shall be filled with light."

These dreams remind us to be authentic rather than phony-holy. Even if you're a confirmed miscreant, it's better to be a conscious miscreant than a pretentious saint. Just try it! When you begin to see these patterns in your journal entries, be painfully honest with yourself. At first, it's probably going to be unflattering. Maybe not, but most likely, yes. Just allow the raw awareness of the facts to operate and go to work on you. If you resist then you'll build a wall between you and your daemon, between you and your subconscious mind. In fact, it's this psychic resistance that creates the Veil! Without any resistance the Veil will simply evaporate.

Psychological

Obviously, all dreams are to an extent psychological. After all, the entire process is a phenomenological process occurring in your psyche. Even Astral travel is registered and interpreted by your brain and mind. So why include a sub-category of dream called *psychological*? Well, there really is a specific kind of dream that centers solely on the dreamer's emotions, obsessions, desires, goals, shadow repressions, and so on. These dreams are very difficult to tease apart from the *psychosocial* dream because our personal psychology is unavoidably situated in a meshwork of social interactions, cultural conditioning, and familial ties. However, I think it's important to treat them separately whenever possible for the simple fact that how you feel as an individual is just as important as how and when you choose to share those feelings with the world around you, just as it's equally important to be open to other views and perspectives coming from the world around you even if that means having to put your own feelings aside. So, a dream about your ill-tempered mother-in-law may not necessarily include how angry she makes you feel, and a dream about how angry she makes you feel may overshadow the various reasons why she's ill-tempered.

It's important to leave room in your dream journal for both *I* and *Thou*.

A common manifestation of the *psychological* dream is that of repressed and unwanted thoughts, urges, and emotions. Because these repressed energies can never truly be banished (they are yours after all), they are projected onto the world around you and appear frequently in dreams as monsters, angels, animals, or people you may or may not know. We can repress our undesirable and desirable traits equally. The technical term for this repository of banished energy is Shadow. For over a decade I was haunted by a recurring shadow-symbol in my dreams: a tornado...

To this very day I'm sometimes revisited by it. I noticed years ago that the tornado would appear in times of insecurity and repressed rage. Today, whenever this symbol appears in my dreams I try to become Lucid and communicate with the twister or, if that fails, run toward it! Also, I ask myself how or if I'm repressing my anger and fear and what I can do to open to these feelings and allow them to flower and self-liberate. I also inquire where I might need to tie up loose ends and create a more stable foundation for me and my family.

Pay special attention to figures in dreams that resist control. In my example of the tornado, the twister would sometimes bend to my will and at other times would conquer me no matter how Lucid I was or how hard I tried to stare the thing down. In the former case, the tornado's stubbornness was an indication that I felt powerless in the face of some pressure from my environment and the powerful emotions triggered thereby. In the latter case, the twister's cooperation showed that these forces had shrunk to a manageable size. Not only that, there's every reason to believe that by facing and subduing these recalcitrant dream figures we plant the subconscious seed of courage needed to face the situations and people they represent.

Lastly, there's a big-picture aspect to the psychological dream. The nature of the overall Self is cyclic, much like seasons. The psyche moves in spirals and often has patterns of regression, obsession, evolution, and plateaus. It's very helpful to be able to spot these patterns. Just think about it. If you know that winter will arrive soon then you can plan accordingly. If you know that a storm is coming, you can take the necessary precautions and psychologically prepare yourself for the challenge. In other words, by paying attention to the patterns in your Dream Journal, becoming Lucid, and gaining control over how you interact with the events and personalities in your dreams, your intuition will grow, and you'll be able to sense and creatively respond to the changing seasons of your psyche.

Psychosocial

The *psychosocial* dream rarely presents itself without at least something of the *psychological* element alongside it. After all, no man or woman is an island, and we are inextricably linked to one another regardless of caste, color, culture, or creed. From the moment we take our first breath we become members of the Order of Co-Creators. As a direct consequence of birth, we can't think a thought, write a grocery store list, plan a career, or have a dream without borrowing from or contributing to the social network that comprises humanity. In fact, even before we're born we exist as one being within another being, in the womb of our mother. Therefore, it's no surprise that our individual psychology is not so "individual" after all.

That's not to say that individuality should then dissolve into the system of intersubjectivity and lose all sense of uniqueness, but we must bear in mind that the individual and the collective arise *at the same time*. We treat them separately because the language of crowds differs from that of individuals. We see this fact even in small relationships. Just look at the differences in "love-language" between a man and a woman! Or the vast differences in the communicative capacity of an adult and a child.

It's a good idea to list the psychological and psychosocial categories alongside each other in your Dream Journal. That way it becomes easy and convenient to contemplate and record them in the same entry. For example, if I'm having a dream about wandering naked through the halls of my old high school in full view of a pointing and laughing audience, then the *psychological* element would be the symbol of my own insecurities (nakedness/being laughed at), and the *psychosocial* element would be that of my old high-school. After a while you'll be able to distinguish between the two intuitively, and this intuition will spill over into your life.

The questions that define the *psychological* dream are: *How do I feel? What do I think?*

And the questions that define the *psychosocial* dream are: *Where does this take place? What are the rules here?*

If you keep these differences in mind, you should have no problem spotting them, teasing them apart, and seeing how they interact.

From there, it's up to you to bring more awareness and care into these areas of your life and apply what's being revealed.

***

Lastly, when dealing with Educational dreams, you're especially looking for:

- Recurring dreams
- Dreams that feature immovable, uncontrollable, and persistent people, places, and things.
- Dreams that contain solutions to creative, spiritual, intellectual, and any other kind of problem.

If these elements are present, you're dealing with the Educational dream type.

The Astral Dream

Out of all the different dream types, none is more misunderstood, debated over, and misrepresented than the Astral dream. Go ahead and scan through any number of books on Astral Projection or Lucid Dreaming and the first thing you'll notice is the uncanny ambivalence of most authors on whether these two are separate or the same phenomenon. Where one author defines Astral Projection as a Lucid Dream in the Astral Body, another will define Lucid Dreaming as Astral Projection in the Dream Body.

Some authors even distinguish between Astral Projection and OOBE, dubbing the latter an "astral dream" and the former a 100% pure Astral journey into the physical world or the so-called Astral Planes. To be honest, I don't think half of them know what to think on the matter. From experience I can tell you that the latter view makes more sense *practically*, but neither of them can hope to make sense *empirically* because there's currently no scientific method to fully measure and qualify the many varieties of OOBE.

But they're all experiences *out of body*…

Whether you're having a Lucid Dream, Astral Projection, or a Near Death Experience, you're still experiencing yourself as existing separately from your physical body. Furthermore, in all of these experiences, you're fully conscious and aware of what's happening.

You're not asleep, at least not cognitively. Also, the only true way to know and apply the differences between an Astral Dream, Astral Projection, and a Lucid Dream is to test the beings, times, and events encountered in each and confirm or refute them as existing solely in the mind or as separate phenomena. For example, I once did this by looking at the time on my stove's digital clock after going Astral. The time read 5:37 am. I then came back to my physical body, woke up, and walked into the kitchen to check the time. The clock read 5:40 am.

The exact amount of time it would've taken me to go from the Astral to waking up and walking into the kitchen is approximately three minutes!

Coincidence? Perhaps. Perhaps not. Regardless, this is the kind of proof one should look for when trying to tease apart the various types of OOBE. Unfortunately, this isn't easy to do, especially when dealing with the Astral Planes. The only exception is the validation granted by Premonition, details given by Astral beings, or situations regarding events beyond the Veiler's knowledge which can be confirmed or refuted.

But what's the difference between the Astral Plane and an Astral Dream? Aren't they two ways of describing the same thing?

Well, not exactly.

Recall the story about the phantom light in the *Introduction* to this book? Well, therein lies the secret key to the *Astral Plane/Astral Dream* conundrum. How so? First, notice that the ghostly light descended from the top bunk as an obvious response to my childish fear of the dark. Due to the obviousness of the thing, this serves as a perfect example of how a psychic element can appear as an Astral apparition, but it doesn't necessarily always happen that way. There are things floating around in the depths of the psyche which, if we were suddenly faced with their externalization, we wouldn't recognize them as belonging to us at all; but they do.

The point?

There exists an "in-between" state in which internal psychic processes appear as external phenomena, and how to tease apart "I" from "Thou" in this regard is one of the most important skills a Veiler can cultivate.

Consider the well-known "exit symptoms" of an OOBE. Most people hear voices and sense presences in the room. Powerful vibrations and sleep-paralysis are also extremely common exit-symptoms. Many people feel hands touching their skin and hair. Some people hear buzzing, banging, popping sounds and sounds that resemble an arcade. Sometimes the voices heard are familiar while others are not. There's almost always a feeling of floating or sometimes falling or sinking. Now, the same exact symptoms often occur as one moves from awake to Lucid Dreaming. These are simply the sensations which accompany going behind the Veil, but are the voices and visions and sensations always Astral? Or are they all just symptoms of a Lucid Dream?

Yes, and yes!

When you visit a new country for the first time the language and customs may appear very strange in some ways and familiar in others. Stay long enough and you'll eventually learn the language and customs and what was once confusing will become common. That's because, despite our cultural differences, human beings have more in common than not. The same goes for the Astral and Dream planes. Let me paint a better picture so that the point is clear.

The dreamscape is a sort of intermediate state between the Physical, Etheric, and Astral realms. The *Physical* has more in common with the *Etheric* just as the *Dream* has more in common with the *Astral*. As one initially transitions from awake to Lucid Dreaming, the sensations of the Subtle Body become more pronounced. Feelings of sinking or floating, of being touched, vibrations, and so forth, are all extremely common. However, once the physical body is completely asleep while the mind remains aware, sensations of the Astral Body become more pronounced. Here's where the well-known exit-symptoms of OOBE often begin. Now, if any attention is given to the voices or visions at this time, then one typically either enters a Lucid Dream (where Astral elements may blend in) or falls totally under the spell of **THETA** and has a non-lucid dream. Become a little more experienced with Dream Control and you'll eventually come to see the difference between psychological and Astral Dream phenomena. It takes time and consistent practice, but this much is clear:

Lucid Dreaming and Astral Projection are two different experiences and render different data.

They might be two expressions of the same dissociative reflex, but in practice Lucid Dreaming belongs to the *Veil of Dreams* and Astral Projection belongs to the *Veil of Ghosts.*

But what if one wishes to bypass the Lucid Dream and have an Astral Projection? The trick is simple but not at all easy. What you must do is this: Ignore the exit-symptoms!

That's right. Pay no attention to the vibrations or the voices or visions. A very difficult thing to do because for most people these are nothing short of hypnotic. I can't tell you how many times I'd lay down in bed, eager to step behind the Veil, only to stop at the brink of success because of good ole' fashioned laziness. It can still be difficult at times, but time has given me an almost cavalier attitude toward exit-symptoms. As with anything else worth doing, fear is just a mask worn by wonder to test your readiness to enjoy her.

Now let's take a closer look at this thing called *Out of Body Experience*, shall we? In the following chapter we'll go somewhat in-depth about some of the more controversial aspects of Astral Projection and Lucid Dreaming. We'll discuss the controversial topic of "entities" and other ghostly encounters. We'll learn a bit more about the differences and similarities between Astral and Lucid. Finally, I'll give some personal examples of where the line between them blurs or disappears altogether.

Let's get started!

CHAPTER THREE

ASTRAL PROJECTION VS. LUCID DREAMING: SIGNS AND SYMPTOMS

As we learned in *Chapter One*, Conscious Sleep has been around for a very long time. Whether in Egypt or Tibet or ancient Greece, we find examples of this art scattered throughout the halls of history. However, the phenomenon known today as Lucid Dreaming was first introduced to the Western scientific community in the year 1913 by a man named Frederik van Eeden.

Here's what he had to say about it:

> "The seventh type of dreams, which I call lucid dreams, seems to me the most interesting and worthy of the most careful observation

and study. Of this type I experienced and wrote down 352 cases in the period between January 20, 1898, and December 26, 1912.

"In these lucid dreams the reintegration of the psychic functions is so complete that the sleeper remembers day-life and his own condition, reaches a state of perfect awareness, and is able to direct his attention, and to attempt different acts of free volition. Yet the sleep, as I am able confidently to state, is undisturbed, deep and refreshing. I obtained my first glimpse of this lucidity during sleep in June, 1897, in the following way. I dreamt that I was floating through a landscape with bare trees, knowing that it was April, and I remarked that the perspective of the branches and twigs changed quite naturally. Then I made the reflection, during sleep, that my fancy would never be able to invent or to make an image as intricate as the perspective movement of little twigs seen in floating by."

Thanks for that, good Doctor!

Then again, in the year 1975, another pioneering scientist named Alan Worsley performed an experiment at the University of Hull in England. He successfully signaled to researcher Keith Hearne that he was Lucid. Upon gaining Lucidity, he signaled Worsley with a predetermined set of eye movements. Finally, in 1978, researcher Stephen LaBerge conducted the same experiment and documented his findings for the greater scientific community.

As you can see, the art of stepping behind the Veil has a bright future!

That's certainly good news, but what about research in the field of Astral Projection? As we learned in *Chapter Two* in our discussion of the Astral Dream category, the Lucid Dream and Astral Projection experience have more similarities than not. Many researchers believe that they're the same thing, and one of their arguments is:

If Astral Projection is different from Lucid Dreaming, then why can't we do it while awake? Why must we first go to sleep as a prerequisite for going Astral?

Well, first, there are some Veilers who insist they *can* do it while awake! Regardless, this question stems from an incomplete understanding of the Gross, Subtle, and Causal aspects of the human bodymind. Asking why one must be asleep to go Astral is much like asking why one must be awake to fly an airplane. To fly an airplane, you need to use the physical body to operate the aircraft, yes? Also, you need to be awake in order to use your physical body, right? Well, in order to access the Astral Body, you need to put your physical body to sleep.

Remember this: To have profound sensory experiences while you're awake you need to fully occupy your Gross Body. To have profound sensory experiences in your dreams you need to fully occupy your Subtle Body. To have powerful sensory experiences on the Astral Plane you need to fully occupy your Astral Body, which is really just the Subtle Body made mobile. Put simply, to have a full-sensory OOBE you need to put your physical body to sleep; otherwise you'll have one foot in the Gross Body and the other in the Astral Body.

However, one's neuronet can be trained and wired in such a way that it becomes capable of housing true Astral Projection. How so, you ask? Well, in the 120-Days Curriculum I'll be sharing with you some methods for doing just that. For now, though, consider the following study conducted by Adra M. Smith and Claude Messierwere of Ottawa University:

In their remarkable experiment, a young woman who claimed to have the ability to leave her body at will, was asked to prove it. What the researchers discovered was, at least from a neurological point of view, quite fascinating.

They found that this woman's brain was lighting up at centers usually reserved for complex kinesthetic image processing, spatial orientation, and body awareness in relation to the environment. In other words, she was *really* experiencing herself as separate from her physical body. Furthermore, she was wide awake while doing so!

The research team concluded that OOBE is a kinetic type of *synesthesia*. The latter is a peculiarity of cognition in which one perceives sound as color, color as physical sensation, physical sensation as smell, and so on. However, what the researchers failed to deduce was whether this young woman was in fact having an Astral Projection experience, or just a Lucid Dream performed while physically awake. (Later, I'll teach you how to do this.) Indeed, the latter could very well be a unique form of *synesthesia*, but the former may not be.

My opinion on the above experiment is that the volunteer isn't an Astral Projector. Rather, what she's doing is playing with her perception in a novel and creative way that paves the way for true Astral Projection. With proper training she'd undoubtedly make a fantastic Veiler, and her unique talent can most certainly be used as an Astral exit technique (more on this later), but my guess is that she's not having a genuine Astral exit during these experiments.

I include this experiment here to illustrate how easy it is to confuse behind the Veil experiences. An experiment on genuine Astral Projection would have to include the test of *real* Bi-Locationality. That is, the volunteer must be asked to project to a place he or she has never been, and then describe it in as detailed a manner as possible. That said, what these two researchers demonstrated is a wonderful example of the type of research that I'd like to see continue.

Another prominent researcher in the realm of Astral Projection is the well-known Veiler, Robert Monroe, founder of The Monroe Institute (TMI) in Virginia and author of the seminal book, *Journeys Out of the Body*.

Monroe was a rather interesting fellow, wearing many hats. He was a musician, a broadcaster, a soldier, a father, a husband, and an entrepreneur. He had his first Astral Projection experience in 1958, describing the ubiquitous exit-symptoms of sleep-paralysis, vibrations, and a bright light shining on him from somewhere above.

In 1978–1983, the United States military sent soldiers to the Monroe Institute to be trained in Astral Projection, the details surrounding which are predictably ambiguous.

Robert Monroe created the successful Gateway Voyage Program, which offers a gradual system comprised of "focus levels" that guides the practitioner into higher and more refined skill in OOBE. The program also features a TMI staple called Hemi Sync, which utilizes binaural beats sound technology for assisting in the OOBE process.

I purchased Monroe's program back in 2000 to research his methods. What I liked about it was the attention he gives to the loosening of the Subtle Body (though he doesn't call it that). In fact, I experimented with his method of inducing an OOBE by conjuring the sensation of "rolling like a log" while entering the first stage of sleep. It works wonderfully, and I use it to this very day. In the practice section of this book, I'll share this method with you so that you might benefit from it as well.

For those of you who are interested in learning Astral Projection, keeping your dream journal up-to-date, thorough, and organized is paramount to avoiding the Astral/Lucid confusion. Remember, both Astral Projection and Lucid Dreaming are equally *Out of Body* Experiences! The major difference between them is that the former involves real Bi-Locationality whereas the latter tends to take place right there in your bed, with the occasional influx of Astral elements ("astral dream"). It's my wish that one of the contributions of this book will be to give clarification regarding this distinction.

Entities, Exit-symptoms, and Imagination

> "There exists an 'in-between' state in which internal psychic processes appear as external phenomena, and how to tease apart 'I' from 'Thou' in this regard is one of the most important skills a Veiler can cultivate."

The reason I'm repeating myself here is because this topic is of the utmost importance, not only to becoming a skilled Veiler, but also so you don't lose your mind in the process. As the *Introduction* to this book has hopefully made clear, ignorance of the mind's film-projector-like nature can lead to all kinds of trouble. Psychologists refer to this "psychic film projector" as a *dissociative state,* and research shows that at least five percent of the world's population are to some extent dissociative. The reflective mind is, after all, a brain-function, the sole purpose of which is to compartmentalize, split, and reflect upon perceived reality. Of course, what constitutes a dissociative *state* versus a dissociative *disorder* is whether it enriches or encumbers your well-being and ability to function efficiently or qualify perceptions accurately. If you encounter something strange or inexplicable during your attempts at Lucid Dreaming or Astral Projection, and if you just take it at face value without knowing how to tell the difference between what's *out there* versus what's simply a projection of your own psyche, then you can very quickly lose all sense of proportion.

To illustrate just how far this psychic film-projector can go, allow me to share an experience that I had with a Ouija board when I was fifteen years old:

I was with a friend of mine in the basement of my house. He had sneaked in a Ouija board that he'd borrowed from his brother, a fact which would've brought out the Devil in my mother had she known about it. But there we were, hands on the planchette, asking if there were any spirits in my house willing to speak with us. Nothing happened at first, but soon the planchette began to move to "Yes." I accused my friend of moving it and he accused me, but then something strange happened. My friend asked the spirit for its name and, because it was close to Halloween, I thought the name "Dracula," and sure enough the planchette moved to "D" and then "R" and then "A," and so on. At that point my buddy *really* accused me of moving the planchette, but I was innocent of willfully moving it. He then asked at what age the spirit died. I thought of the number "thirty" and again the planchette mirrored my thoughts.

The peculiar thing about the above account is that I truly wasn't moving the planchette. And yet it still moved according to my thoughts. There were even times when it seemed to move ahead of my fingertips! How can this be? Subsequent research I did on the subject revealed one plausible explanation. According to this theory, minute electrical impulses coming from the nerve-endings in the fingertips are responsible for Ouija board phenomena. This makes sense as thoughts are also electrical impulses. Years later my mother introduced me to a hypnotist who demonstrated this for me in real-time. She took a piece of paper and drew the words "Yes" and "No" on it. She gave me a small pendulum and asked me to dangle it above the paper, using my dominant hand, between the words YES and NO. She then asked me to hold it steady while rapidly moving my eyes sharply from YES to NO. Soon the pendulum began to move from side to side without any conscious volition on my part. She then asked me to stop moving my eyes and focus only on the "Yes" side of the paper. To my surprise, the pendulum began to *pull* in that direction!

So much for communing with the dead…

In this section, I'll introduce you to some of the more common "entity" encounters experienced by most Veilers as well as a few of the more uncommon ones. Rest assured that at least seven out of ten reported entity encounters are without doubt a product of what I've called the "in-between" state of the psyche. Like a movie projector, the clandestine activities of the bodymind normally suppressed by wakeful consciousness are externalized and projected whenever your brainwaves drop down from **BETA** to **ALPHA** to **THETA** until they're terminated at **DELTA** or *actualized* at **GAMMA**. This is also the same mechanism used by hypnotists. These psychic projections can be so convincing that hypnotized subjects can even be physically burned and scarred by convincing them that they're holding something hot!

After all, seeing *is* believing.

For the same reason, someone having a nightmare about drowning will gasp for air just as someone might dream of going to the bathroom and wet the bed. The only difference between a Vivid Dream and a Lucid one is that in the former you're reasoning mind is unconscious whereas in the latter it's at least 40% involved in the experience. The same holds true for Astral Projection: *you must pass through the Dream Plane to get to the Astral Plane.* You're making these transitions *consciously* and are therefore exposed to the phenomena of these liminal states. Consequently, you'll experience many of the same phenomena whether going Lucid or going Astral, as we've seen.

But the question remains: How can one tell the difference between an entity and a psychic projection?

First, let's assume for the moment that entities do in fact exist. And for the sake of avoiding any religious or spiritual connotations, let's avoid words like *angel, demon,* or *ghost.* And let's also be assured that these experiences are, quite often, projections of the mind. That said, let me now list the various forms these experiences might take and then offer some personal experiences to demonstrate just how slippery this issue can be and how you might gain clarity. My hope is that you'll get an inkling, by way of illustration, of when you're dealing with a psychic projection and when you might be dealing with something altogether different.

Being Physically Touched

One of the most common "entity" experiences involves being physically touched. Sometimes this takes the form of being poked, or of one's hair being stroked, or head patted, someone kicking the bed, or even being slapped! Sometimes there are sexual elements to the experience. The usual response is, understandably, terror. I mean, if something can stroke my hair then what's to stop it from punching me in the face, right?

What you're experiencing, 99% of the time, is nothing more than a sort of groggy Lucid Dream.

You'll recall, in our discussion of the *Seven Categories of Dream*, the Physio-Etheric dream and its symptoms. Well, what you're typically experiencing when you feel like someone's touching you as you fall or wake from sleep is the bodymind relaxing and throwing off stress. They're in the same class as myoclonic or hypnic jerks and spasms. Because your mind is entering or just exiting the dream state, you interpret these sensations as being physically touched, poked, and prodded. Sometimes these sensations indicate an approaching Astral Projection, but more often than not they're nothing more than the symptoms of a Physio-Etheric dream. Depending upon your degree of Lucidity at the time of their occurrence, these sensations range from being rather vague to quite real.

Another explanation, barring neurological disorders, is digestion. In my experience, sensations of being poked in the lower back and abdomen are almost always a direct cause of gas or some other digestive issue. Once I even felt someone sticking their finger into my navel! Again, this is probably not some evil entity trying to possess your body or steal your soul. Chances are it's just an undercooked potato or an undigested bit of beef, to quote Mr. Scrooge.

Lastly, the sensation of being stroked is typically the rebalancing of *Qi* in the Meridians. However, I've often experienced this sensation when there was someone in the room. I often sleep with earplugs in my ears because my wife's an insomniac and frequently moves about the house throughout the night. I wake up for work every morning at 5:30 am, hence the earplugs. Well, there have been a few times I've been awoken from sleep because of the "skin stroking" sensation only to find that my wife had just walked into the room. It wasn't the wind because I sleep with the covers on, so my Etheric energy was probably reacting to her presence. That said, you'll probably notice that the sensation of being stroked is strongest during the Autumn and Winter seasons or in any cold and dry climate. This seems to have something to do with the peculiar relationship between *Qi* and bioelectricity. Also, if there are any powerful Electromagnetic Field (EMF) sources near your sleeping space such as WiFi, a cell phone, an electrical outlet in use, a digital meter on your home, or a plugged-in laptop, those will also produce much of the phenomena associated with entities.

So, until your bed sheets are ripped off of you by unseen forces or you wake up with your bed levitating five feet in the air, don't worry! You'll be okay.

Feeling Presences in the Room

In his classic book, *The Varieties of Religious Experience,* William James describes the experience of felt presences in the room as told to him by one correspondent. He writes:

> "An intimate friend of mine, one of the keenest intellects I know, has had several experiences of this sort. He writes as follows in response to my inquiries:
>
> " 'I have several times within the past few years felt the so-called 'consciousness of a presence.' The experiences which I have in mind are clearly distinguishable from another kind of experience which I have had very frequently, and which I fancy many persons would also call the 'consciousness of a presence.' But the difference for me between the two sets of experience is as great as the difference between feeling a slight warmth originating I know not where and standing in the midst of a conflagration with all the ordinary senses alert.' "

In other words, the feeling that you're being followed or stared at from across a crowded room is quite different from the feeling of an unseen presence in your room at night. Curiously, this type of "entity encounter" is one which happens not only while in bed but also while awake. More than any other version of the entity phenomenon, the feeling of a distinct but unseen presence is the one most often reported by people.

The thing which makes the *presence* so alarming, besides the obvious invasion factor, is that it's almost always accompanied by a specific ambience or mood. Sometimes the feeling is one of unutterable peace, sometimes joy or love, and at other times the mood is quite malicious and evil. Rarely, one first feels the presence and is then physically touched or spoken to. In such a case one's nerves are justifiably shaken. Whether pleasant or terrifying, the awareness of an unseen presence coupled with the sound of a voice or the sensation of being touched, leaves quite an impression on even the soundest of minds.

Are we dealing with an entity in these cases? Or is this just the good ole' film-projector playing a new movie? Should we contact a spirit medium or priest to come "cleanse" our home? Or maybe burn some sage and recite the rosary? Well, to be honest, it's when those methods *don't* work that you should begin to worry! Why? Because if what you're dealing with is truly a projection of your own mind then by your mind it can be dispelled. It's that simple. However, if what you're dealing with isn't a product of your psyche and does exist apart from you, then chances are it's going to resist a little. Think about it: if someone's robbing you or invading your home do you think praying will convince them to stop? No! On the other hand, if the presence is a product or your mind, then it will almost always flee or dissolve when confronted by a firm and fearless command. In fact, the test which I give to determine whether I'm dealing with a genuine entity or just a chimera of my psyche is this: *project a feeling of compassion and joy towards it!* Even if the presence doesn't disappear altogether it'll change its form to fit your mood.

I've been confronted by monsters that I was certain were real. I've projected kindness towards them only to watch them transform into sorrowful and wounded creatures. How can this be? Well, my conclusion is that the so-called monsters were really just projections of my own wounded self, hiding sorrow behind malice. To be sure, that hasn't always been the case, but often it has.

The *presence* experience is one of those things best evaluated by two people. This is where sharing a bed with someone can help. If you both feel a presence in the room at the same time, then you might be dealing with a genuine entity. Alas, this is very rare.

Hearing Disembodied Voices

Hearing voices is one of those things that tends to make people question their sanity before they question their spiritual safety. Be that as it may, when one is dabbling in practices such as Astral Projection, Lucid Dreaming, and other behind the Veil activities, hearing voices can be especially frightening. This is usually due to the association of psychic skills with unseen forces. Many people have an ingrained belief that Subtle Body practices evokes denizens from unseen realms. This isn't altogether untrue. However, most of these encounters are harmless. To be frank, most genuine supernatural encounters are misinterpreted by the experiencer. Because we don't know exactly what we're dealing with when such things occur, we imagine the worst and therefore tend to experience exactly what we expect to see, hear, or feel.

There's an interesting facet of the disembodied voice phenomenon that bears more of a resemblance to picking up radio frequencies than it does to unseen forces. Once you get past the psychic noise of your own thoughts-made-audible, there begins an entirely different experience that can only be described as broadcasts of some sort being picked up by the brain. Anyone with long-term experience of the voices phenomenon will recognize what I'm talking about here. Sometimes it appears that you're picking up actual radio or television broadcasts by some unknown mechanism of the brain. At other times it seems you're hearing the thoughts of other people in your neighborhood or the building you live in. Sometimes the voices are of people you know, and at other times they're completely unfamiliar. At any rate, the voices sound and feel like they're coming from the center of your brain and not from somewhere in the room.

Then there are other times when you're hearing voices, not in the center of your brain, but from somewhere in the room you're sleeping in. I've often heard these voices while in deep meditation. Sometimes they're malicious or give bad news and admonitions, and at other times they're quite funny or even angelic. They usually occur alongside the feeling of a presence in the room, which makes the experience even more spooky. Sometimes the voices will be accompanied by loud sounds as if there were a party happening right there in your bedroom or meditation space. There may be the sound of chairs being moved around and people having loud conversations. Medical science has given this phenomenon the unflattering title of "Exploding Head Syndrome," the true causes of which remain unknown.

Depending upon your goal at the time when they occur, you can deal with auditory phenomena in a few ways. If you're just trying to get a good night's sleep, I find that sitting up and doing some deep breathing for ten minutes helps clear the air. Make sure all WiFi is brought to a minimum and that you're at least eight feet away from any plugged-in laptops or cell phones. Also, never meditate or sleep next to an electrical outlet that's in use. But if your goal is to gain something from the experience, then try to hear what the voices are saying and even ask questions! Then write down in your dream journal everything you hear. However, if you're trying to go astral, ignore the voices and sounds *completely*. I know it's difficult, but it's important to ignore exit-symptoms during the initial phase of Astral Projection. If you pay attention to the sounds and the sights, then you'll just end up having a Lucid Dream and your projection attempt will fail. Also, if you're meditating, obviously you want to remain centered and unaffected by voices or anything else for that matter.

Whether or not you're dealing with an actual entity, I find that the usual approach of kindness, courage, and joy works to silence them. Wake up if you must and change your focus from one of fear to one of courage and compassion and just watch what happens. This is difficult, I know, but once you see how effective it is you'll never be afraid again.

Apparitions

This is one of the most feared of all entity encounters. When they occur in Astral Projection or Lucid Dreams they're almost always projections of the psyche. Due to the mind-split effect, these visions can sometimes appear external as you transition from wakefulness to sleep or *vice versa*. These are simply hallucinations. Regardless, they can still be very frightening and alarmingly real. So real, in fact, that you can sometimes even feel body heat or smell perfume! This is just one of the reasons why many people confuse Lucid Dreaming with Astral Projection and sometimes equate the two. It takes time and experience to be able to tell the difference.

As far as genuine apparitions go, they usually don't take the form of dead relatives, spirit guides, or mythical creatures. They're often much less dramatic than that. Also, they tend to happen while fully awake and not while you're sleeping or just waking up. Sometimes they appear as fleeting orbs of light. I recall one experience from 2011. I was sitting on a couch opposite my roommate's cat when suddenly a bright blue orb floated in front of me for a moment, and then slowly drifted toward the hallway and out of view. The thing that assured me if its authenticity was the fact that the cat saw it, too. He followed the orb with his eyes and his hair stood on end.

I had another similar experience in 2006 with my ex-girlfriend. We were lying in bed watching TV when a bright golden light that looked like it was made of liquid slowly floated through the room and toward the window! My girlfriend turned to me and asked, *"Did you just see that?"* I said, *"Golden light? Floated across the room?"* To which she responded, *"Yeah. What the fuck was that?!"*

I had no answer for her…

Apparitions can also take the form of something that resembles heat waves rising from asphalt. If you've ever been on a highway during a hot Summer day and have seen the squiggly waves of heat emanating from the blacktop, then you know what this species of apparition looks like. Curiously, this is also what Auras look like when you first start to see them. Before you begin to see colors in Auras you'll see colorless emanations radiating from the object. Well, sometimes these emanations can be seen unattached to any body or object. They behave as if they have intention, which is the most bizarre quality they possess. I've sometimes sat and observed them for hours, trying to make sense of their behavior. Sometimes they'd behave much like fish, swimming through the air or hugging the floor as though searching for food. At other times I've seen them hovering around plants and people. They seem harmless.

Then there are other apparitions that portend ill fortune. Years ago, I began seeing what I can only describe as *black light* darting through the air or surrounding certain people. They resemble ravens but without wings, are black as coal, and move very quickly. What was strange about their appearance was the immediate disaster that *always* followed in their wake. These little nasties became such good prognosticators of ill fortune that I began to rely on them as warning signs. Whether it's a car crash, an argument, or an illness, these dark denizens never fail to deliver. My wife began to see them too, and to this day if we see them we'll cancel our plans or be extra vigilant. If you see these black lights before your Subtle Body practice, postpone practice for a later date. Play upbeat music and surround yourself with positivity. Avoid negative thoughts and feelings at all cost, and make sure that you're healthy and in good company.

To see a full-bodied apparition is rare. Sometimes it happens that you see other people who are Astral. Most of them are asleep and are unaware of your presence. Sometimes animals and pets are seen while they're Astral. There's nothing to fear. Just enjoy the show and embrace it as a sign of progress.

Possession

This is without doubt the most feared of all entity encounters. To see, hear, or even feel some unseen force is one thing, but the thought of being possessed by it is quite a different matter. Looking back at my childhood and adolescence, this was by far the most traumatizing thing that happened to me. I've not found a satisfactory explanation to this very day, and I've done tireless research on the subject. As I began to say in the *Introduction* to this book, I used to suffer from a terrifying waking trance in which I had little control over my body, mind, and voice. At times I couldn't even recognize my own mother or remember my own name!

But that's not what made these episodes (let's call them that) so strange.

There were psychic elements to many of these episodes; elements that simply can't be explained in any logical way that I know of. Two events come immediately to mind. The first occurred when I was about ten years old. I had a childhood friend at the time named Andy. He seemed every bit the normal kid, but something happened that revealed a darker side to him. When I think back on this experience, there's no way I could know what I came to know while under the influence of this trance state.

One night I was awoken from sleep by an indescribable sensation. To this day I can't find words that adequately describe the feeling. The image of a huge boulder rolling over a toothpick comes to mind, but that's still not quite it. It's as if your very soul is rapidly shrinking to the point where at any moment it'll be extinguished. In its place grows a terrifying feeling of fear and amnesia followed by blackouts and a pervasive sense of danger.

This night found the ten-year-old me in the grip of this psychic hell. I can't recall how she was alerted, but my mother came into the room and was trying everything she could to snap me out of it, all to no avail. Then it happened...

I started screaming, "Andy, don't do it! Stop! Andy don't!!!!"

My mother eventually managed to calm me down and put me back to bed. But the next day she hit me with some shocking news. My friend, Andy, had been locked up in a facility for disturbed children because he was caught attempting to violently rape a five-year-old girl. My mother was alarmed, first at the horrible crime committed by a friend of her ten-year-old son, and second because I seemed to have dialed into it during my trance the night before.

These episodes ended abruptly when I turned sixteen, but they went out with a bang. The second to last episode occurred when I was fourteen years old. My brother had decided that it would be a fun idea to sneak three of his friends into the house while the adults were sleeping. His bedroom was in the basement of the house, so it was easy to sneak them in through the hatch way without making too much noise. My brother asked me to stand guard for a little while, and to alert them should our mother wake up and come downstairs. He asked me to do this by whispering through the floor vent that ran from the hallway floor into the basement.

I agreed...

After my brother had successfully sneaked his friends in, I fell asleep on the couch in the living room. Then, suddenly, I awoke to find myself walking slowly up the stairs to my mother's bedroom. I was covered in sweat and my body felt like it was being dragged up the stairs by some foreign energy. I felt like I was lost inside myself, in some dark cavern of my being.

I was terrified...

When I reached my mother's bedroom, I opened the door and begged my mother to wake up. I kept saying, *"They're downstairs! You need to go downstairs now!!!"* At this point my stepfather, who had to wake up for work at 4:00 am, was angry, but my mother got up and ran toward me. Something about my demeanor must have alerted her to what was happening to me because I can remember her trying to shake me. For some reason, though, it hurt me when she touched me. It wasn't a physical pain either. It was something else I can't describe. To this day she insists that it was because whatever was inside of me sensed the Holy Spirit inside of her, but I digress.

As soon as my mother opened the basement door I snapped out of my trance. I remember my muscles twitching violently as though an electrical current was passing through my body. I was sweating profusely, and my skin felt clammy. My brother's friends were promptly kicked out of the house, my brother hated me for it, and suffice it to say I had trouble going back to sleep that night.

Then the following morning brought news that caused a chill to run down my spine.

As it turns out, my brother's friends had brought a few occult books in with them the previous night and were experimenting with incantations designed to contact the dead. Using a Ouija board, one of them would recite the incantations while the other two manned the planchette, and I was busy sleeping on the couch in the living room above them. Apparently they were successful, and whatever they summoned came to me to put a stop to it! Whether or not this was a genuine case of possession, I can't say for certain. Still, you must admit, that's quite a coincidence.

As many sufferers of somnambulism will tell you, the feeling that you're not in control of your faculties while in a hypnopompic trance is rather common. After all, if I gave you a few sleeping pills and a strong cup of Espresso at the same time, you'll probably say, do and feel some strange things that are out of character for you. That said, and as you can see from the above accounts, there are times when logic fails, and mystery begins. However, these experiences are rare. They do happen though, and the only advice I can give you is this:

Raise your energetic vibration to that of health, happiness, and above all, compassion!

Your health will insure you against the nervous shock of unknown experiences. Your happiness will shield you against the type of negative thoughts and feelings which tend to attract dark energies. Finally, compassion will transform your heart into an alchemical furnace capable of turning dark energies into lighter ones. That way when thorns are thrown into your heart, roses will come out of it. You'll be pleasantly surprised to find that some of the malicious encounters are subdued by a good hug. I know that sounds corny, but it happens to be true.

One Final Word

In a future publication, I'll offer an exhaustive discussion on Astral Projection. I'm addressing the issue here, in a book about Conscious Sleep, because the two abilities are so inextricably linked, and a discussion of one without the other would be pitifully incomplete. Also, in my forays into the myriad online discussion groups on Lucid Dreaming and Astral Projection, I've noticed a bit of confusion and misinformation on OOBE. As I've said, this confusion is an understandable one. Still, someone needs to clear the air and take the square peg out of the round hole, so to speak.

Lucid Dreaming is an advanced yoga when taken into higher levels of skill. It requires a subtle mind and an indomitable willpower, but alas, it's an ability that's at least 70% psychological and *personal.* The other 30% accounts for the occasional influx of Astral, precognitive, and preternatural elements. Whereas Astral Projection, on the other hand, is 70% preternatural and Astral with the remaining 30% being the psychic projections of one's own biography.

As you've probably guessed, being an advanced Veiler means that you're capable of both Lucid Dreaming *and* Astral Projection. Few, but some, achieve Astral Projection first and Lucid Dreaming second. Most people, however, will achieve dream Lucidity well before Astral Projection. If you keep trying, follow the methods outlined in this and other books, and consistently ponder and explore, it's my firm belief that you'll eventually succeed in one or both of these skills.

Lastly, when it comes to serious attempts at Astral Projection, the best advice that I can give you is this:

Don't be afraid!

Fear is the number one culprit for unsuccessful attempts at OOBE. If this fear goes on long enough then the Veil will close, and you may never get another chance to open it again. This is why I place so much importance on being healthy, happy, and compassionate. If you don't have these three keys, then you'll probably have some frightening experiences and may give up on your quest. The best way to cultivate these three keys is entirely a personal affair. For me, it meant a complete lifestyle change. I switched to an organic diet, moved out of the city and into a more rural environment, surrounded myself with positive people, and started a balanced exercise routine. I even changed the way I breathe! This isn't necessary for everyone, and being a Veiler wasn't the primary reason I made these changes, but it revolutionized my Lucid Dreaming and Astral Projection practices.

What do you have to lose?

CHAPTER FOUR
PAVING THE YELLOW BRICK ROAD: NEUROPLASTICITY AND CONSCIOUS SLEEP

Neuroplasticity

The brain's ability to reorganize itself by forming new neural connections throughout life is called Neuroplasticity. Neuroplasticity allows the neurons (nerve cells) in the brain to compensate for injury and disease and to adjust their activities in response to new situations or to changes in their environment.

That's the medical definition of Neuroplasticity, a hot-topic nowadays getting press from virtually every field of endeavor. Whether we're talking about sports, spirituality, business, art, physical therapy, or dog training, the discovery that the bodymind, especially the brain, is capable of creatively rewiring itself in new and undreamed of ways is currently stealing the show.

One of the most fascinating discoveries in Neuroplasticity research involves the power of imagination. In 1985, a neuroscientist named Alvaro Pascual-Leone performed an experiment that proved the power of imagination over synaptic development in the brain. The experiment involved two groups of volunteers. The first group was given a five-finger piano exercise to practice for two hours every day for a predetermined period. When the time was up, the volunteers were brought to the lab and their brains scanned for any cortical changes that may have occurred because of the piano practice. They found that the areas of the cortex responsible for learning the piano exercise had not only been refined, but had also spread to surrounding areas of the brain, essentially rewiring it to "house" the newly acquired piano skills.

But wait, there's more!

Pascual-Leone then took another group of volunteers and gave them the same piano exercise, only this time they weren't given pianos to practice on. Instead they were told to simply imagine, as vividly as possible, what it might feel and look like were they to practice the exercise on a real piano. The results were astonishing. When the volunteers were brought to the lab, and their brains examined for cortical changes, the same synaptic refinements observed in the group of volunteers that had practiced on real pianos had also taken place in the brains of those who had only imagined doing so!

And just like that, Alvaro Pascual Leone proved mind-over-matter.

This remarkable finding soon spread to Sports, then to Physical Therapy, then to Academic Performance, and finally to Spirituality and the Arts.

Hypnotists also utilize this mechanism with clients suffering from addiction, obsessive compulsive disorder, learning disabilities, social anxiety, and so on. Granted, they may not think about it in those terms, but that's exactly what they're doing. The interesting thing about hypnotism is that it's essentially a Lucid Dream in which the Hypnotist guides the client into low-grade Lucidity. Hypnotism works by utilizing what neuroscience refers to as the "top down" affect, which is simply their way of saying "mind over matter." In other words, *intention and vivid imagination come together to influence physical changes in the nervous system.*

When this volition is carried through both awake and sleeping states then the effect is doubled!

Remember when I said that Veilers have a unique anatomy? Well, the anatomy I was referring to is acquired through neuroplasticity. That's the *physical* part anyway; but you must start from there or you'll have no foundation upon which to build your skills, whether your goal is to dream vividly, lucidly, or to go Astral. So, the take-home message is this:

Unless you rewire yourself to make it happen, you won't succeed.

In this chapter, I'd like to bring *Part One* of this book to a close with an in-depth discussion of the topic of Neuroplasticity and Dream Mastery. It's my belief that human beings, sometime in the distant future, will generally have access to skills such as Lucid Dreaming and Astral Projection. When enough people acquire these abilities they'll soon be shared by the collective humanity.

Neuroplasticity and OOBE

What if I told you that, in your entire lifetime, you'll probably spend up to 229,961 hours of your life in unconscious sleep? If you'll meet the average life expectancy, and if you'll get a healthy eight hours of sleep per night for the rest of your life, then that's about how many unlived hours of your life you'll be left with. Why?

Because that's an estimate of how many hours we spend sleeping in a single lifetime. Think about it for a minute.

That's one-third of your life!

That's roughly twenty-six years of unused potential squandered in unconscious sleeping and dreaming. Granted, a full eight hours of rest is essential and difficult enough for most people in today's jet-set world, but just think about what you could accomplish in twenty-six years of willful and productive activity.

My first-hand experience of Neuroplasticity began in my second year of Internal Martial Arts training. After years of using my body in an unskillful manner, the basic body-mechanics of *Taijiquan* (popularly known as Tai Chi) came as something of a culture shock. In *Taijiquan,* the use of muscular *contraction* is brought to a minimum and is replaced by muscular *extension.* This requires a profound relaxation of the musculature of the body so that the connective tissue can unify the body's structure from head to toe. Anyone who's ever seriously confronted this training knows just how difficult this can be.

When I first began studying *Taijiquan,* I was in awe of my teacher's abilities. With little effort he could send powerful shockwaves through my body, sometimes targeting specific organs, while leaving the rest of my body completely unaffected. It was as if his body were made of some sort of powerful rubber; that is, there wasn't any hardness or rigidity in his movements to signify martial intent. Rather, it felt as though he had powerful waves of force rippling through his bodily structure, and he was issuing that force into my body with an invisible whip-like power. When I asked my teacher how he was accomplishing these feats, he asked me to perform the opening movement of my *Yang*-style Tai Chi form, but with one proviso: he wanted me to perform the movement without using the muscles in my shoulders and arms.

Um, okay. There's just one problem with that request. The opening movement of the form *is* a movement of the shoulders and arms! Naturally, I thought this was an impossible request; so, I just stood there motionless, feeling like a damn fool.

My teacher just laughed and shook his head…

It took two years of unflinching practice and commitment, but eventually I performed that opening Tai Chi movement, and I didn't need to use my arms or shoulders to do so. Now I not only perform the entire Tai Chi form using "internal" force, but I perform *every* movement of my life in that way.

So, what's my point?

For me to learn how to move my body according to Tai Chi principles, I had to first *unlearn* my former way of using my body. On top of that, I had to maintain a constant and unflinching certainty that this new, and seemingly magical way of moving my body was indeed possible. In other words, I made the firm decision to perform every single moment of my waking life according to Tai Chi principles. Furthermore:

I began to practice these skills in my dreams!

I'd have all kinds of dreams in which I'd be studying with my martial arts heroes, and I'd perform each movement using internal force rather than muscular force. I even learned, by way of Lucid Dreaming, a few secrets that would be confirmed years later in books or by my teachers. Eventually, as time passed, my body began to move according to these new principles all the time. My body even rewired itself around previous injuries! It literally began to feel as though I had created a new body underneath and around the old one.

Eventually, I applied this same method to my piano practice. I had played by ear for twenty years before finally deciding to teach myself to read musical notation. At first it was incredibly difficult, as you can imagine, but as soon as my studies began to pop up in my dreams I knew I was well on my way! In the same way I learned Taijiquan, I found ways to include my piano practice throughout the day and night, even when there wasn't a piano to practice on. While on lunch at work, I'd practice reading musical notation. Sometimes I'd do a mental scan of the Bass and Treble Clefs. And when the day was done, and my head hit the pillow, I'd step behind the Veil and continue my lessons.

Dreaming was and still is one of my most productive times for practicing piano!

As soon as I feel my consciousness slipping into an **ALPHA** state, I picture and really feel myself sitting or standing in front of my piano. I'll conjure up the feeling of my fingers against the keys, vividly hear the notes being played, and as my awareness passes into **THETA** it becomes fixed in the Lucid Dream state (**GAMMA**) and I practice everything from scales to chord progressions to pitch recognition. It's important to be in an **ALPHA** state before doing this, otherwise the mental stimulation will keep you locked in **BETA** and prevent you from falling asleep.

Long story short, I learned how to read and play musical notation in under three months!

The area that I really noticed especially rapid progress in was my technical skills on the piano. I noticed that I'd wake up the following morning and could play faster, more accurately, and in a more relaxed and leisurely way. When I look back on it, I'm left in awe at just how much can be accomplished in those eight hours when most people are snoring and drooling on their pillows!

Neurons that Fire Together Wire Together

In the year 1949, a Canadian neuropsychologist named Donald Hebb coined the phrase, *"Neurons that fire together wire together,"* to summarize the process of Associative Learning, an exercise in neuroplasticity designed to skyrocket academic performance and overcome learning disabilities. Technically speaking, the brain learns to recognize, repeat, and build upon previous experiences (lessons) through the synaptic firing of neurons. The brain sends out a neuro-transmitter on one end and on some other end of the brain awaits a neuron capable of absorbing it. You can think of it as the *Yang* and *Yin* of brain chemistry.

What this means in layman's terms is that whenever we repeat a task or experience the brain recognizes it and responds by reproduc-ing the same biochemical elements needed to respond to it. This can either be a positive or negative thing. For example, for someone suffering from PTSD, just the sound of a door being slammed can trigger the "fight or flight" response. On a lighter note, the scent of burning leaves in Autumn might trigger a flood of memories and emotions associated with one's first love.

In a sense, this is common knowledge. We all recognize this process whenever we remember a person's name or build upon a skill. However, utilizing neuroplasticity to build upon our strengths is one thing; using it to work out our weaknesses is quite another! Let's take as two specimens my above examples of the PTSD sufferer and the unrequited lover. In the former case, we're presented with an individual whose quality of life is severely impaired due to the effects and limitations of chronic trauma. She or he may be perfectly fine and functional in every other way, but the constant anxiety and high levels of cortisol (stress hormone) suffice to keep this poor soul tied to the whipping post, and how to unlearn that programmed response is where neuroplasticity truly comes into play. This requires a firm commitment to revisit the original trauma and the feelings associated with it. The difference is that the sufferer must now *respond* rather than *react* to the familiar triggers, allowing every feeling to come up without censorship, only this time looking at and behaving towards it in a completely novel way. Furthermore, this new response to an old wound must become a trend in the sufferer's daily life. Eventually, according to the law of Neuroplasticity, the neurons associated with the original trauma will dissolve and rewire themselves to the new and healthier responses.

Neurons that fire together wire together.

This is simply a modern expression of the ancient Alchemical adage: "*Solve et Coagula*" (Dissolve and Bind).

You might think that there's nothing particularly "bad" about remembering one's first love, but what happens when every subsequent love affair is measured against it? What if every time you're on a date, or strolling with your wife or husband through the park on a cool Autumn afternoon, you're swept away by nostalgia to such an extent that you become blind to the person walking besides you? To make matters worse, what if every time you hear a love song on the radio you think of your old flame? What if your first experience of romantic love was so powerful that you see, in every sunrise and sunset, the "one that got away"? You might say that this gives new meaning to the Shakespearean line, *"O what tangled webs we weave!"*

Tangled webs, indeed...

In our brains, those tangled webs are the synaptic connections of our *neuronet*. In our daily lives, they're the behavioral patterns that keep us running on the hamster wheel of our past trauma and psychological conditioning. In the example of our pining lover, the experience of first love left such an emotional impression that all potentially new romantic encounters were over before they began. In this case love, as beautiful as it may have been, constitutes a genuine trauma.

How to unlearn that?

A similar mechanism is at work for many practitioners of the psychic arts. A common problem for many would-be Veilers has to do with something that I call the "psychic moat." I'm referring to the psychological wall that forms between that part of the brain capable of perceiving subtle-realm phenomena and that part of the brain capable of interpreting those perceptions. As I've said elsewhere, children typically have access to many subtle-realm experiences. They haven't yet developed the higher cortical brain structures capable of filtering them out. Those bricks haven't yet been laid and the wall that separates the conscious from the subconscious mind hasn't been built yet. Consequently, and for better or worse, the moat that protects most adults from the shadowy figures looming in the outer darkness is something that most children swim in until they're taught or learn to be wary of the real or imagined sharks lurking in those waters.

Usually, by the time we reach adolescence or shortly thereafter, the psychic moat has been constructed and we're safe behind our castle walls, locked inside the ivory tower of conceptual and ideological thought. This is often a necessary milestone. After all, the ever-increasing demands of adult life are almost always at odds with the clandestine activities of one's Subtle Body.

But there's another, far more pernicious, reason for the emergence of the psychic moat. I'm referring to the learned and repeated response of fear to the confrontation with the *Unknown*. As I pointed out in the *Introduction* to this book, my own experience was exactly that. This terror continued up to the age of sixteen, at which time the psychic moat was well under construction. It took years of diligent employment of neuroplasticity to rewire my neuronet to regain and sustain Subtle Body experiences. Of course, I didn't think about it in those terms then, but I now know that this is what happened.

Once the third eye closes, as it were, it can be near impossible to open it again.

The psychic "block" happened despite ourselves and can't simply be removed by an act of will. Like all trauma, one may sincerely wish to gain or regain access to the subtle-realms, but the reaction of fear can be so primal and visceral that any *behind the Veil* encounter is reflexively rejected by the very core of one's self.

Neurons that fire together wire together.

This is where the exercises in *Part Two* of this book can help. They're the methods which I used to build a bridge across my own psychic moat, and many other people have done the same to great effect. It just takes a little courage, a little natural talent, and a lot of perseverance.

Mirror Mirror on the Wall: Marriage of the Conscious and Subconscious

So that's the *physical* aspect of Conscious Sleep. Alas, though, nobody wakes up in the morning and says, *"I'm going to have a very neuroplastic day today!"* Often, we as human beings interpret our experiences in a deeply personal way. We don't, for example, experience love as a neurotransmitter called *Serotonin*. We experience it as elation, regard for the beloved, bonding, joy, and emotional communion. Similarly, we don't experience a Lucid Dream or Near-Death Experience as a **GAMMA** brainwave or a series of neuronal firings. We don't experience our Astral Body as a "neuronet": we experience it as a *body!*

This distinction between the psychological, spiritual and, in short, the *personal* aspects of rarified experiences and their physical embodiments in brain chemistry is very important on the one hand and totally unimportant on the other. It's important because, all too often individuals desiring to cultivate Subtle Body skills focus overmuch on the phenomenological aspects of the training and totally ignore the importance of exercising, nourishing, promoting, and protecting the physical structures that house these capacities. However, it's also *not* important past that point. In other words, the real action and fun is to be had in the cultivation and experiencing of these skills. In a very true sense, the repeated experience of Lucid Dreaming, Astral Travel, and so on, is the very exercising and creation of the anatomy required to perform them. That said, without a balanced and healthy bodymind, and without an appreciation for the organic unity between all levels in the garden of your being, as well as your compatibility with the environment in which you cultivate that garden, your growth as a Veiler will be lopsided, and possibly even dangerous.

As in all alchemical operations, Conscious Dreaming is a skill resulting from the pairing of two opposite elements to create a third element. It's the classic formula of *Thesis, Antithesis,* and *Synthesis,* only applied to the realm of the human spirit. In evolutionary terms, abilities such as Lucid Dreaming and Astral Projection are developmental *Emergents* in the psychic unfolding of human potentials. In a universe of seemingly limitless possibilities, as evolution unfolds, new and undreamed-of capacities emerge out of the dynamic interplay of opposites. When it comes to higher cortical functions of the human brain, we're dealing with a hardwired (and hard earned) method of learning. We call this unique function of the brain, *reflection.* That is, we can think about thinking. We have evolved brain structures capable of sending out a call, as it were, with the bonus of being able to listen to the echo, and sometimes a genuine response. Because of the unique physiology of our brain, human beings have a remarkable capacity for learning, reflecting upon and combining what we learn into new and exciting inventions, and then digesting all of it to use as fuel for future creations!

When it comes to dream Lucidity, to give one popular example, what we're essentially doing is taking our conscious mind—with its higher cortical reflection abilities—and we're turning it around to face our subconscious mind. The subconscious mind is the repository of all our digested and undigested knowledge and experience. It's also the fastest route to the Collective Unconscious of our entire species past, present, and future! Thus, by *binding* our conscious and subconscious elements in a new way, we're setting the stage to create something new; an *emergent* called Lucid Dreaming. To be sure, *Vivid* Dreaming has probably been around for quite some time now, but *Lucid* Dreaming? There are many ancient references to

Lucid Dreaming in Egyptian, Hebrew, Babylonian, Arabic, and Greek literature (to name a few), but this skill was probably limited to only a handful of people. Such people, as we've already discussed, were often the Sages, Priests, Shamans, and Mages of their respective societies. Furthermore, if you wanted to learn Lucid Dreaming or Astral Projection in those days, you had to first be accepted as a student, have some natural talent, and even then, you were often sworn to secrecy. Some people even paid with their lives!

Today, we have an open exchange of information the likes of which has never been seen. Interest in the realm of dreams, visions, psychic powers, OOBE, and other rare capacities of the human spirit, are at the epicenter of a sort of Renaissance. In such a climate, the appearance of evolutionary *Emergents* are sparking and fizzing up from the depths right before our eyes. We experience these novel capabilities as adventures of the soul, expansion of the mind, and sometimes total loss of egoic boundaries (for better or worse!) As more and more people step behind the Veil, as more and more people transform their anatomy to house these new abilities, as more and more people share their knowledge openly and without fear or dishonesty, humanity reaches new heights of grandeur, and hopefully, new depths of humility.

So, there you have it! You now know the rudimentary details of Conscious Sleep. We've covered the role of dreams and OOBE in Art, Culture, and Science. We've learned about the Seven Categories of Dream and how we can spot them. We discussed the importance of Journaling. We've been introduced to the roles which the seasons, times of day and night, bodily processes, geomagnetic tides, and bioelectricity play in Subtle Body development. We shed some light on the so-called "entity" phenomenon, the differences and similarities between Lucid Dreaming and Astral Projection, and some of the more controversial aspects of being a Veiler. Finally, we took a quick look at the importance of neuroplasticity and the grounding of psychic and Subtle Body development in physical structures and processes.

Before moving on to the practical section of this book, I'd like to reiterate the importance of a balanced, open-minded, and healthy approach to skillful Dreaming. Too often a person begins a practice like Lucid Dreaming or Astral Projection without first checking in with all the other parts of her or his bodymind. I can't count how many times I've spoken with frustrated students who've read a book or two on OOBE and have either had minimal success, or worse, a great deal of success accompanied by psychological and spiritual disturbances. Students are often shocked to discover that something as simple as drinking too much coffee, or consuming too much alcohol, or eating too close to bedtime was the one thing keeping them from successful Lucidity or Astral Projection. Sometimes it's something as simple as how one's sleeping space is oriented, or how stressed out one is, or even how close one sleeps to a plugged-in laptop! (I can't stress this enough.)

Lastly, the importance of establishing a psychological center can't be overstated. Making meditation a part of your daily life will quite literally skyrocket your development as a Veiler. Also, it'll keep you from losing your grip on reality when you reach a certain height of skill. There are countless methods of meditation on the market today, and each of them has something to offer, but the best meditation method for Lucid Dreaming and Astral Projection is one that centers the practitioner at the root of consciousness itself. As we'll see later, this is also the method by which one learns the art of *Pellucid* Dreaming and represents the emergence of the goal of being a Veiler:

The continuity of consciousness...

PART TWO

INTRODUCTION
FALLING AWAKE: STEPPING BEHIND THE VEIL

Now we come to the heart of this book. The practices I'm about to share with you are the result of over twenty years of personal experience. They represent the very essence of my own spiritual path and I trust that you too will benefit from them. The material will be presented in a cumulative fashion. I'll introduce you to some powerful techniques to develop the proper anatomy for Vivid, Lucid, and Pellucid Dreaming, Astral Projection, and other subtle-realm activities.

Unlike many other books on the subject, we'll be taking a full-spectrum approach to Conscious Sleep, one not limited to bedtime. After all, and in a very real sense, we're dreaming all the time! This is not a book written solely for those wishing to learn Lucid Dreaming or Astral Projection, but rather, for those seeking a genuine transformation of consciousness and a more intimate acquaintance with their hidden potentials. Some of the practices require a level of commitment not everyone reading this will be willing to make.

That's perfectly okay!

Not all practices are suitable for everyone and there's no "one-size-fits-all" approach to, well, just about anything. Simply proceed at your own pace, choose the practices that pique your interest, and have fun! How deep down the Rabbit Hole you go is largely up to you. There comes a point, however, when your experiences will gain momentum and occur at a pace beyond your ability to digest them. This is where meditation and the *integral* approach offered in this book can serve you:

There are checks and balances built into the system I'm about to teach you...

Many of the methods offered here are pulled directly from the Taoist, Yogic, Tibetan, and Tantric traditions I've personally used in my own quest. Others are the result of my own spontaneous break-throughs. Regardless, I've personally experimented with every method taught in this book, and with great success, for many years now. I've taught them to many other people, too.

I'll teach you the ideal diet for Subtle Body development, the best nutritional supplements and herbs for enhancing Vivid and Lucid Dreams, the healthiest sleeping arrangement for Astral Projection and Dream Yoga, powerful meditation practices, mind-blowing mental gymnastics, and a powerful sexual method that'll catapult your Lucid Dreaming skills into undreamed of territory!

The only thing you're going to need is an open mind, a quiet bedroom, and a strong commitment to practice. Also, a community of like-minded individuals is indispensable. I didn't have that luxury for a long and lonely time so I know how much of a blessing it is to have people you can turn to when things start happening. In the *Bibliography,* I've listed several links to various online forums and discussion groups, including my own sites on Lucid Dreaming, Astral Projection, Meditation, and so forth.

The practical core of this book is built on what I call the "120-Days Curriculum." Research shows that it takes roughly ninety days for most of us to acquire a new habit. Many systems, like Tai Chi or Taoist Internal Alchemy, have what they call "100 Days of Building the Foundation," which is just another way of saying that it usually takes about three months to learn and digest the basics of a new skill. In the first four weeks I'll teach you *Vivid Dreaming.* During this time, you'll learn time-tested methods to dramatically enhance how colorful your dreams are, eventually incorporating all five senses into your dreams. Vivid Dreaming is really the gateway to successful Lucid Dreaming, so in the second four weeks you'll learn *Lucid Dreaming*, which is the gateway to *Pellucid Dreaming* (week three), which is the gateway *to Astral Projection* (week four). Each of these four skills proceed in a "transcend and include" fashion, with each new skill including, building upon, and transcending the former skills. The greater portion of this training aims at carrying awareness deeper and deeper into the sleep cycle. The reason for this emphasis is simple:

The ability to remain conscious throughout the sleep cycle holds the key to all the treasures hidden behind the Veil! Everything from Vivid Dreams to Lucid Dreams, to Prophetic Dreams, to Astral Projection, to psychic abilities in general.

The crucial point to remember is consistency and perseverance. Without these qualities, your development will be shallow. Follow the instructions as closely as possible. If you have trouble with a certain practice, try to modify it to fit your current situation, but *do the practice!* Also, if you get stuck on any point or practice, feel free to contact me directly and I'll assist you or direct you to someone that can. Get creative, stay light-hearted but sincere in your efforts, and you *will* be successful.

Let's get started!

Your Fellow Traveler,

Daniel Kelley
http://behindtheveil.simdif.com
27 April 2017, 10:00 am

CHAPTER FIVE

MAPPING WONDERLAND:
FORMATTING YOUR DREAM JOURNAL

At this point, you should start keeping a daily record of your dreams. If you already have your own method of recording your dreams, then continue. If you see anything in the following format that you'd like to add to your existing format, do so. In fact, you may wish to dispense with jotting down your experiences and record your voice instead. This is an excellent method of journaling, and I personally utilize a combination of the written and audio approach.

The following format is one that I personally developed. I find that it truly covers most of the dream Categories experienced by most Veilers. I offer it here as just one of many options for recording dreams and Astral experiences, and I trust you'll find it very useful.

If the information presented in *Chapter Two* is still unclear, I urge you to go back and re-read the section on the Seven Categories of Dream. Remember, your journal can be as simple or as textured as you wish it to be. However you decide to record your dreams and Astral experiences, be sure to be as descriptive as possible. All variables should be included. For example, the current moon phase, the weather, the season, what you've eaten, etc., all influence dreams and Astral Travel. Your goal is to spot patterns over time, thereby discovering which set of circumstances and conditions are best, or detrimental, to Conscious Sleep.

Let's begin!

The Dream Journal

The following is an excerpt from my own dream journal. This should give you a fairly good idea about how to format your own:

ENTRY ONE

DATE: 28 December 2016
TIME (of entry): 12:48 PM
MOON PHASE: waning crescent
SOLAR ACTIVITY: coronal hole sending enormous solar
    winds toward earth.
DIET: Organic vegetarian soup: kale, lentils, tomatoes, garlic,
    onions, cayenne pepper.
EMF: Smartmeter. WiFi from other apartments.
WEATHER: Cold. Cloudy and windy.
SEXUAL ACTIVITY: Abstinence (from ejaculation) five days.
    Yi Jin Jing stimulation (a Taoist practice).
STRESS LEVEL: (1–10 scale): 6
HEALTH: Feeling under the weather. Dizzy. Lethargic. Heavy.
    Loss of motivation.

The Dream

I had a spontaneous Lucid Dream last night, one that happened despite myself. I awoke inside the dreamscape lying on the floor in the same physical posture as my sleeping body. I was attempting to lift myself into the air upward until I could feel the ceiling against my back. Although I did manage to become airborne, I never did feel the ceiling. This lift-off method is just one technique I employ in Lucid Dreams to induce an OOBE. The sensation of floating became so strong at one point that I thought that my physical body might begin to levitate! One thing worthy of jotting down here is that I had *dual access* to both my dreaming and physical selves. It's hard to describe. It's a sort of mirroring effect, much like what happens when you have two mirrors facing each other and the illusion of an unending tunnel is created.

The other dream I had featured anxiety about the upcoming work day. I had to go back to a job that I thought was already finished. The painter was unhappy with the work and my boss was unhappy with me. In the dream, the building was enormous and unlike the actual job site, although it is in the ghetto and the building in my dream resembled a dilapidated slum house. It was extremely dark inside and people from every indoor phase of construction were working in separate rooms with halogen lights on. Only I didn't have one and my job requires that I do. Also, there were unsolvable issues on the job, and in the dream—at this point not Lucid, just Vivid—I recall feeling nonplussed about just how I was supposed to get out of this without losing my job.

As I wandered through the building on the lower level, I noticed that there were families living in finished areas of the job site. I asked a woman if she had a flashlight I could borrow, and she said yes. She reached into the top drawer of her dresser and handed me a Maglite flashlight. I thanked her and started to go back upstairs to where my work was to be done, when I was distracted suddenly by the sound of music coming from down the hall. I followed it to an outside area where some tenants had made a makeshift recreation area. There was no finished floor, just the ground and some furnishings they had brought outside for the occasion. A group of four or more tenants were playing in a little honky-tonk band and performing for the gathering in a very lively and spirited manner.

Then I zeroed in on the man playing piano. The piano was a crudely built stand-up with several white keys missing from the upper register, and some of the keys were cracked, and yet this guy was playing in such a way as I have rarely witnessed! I was blown away by his skill and the fact that he looked like a rough sort of man;

the sort you'd never imagine could play Brahms. I decided that I had to speak with this man, since I'm a pianist, and I'd be remiss if I failed to pick the brain of this virtuoso.

So I waited...

After the show had ended, I approached him. He offered me some whiskey and I accepted, even though I care little for whiskey. Anything to convince this man to teach me a few things. But just then he was bombarded by people asking him to fix this and tend to that, all shouting his name (I can't remember it, though the name Dwayne keeps popping into my head). I got the impression that this guy was incredibly liked by the community. Children especially were drawn to him.

Finally, I was able to convince him to give me his undivided attention. I asked if he had gone to Julliard School of Music or something. He said "no" and that his mother taught him to play and that she gave him that piano as an heirloom. He mentioned that he and his wife (the woman who gave me the flashlight?) used to travel the world together playing music.

The dream then shifted to my grandmother's house (a recurring symbol in my dream for years). It was haunted (as it always is). There were some adolescents across the street making a commotion, like a high-school gathering of sorts. I got into my car and drove away.

The next thing I recall is becoming Lucid in the manner I described above. I eventually woke up in a cold sweat.

Psychological: obviously this dream was psychological in nature. Anxiety about work. The Biographical element of my grandmother's house.

Educational: I never did get those tips from my pianist friend, but I did notice that what he played was in the chromatic scale. As it turns out honky-tonk piano is largely in that scale and incredibly difficult to play.

Dream Recall

One of the most common obstacles to Conscious Sleep is the inability to remember one's nightly adventures. Whether we're talking about Lucid Dreaming, Astral Travel, or just good old-fashioned

Vivid dreaming, without the ability of Dream Recall we're just drooling on the pillow for eight hours every night. Remember, we all go *out-of-body* every time we sleep, only we're unaware that we're doing so, and Dream Recall is the initial step to bringing awareness into these unconscious escapades.

So how to do it?

Well, there are a few things you can do to get started, and it begins while you're *awake*. First, you'll need to sharpen your memory of daily events. I'm not only talking about those things which leave an emotional impression, but also those minor details you'd typically omit from memory. For example, remembering that jerk who rudely cut in front of you in the checkout line of your local coffee shop is easy to recall; but what were the color of his shoes? Or you had a casual conversation with the postman about the weather. What was his name? What color were his eyes?

Another thing you can do is to take a nutritional supplement called *Huperzine* before bedtime. It dramatically increases Vivid Dreams and Dream Recall. Of course, this shouldn't replace the work of exercising your memory, but should be used as an adjunct to it. Also, L-Theanine, which is an amino acid found in the brain, increases dopamine and often assists in making dreams more dramatic. Lastly, smoking *Mugwort* or *Calea Zacatechichi* just before bed can be an incredibly powerful OOBE inducer. These supplements are categorized as *nootropics,* a term that literally means "toward consciousness."

Another great exercise for increasing memory requires nothing more than a rubber band and a commitment to practice. Place a rubber band on the wrist of your non-dominant hand. Next, choose a thought, word, or behavior that you tend to employ often, and make a mental note that you'll avoid saying, thinking, or doing the chosen thing. Now, every time you slip, sharply snap the rubber band on your wrist. Not too hard! We're not trying to punish ourselves. Rather, the goal here is to use this biofeedback device to encourage vigilance of mind. I've used this method for years and I promise that it works wonders!

Lastly, pick an activity you do often and retrace your steps upon completing it. For example, after you return home from grocery shopping, sit down and mentally retrace your steps *in reverse,* starting with putting away the groceries and ending with the trip to the store. It's important to imagine as vividly as possible and to include all five senses in the visualization. If you have trouble doing this, no worries! Just do the best you can. Later I'll teach you some powerful methods for developing your visualization abilities.

So that's what you can do during the day to increase your Dream Recall skills. In fact, you may come to find that the above exercises suffice to induce Vivid and Lucid Dreams! If so, that's great. Keep practicing, and don't be afraid to get creative and come up with your own practices to increase the power of your memory.

So, what else can be done to develop Dream Recall? What to do in those moments when you're sitting there with your journal in front of you and you can't recall a single detail of last night's dreams? Isn't there a way to just tap into a state of consciousness where dreams are there at a touch? Isn't that what this book is all about?

Absolutely! Try this on for size:

First, you should never wake up and just hop out of bed, as we've already discussed. Lie there for a few minutes and hang on to the twilight state between awake and asleep for as long as possible. Second, if you must use an alarm to wake up, use one that slowly increases in volume rather than a loud one that jolts you from sleep. Third, while still lying in bed, gently turn your thoughts toward the prior night's dreams. Please note the word "gently"! Dreams are composed of Etheric energy. Like all Etheric energy, if you become aggressive or tense, it will stagnate and prevent Dream Recall. Lastly, get out of bed gracefully with your mind still on last night's dreams, and sit down comfortably with your journal.

If at this point you still have trouble remembering your dreams, try this:

Do a mental scan of the seven Categories of Dream. Because at least 80% of all dreams are biographical, begin with that Category. Simply conjure up some images, people, experiences, and places from your life which carry the most emotional charge and allow them to occupy your mind for a moment. This often suffices to stimulate Dream Recall. Continue this same thought process with the other six Dream Categories and see what pops into your mind. Be sure to leave nothing out! This holds true especially for dreams of a less flattering nature, whether you're dreaming of saving the whales or of sleeping with your college professor.

Be as descriptive as possible and omit nothing. No detail is too small or insignificant that it shouldn't be included in your journal entries.

A common issue for many people is privacy. Some dreams can be so bizarre and unflattering that the prospect of someone stumbling upon one's journal often prevents people from journaling. At the very least, it can prevent you from being honest and thorough in the description of your dreams. Nowadays, this problem can be easily remedied by keeping a digital journal and protecting it with a password. If this still doesn't put your mind at ease, then you can get a little more creative. For instance, in place of the actual names of people you know, you can use pseudonyms. Also, instead of writing in a journalist-type style, you can record your dreams as if writing a fictional story. This can be fun to do. In fact, I know of several writers who record their dreams and Astral experiences in this manner and have used them to write novels!

However you decide to record your adventures behind the Veil, there are four guidelines you should always follow:

- Be descriptive.
- Be thorough.
- Be consistent.
- Be creative.

After a while, you'll notice patterns in your journal. This is when your journal truly comes to serve you. You'll begin to learn which conditions promote and preclude Conscious Sleep. These may not apply to other Veilers, but they do represent *your* unique fingerprint as a navigator of these realms. Of course, there are some universal principles that affect all Veilers in some way or another, but it's to your own unique nature that you must be true. Also, you'll notice patterns in your dreams themselves. Recurrent dream scenarios and symbols will begin to reveal themselves, weaving in and out of the narrative of your journal. Synchronicities will appear in your daily life as the barrier which separates your Gross, Etheric, Astral, and

Causal Bodies begins to break down. Premonitions begin to emerge, and your psychic abilities will sharpen.

Why does this happen?

The answer to this question holds half of the key to behind-the-Veil access. You see, when you consistently pay attention to your dreams, you're sending a message to your subconscious mind that you mean business. In fact, there's nothing mysterious about this. You probably do it all the time without giving it much thought. For example, every time you tell yourself that you *must* wake up at a certain time in the morning, your subconscious mind responds by waking you up at that time! It oftentimes does this by sending you a dream that signals you to wake up. Similarly, if you consistently tell yourself before going to sleep that you *must* remain Lucid in your dreams, then you'll eventually succeed in doing so. The same holds true for Astral Projection.

It's your consistent and firm intention to step behind the Veil that unlocks the mysteries behind the it!

Lastly, whenever your dreams are pointing towards something important about your life, be sure to take them seriously and follow their advice. This builds a powerful bridge between the conscious and subconscious regions of your mind and cultivates your intuition in ways you'll have to see to believe. Should you repeatedly ignore these messages coming from behind the Veil, you'll see minimal progress in your quest as a Veiler.

Your Dream-Language

As you pay more and more attention to your dreams, your subconscious mind begins to speak to you in many unexpected ways. This amounts to nothing less than a dream-language shared by you and your deeper (or higher) self! Some dream-symbols are universal, such as the Archetypes, as we've already discussed. For the most part, though, the symbols used by your subconscious mind will be unique to you. There exists no book on the so-called "Interpretation of Dreams" that can substitute for your direct understanding. Furthermore, this is a language that evolves! For example, because I've read Tarot cards for many years, I'm pretty good at understanding the innumerable meanings of each card and combinations of cards. Consequently, my subconscious often speaks to me by sending me dreams with themes pulled straight from a Tarot deck.

There truly is no limit to how creative you can get regarding the development of your own dream-language. Symbols tend to work best for most people. At first, try to keep the symbols as simple and non-abstract as possible. Tarot is a great place to start, particularly the twenty-two Trumps of the Major Arcana. However, don't feel limited to my suggestions. Experiment with different methods until you find one that works best for you. Just remember one thing:

The making of your dream-language is a two-way street!

On the one hand, your subconscious mind is continuously pulling data from the environment and converting it into symbols and scenarios to communicate with you as a Veiler. Your job is to spot them and decode what they mean. At the same time, you can refine those symbols and enrich them with subtler levels of meaning. What you're then left with is a living, dynamic, and multi-textured language with which to commune with the deepest layers of your being.

This takes a certain amount of time to develop, but once you do you'll be amazed at how honest your subconscious mind can be, sometimes painfully so. There truly is no pretension or tact involved in the conscious/subconscious interface! Psychologists have known this for decades. Sigmund Freud was always on the lookout for slips-of-the-tongue, disparities between verbal declarations and body-language, and especially contradictions between one's social image and the symbolic manifestation in dreams of one's true personality.

Another excellent, but admittedly rarer, form of dream-language is what's known as automatic-writing (Spiritism) or free-association (Psychology). In this method, one sits down with a blank piece of paper and, with pen in hand, enters Trance and begins casually scribbling words onto the paper. At first, this amounts to little more than a sort of mystical doodling. Soon, however, and with practice, words begin to emerge. Sometimes the words appear to be a different language. At other times it's in one's native tongue.

Speaking of tongues, another rare form of dream-language is called Glossolalia, better known as "speaking in tongues." In this rather entertaining form of dream-language, the adept begins by muttering incoherently in a mantra-like fashion. As the state of Trance is entered (called "grace" by Pentecostals), the adept then begins to utter words that are believed to be prophetic at best, educational at the very least. Personally, I believe that it's more commonly the case that Glossolalia produces utterances from one's subconscious mind. That's not to say that these utterances are never prophetic. Sometimes they are. Still, most of the time they're entirely biographical or psychosocial. At any rate, why not give it a try?

Personally, my favorite method of *daytime* communication with the subconscious and superconscious regions of my psyche involves the combined use of Tarot, Trance, and a Pendulum. I call my method of divination *Animitariomancy*. Readers interested in a full discussion of this method are encouraged to read Book Two of this series, called *Tarot for Lucid Dreamers: The Animitariomancy Method.*

So, what's your dream-language? The best way to find out is to keep your dream journal up to date and always be on the lookout for patterns, synchronicities, and recurring scenarios in your dreams, reveries, and life in general. Once you spot them, they can be refined, and you're left with a living and dynamic language shared by you and the deeper you.

CHAPTER SIX

CLEANSING, STRENGTHENING, AND LOOSENING THE SUBTLE BODY

You may be wondering what Taoist and Yogic practices have to do with Conscious Dreaming and OOBE. After all, isn't Conscious Dreaming a strictly cognitive skill? Isn't Astral Projection just, well, an Astral skill? Why bring in all this meditation stuff? What's the big deal? Can't we just focus on what happens while we sleep and forget all about these other practices?

In this chapter, we'll discuss the importance of meditation and Subtle Body development. In my own system, these practices belong to the *Veil of Breath*. As such, they focus specifically on the cultivation of Etheric energy *(Qi)*. You may not yet see the significance of these practices, or how they pertain to Conscious Sleep, but by the end of this chapter it'll all make sense. (I use the terms *Qi,* Bioelectricity, and Etheric energy interchangeably as they're three different words describing the same thing.)

I'm going to introduce you to two powerful methods of meditation that combine Subtle and Causal Body cultivation. Both techniques are one technique broken into two parts. The first technique is known as *Embryonic Breathing,* and is an ancient Taoist method for storing Etheric energy. It has several other applications, but we'll be using it primarily to gather, store, and generate bioelectricity. The second half of this method is known as the *Microcosmic Orbit* (in Yoga) and Small Circulation (in Taoist Qigong). This not only cleanses the six *Yang* and five *Yin* meridians and their corresponding internal organs, but it also strengthens the Etheric energy and *loosens* the Astral Body. As I've said, it seems that one must first travel through the *Veil of Dreams* (the Dream Plane*)* before one can reach the *Veil of Ghosts* (the Astral Plane), and one's "dream body" is just one's Astral Body travelling through the realm of dreams. With that understood, you can see how the Microcosmic Orbit practice might have countless applications for Conscious Dreaming and other forms of OOBE.

The Importance of Trance: The Wuji state of No-Extremity

The word "trance" immediately conjures up images of hypnotized subjects following the suggestions of a hypnotist. Or perhaps some Indian holy man sitting cross-legged in a cave, endlessly chanting mantras. However, the Trance which I'm referring to here is a transcendental state brought about by a cessation of the willful mind combined with a steady flow of attention.

What does this mean?

In the Zen Buddhist tradition, there's a practice known as *Zazen* that serves as a perfect example of what Trance is and how to enter it. Zazen is usually translated as "sitting for Zen." What exactly is Zen? Well, to put it plainly, Zen is the state where there's no separation between what you're doing, what you want to be doing, and who and where you are. In other words, if you're washing the dishes, then that's exactly what you're doing: *you're washing the dishes.* There's no hankering to *not* wash the dishes. In fact, you're so absorbed in washing the dishes that you *are* the act of washing the dishes.

The British philosopher, Alan Watts, once described Zen by giving the analogy of a rider and a horse. A good horse and a skilled rider are almost one body, and it's sometimes hard to tell who leads and who follows. Similarly, when you're practising Zazen, you're literally *just sitting.* You're not "meditating" or "practicing" or "trancing" or really *doing* anything at all. You're just sitting there with whatever is or isn't arising in the moment. You're just *being.* If thoughts and emotions arise, you don't engage them, but rather you simply sit with them until there's no difference between you and what's arising. The Indian sage, Jiddu Krishnamurti, was referring to Trance when he advocated what he called "choiceless awareness" as "the first and last freedom," although he himself would probably shudder at the association. Still, if you can do this perfectly, then you enter the Trance state. From there, lots of interesting things can be done!

Acquiring the skill of Trance is not easy, and mastery depends upon a variety of factors. The two most common obstacles to entering Trance are physical discomfort and mental restlessness. The posture you'll be adopting for most of the exercises in this book is the supine posture (with a memory foam wedge, if possible). However, the practices of Embryonic Breathing and Microcosmic Orbit utilize a specific sitting posture (at first), and it takes a little time for the body to adjust. Also, the mind initially tends to resist the stillness of meditation, with some sessions being easier than others. Oftentimes a more creative approach is needed before you can "just sit." This is where the method called "mindfulness meditation" can help.

In the mindfulness approach one doesn't just sit passively like an immovable mountain of attention, but rather actively notices and feels into all that's arising. In mindfulness methods, one brings an active curiosity to one's thoughts and feelings without getting swept away by them. For example, if you feel restless and irritable during a meditation session, the mindfulness approach is to allow the restlessness without any censorship or attempt to eliminate it. Instead, observe the feeling of restlessness with an active and almost tactile curiosity that, without words, asks:

"Where is this restlessness arising?"
"What effect is this restlessness having on my body?"
"What conditions are giving rise to this restlessness?"

And so on with anything else that arises during meditation.

Success in meditation of any variety is won the instant the practitioner stops trying to see the meditation session from the *outside*. What this means is that one ceases to objectify the moment, the *Now,* which is where meditation takes place. At first, depending upon the type of meditation you're doing, this requires an orientation process on the physical, mental, emotional, and spiritual levels of the practitioner. It's like learning to drive a car. At first, you've got to be very aware of the stick-shift, the pedals, the steering wheel, and the rules of the road. After a while, though, you get to a point when you can just focus on driving the car, maybe listen to the radio, or have a conversation with someone in the passenger seat. Similarly, once you become accustomed to the physical posture of meditation, the proper breathing, the correct mental attitude, and so on, then you can simply meditate. Then you can focus on things like storing and circulating Etheric energy, deeper levels of absorption, and other forms of Subtle and Causal Body work. In Taoism, they call this the stage of "regulating without regulating." This simply means that now you can truly begin to meditate without having to check in to see if you're doing it properly, which only serves to divide your attention and, therefore, your energy.

However you decide to enter it, the beauty of Trance is that it's just another word for meditation. Unfortunately, the word "meditation" has been given dozens of conflicting definitions. Truly, most of this confusion stems from a one-sided view of what meditation is and what its purposes are. The type of meditation you do depends upon your goals. For our purposes, there are two sides to meditation: a *Passive* side and an *Active* side. In other words, there's a *Yin* and a *Yang* side to meditation, and doing one without the other is like eating without digesting your food.

So, the first tenet for acquiring the skill of Trance is *non-doing,* and there are a few ways to create the situation for non-doing to arise. In Taoist Qigong, this is known as the "Wuji" state of No-Extremity. Another way of putting this is to say that energy isn't moving outward, but rather is pooling within and around your body. Because you're *being* rather than *doing,* your energies come to rest and begin to accumulate. Furthermore, when you successfully enter the Trance state, the Etheric part of your Subtle Body is *stimulated,* and your Astral Body is *loosened*; and once your Etheric energy is stimulated, it can be made to move and *breathe*! This is important, because when you lie down in preparation for Lucid Dreaming or Astral Projection your success is dependent upon your ability to enter this Trance state successfully and with minimal effort. If you make too much of an effort, then you'll interfere with the Trance state. If you make no effort at all then you'll just fall asleep. Remember, this isn't an unconscious state we're talking about here. Quite the contrary:

The state of Trance is like a flame of attention burning in a windless room.

When trying to grasp the Trance state it helps to know that *intention* isn't the same thing as *effort*. An intention carries its own energy, and that energy has a movement all its own. Effort, on the other hand, is a form of tension. Obviously, there's a place where effort is needed, but when it comes to attaining Trance, manipulating *Qi,* or going Astral, effort only gets in the way.

Another way of looking at non-doing is that it loosens the grip of the **BETA** brainwave and allows for the smooth transition to **ALPHA**, **THETA**, **DELTA**, and **GAMMA** brainwaves. In other words:

Trance is the key to behind the Veil access.

There are many situations when we enter Trance *naturally*—which is really the only way to enter it when you stop and think about it. Trance can't be contrived or premeditated, and it's only when this fact gets through the ego's thick head that one can truly begin to meditate. If you've ever lost track of time listening to the sound of the rain, or staring at a sunset or into your lover's eyes, then you've experienced one version of the Trance state. The only difference is that, in meditation, you're including in this global attention your own thoughts, feelings, and consciousness itself. So, the passive side of meditation is just a training in developing a deep enjoyment and appreciation for consciousness itself, for the simple feeling of being, for the mystery of being aware in the first place. Take this heightened feeling of "I AM" deep enough and you'll attain the continuity of consciousness.

Lastly, success in meditation is dependent upon your lifestyle. This includes your diet, your social life, your job, your overall well-being, and even how much sex you have! Like any other aspect of being a Veiler, meditation is an integral and holistic affair. If you truly want to access the deeper secrets of the following methods, then there's a few things you'll want to seriously ponder and implement. Please note that everyone is different. Do your own research and experiments to find the right balance for your needs.

The first thing is diet. The best diet for the Etheric side of Subtle Body development is organic, non-GMO, gluten free, and low carbohydrate. Depending upon factors such as how labor-intensive your job or workout routine is, small but well-rounded meals are ideal. Also, too much caffeine is a no-no. Many seasoned Veilers will tell you that OOBE can be stopped in its tracks due to excessive caffeine intake. I'm not saying that you've got to give up your morning cup of Joe. I love coffee myself! But if you're going to have a second cup, make it green tea or yerba mate instead. Alcohol doesn't tend to negatively impact dreaming, but it does delay it. Since alcohol has been proven to delay **REM** sleep, your dream work will begin later in the sleep cycle if you consume too much alcohol before bedtime. Not only that, but excess alcohol consumption also ties you to the lower Astral Planes. I find that if I go Astral after consuming alcohol, the exit-symptoms tend to be more pro-nounced and uncomfortable.

The second thing is your social life and the overall environment you find yourself in. Toxic relationships, an overly stressful lifestyle, and lack of personal space are detrimental. This is a no-brainer. After all, too much on your mind distracts you from the moment, and lack of solitude means lack of training space. It also muddles your energy. As for your job, that's obviously a little more complicated and most of us can't just quit earning paychecks. So, the job thing is something we've all got to decide for ourselves.

Lastly, and this one's especially important for men past the age of thirty, too much ejaculation of semen drastically weakens the Etheric Force. I know, bummer, right? Be that as it may, it's quite true. Still, notice that I said it's *ejaculation* that weakens the Etheric Force? I didn't say that *sex* weakens it! It took me a few years to grow to a point where I could enjoy sex without having to ejaculate every time, or go without sex entirely for a prolonged period. Traditionally, a man must wait at least ninety days without sex before he can begin the following practices. Unfortunately, I'm not sure how, or if, this applies to women. The standard for men seems to be no more than two ejaculations in a thirty-day period, but everyone's got a different level of sexual force. Taoists call this natural level of Libido *Jing.* Some Taoist and Buddhist masters even claim to be able to orgasm without ejaculation! In the *Bibliography,* I've listed some excellent books on this subject should this topic interest you.

Embryonic Breathing: How to Gather and Store Etheric Energy

In this section, I'm going to teach you the fundamental skill of gathering and storing *Qi.* This isn't necessary for all aspects of Conscious Sleep, but it's crucial for Astral Projection. It also plays a part in how lucid your Lucid Dreams are. Equally important is Embryonic Breathing's power to ground one's energies and set the stage for Microcosmic Orbit practice which, among other things, serves to loosen one's Astral Body.

So let's get started!

Below are the instructions for Embryonic Breathing practice. Be sure to take your time, and don't expect quick results. If you follow the instructions to the letter, then you're sure to have success. Like all skills worth cultivating, Subtle Body development takes time, patience, perseverance, and an indomitable will. I've been practicing Embryonic Breathing for ten years now and can personally attest to its power. I learned it from Dr. Yang Jwing Ming and highly recommend his work to those readers wishing to cultivate higher levels of this skill. Please note that there are elementary, intermediate, and advanced levels of these two practices, and two separate volumes would be required to fully discuss them. Here, I'm simply offering you the basics.

The Practice

The practice of Embryonic Breathing begins with the correct sitting posture. Proper posture, as well as the care and attention you give to it, accounts for at least half of the health and cultivation of your Etheric force. Therefore, a good Chiropractic adjustment to your spine can help to realign your Chakras. Please note that you don't have to sit in full *Lotus Posture* or bend yourself into a human pretzel to reap the benefits of this exercise, but if you're capable of Full Lotus then by all means use it. Just know that you'll be sitting in that posture for upwards of forty minutes or more. The following picture will give you an idea of how to sit for this practice:

Notice that the spine is straight and the legs are crossed. Whenever possible, your hips should be elevated slightly above the level
of your knees. Placing a cushion under your butt can accomplish
this. This helps keep your spine straight by forming a tripod out of
your torso and lower body. Your spine mustn't be held rigid or
ramrod straight. Rather, the chest is slightly concave, and the
thoracic region of the spine maintains its natural curve. Be sure that
your tailbone is straight and in line with the lumbar region of your
spine and not jutting out or collapsing inward. Your mouth should be
closed, and your jaw drawn gently inward toward your throat. Your
head should feel as though it's suspended from above by a string.
This takes the weight of your head off your spine. Your shoulders
should be in line with your hips and relaxed downward naturally.
The tip of your tongue should gently touch the upper palate of your

mouth. This connects the *Governing* and *Conception* meridians, helps to silence inner chatter, and generates saliva to swallow at the end of the session. Certain healing enzymes are generated during Embryonic Breathing that infuse the saliva, which is then swallowed for healing purposes.

Your forearms should rest on your thighs and your hands should be placed in front of your navel.

If you're left-handed, place your left hand under your right, and *vice versa* if you're right-handed. The hands should feel relaxed and comfortable with your thumbs very lightly pressing each other. If you find this hand posture uncomfortable, you can simply let them rest folded on your lap. Folded in this manner your hands create a circuit of energy and helps to keep your awareness on your lower abdomen where Embryonic Breathing takes place. At first, you may keep your eyes open slightly if you experience eye-twitching and other symptoms of a restlessness mind. Zen monks will sometimes meditate while facing a blank wall or the floor a few feet in front of them, or at the tip of the nose, until the mind settles at which point they close their eyes.

That's it! Now you're ready to begin Embryonic Breathing meditation. When possible, face East while meditating in the morning and West when meditating at night. Later, as you advance in skill, you can practice while lying down in alignment with Earth's magnetic field. For books offering a complete discussion on orientations for practice, see the *Bibliography.*

Now that you're in the proper posture for Embryonic Breathing, the next step is to regulate your breathing. During this time, you still regulate your body to make it more and more relaxed. Be sure that you don't slouch or hunch over as this destroys the energetic integrity of the posture, puts undue pressure on your internal organs, increases the likelihood of falling asleep, and distracts the mind with discomfort.

Start by entering the Trance state by accepting all that is arising in the moment with a deep and total YES from the very core of your being. Really feel as though every problem has been solved and there's nowhere to go and nothing to do. Next, become aware of your breathing. Don't do anything with the breath at first, but simply watch its rhythm. Eventually, as your body adjusts to the training, you'll slowly deepen your breathing and establish a rhythm that's deep, silent, slender, steady, and slow. For now, simply breathe naturally and focus on *freeing* the breath by relaxing the physical structures around your lungs and diaphragm. Scan your body for any feeling of tension and, with every exhalation of breath, feel the tense areas relax and melt downward, following gravity. Do this until you feel completely relaxed. The attitude that you adopt here is very important. It should be one of alert curiosity as well as love and care for your bodymind.

Next, and without any force or rigidity, try to feel yourself becoming more and more physically motionless. Without sacrificing the relaxation and integrity of your posture, remain motionless like a stone Buddha. Focus on this stillness for a few moments while maintaining awareness of your breathing. Pay attention to the full course of breathing, including the turning points when inhalation becomes exhalation and when exhalation becomes inhalation. When your mind wanders (and it will), *gently* bring your attention back to your body and breath.

You'll probably notice that by simply becoming aware of your breathing you change its pattern. Allow this to happen. Take note of where your breathing is occurring, that is, are you breathing from your chest or from your abdomen? If you're breathing from your chest, try to relax your chest, upper back, neck and shoulders with a few natural exhalations. Remember, the goal here isn't to force your breathing into a certain pattern, but rather, to relax and open the physical structures of your body to *allow* the breath to return to the same pattern seen in sleeping babies. This is especially true of the muscles, fascia, ribs, etc., surrounding your lungs and diaphragm. You want to relax these areas to allow your breathing to move from your chest to your abdomen without forcing it to do so. You want your lungs to be still and silent and to breathe using just your diaphragm. This takes a lot of practice and should *never* be forced.

(To help relax the physical cage surrounding your lungs, diaphragm, and other internal organs, I suggest you purchase a quality Magnesium supplement. The health benefits of Magnesium are profound and its ability to assist in breathwork can't be overstated.)

Go ahead and enjoy this relaxed state for a few moments. Then, gently, and without "searching" for it, simply become aware of the fact of your *beingness*, your "I Am," the very fact of your consciousness itself. If there are any thoughts floating around in your mind at this point, notice that *you're not your thoughts*. Rather, you're the space in which thoughts are arising. Maintain awareness of your breathing and simply rest in the wonderfully obvious fact of your own presence. Most people feel this "I Am" in the center of their head. In Taoism, this is called the Upper Dantian" and the location of *Shen* (spirit). Do this while focusing more on the inhalation phase of your breathing. This condenses *Qi* inward toward the *Yin* center of the Upper Dantian. Taoists call this spot the "Mud Pill Palace," which refers to the Pineal Gland. When you exhale, simply relax your concentration and allow the air to expel naturally.

So, the rhythm you're seeking to establish is a concentrated awareness of your "I" upon inhalation and, upon exhalation, a relaxing of that concentration. Eventually, you'll begin to feel as though you're breathing from your Upper Dantian. This is called "Spirit Breathing" in Taoist Qigong. Continue this for a few moments and then, while maintaining an awareness of your "I" at the Upper Dantian, include in your awareness the center located at your sternum, called the Middle Dantian. Continue to focus more on the inhalation phase of breathing. This cools down the fire *Qi* located in this region as well as condenses *Qi* inward.

At this point, both your Upper Dantian and your Middle Dantian are breathing. Your "I" is concentrated upon inhalation with a simultaneous awareness of the center of your sternum and, upon exhalation, relax your concentration. This should be done gently and very relaxed. Continue this for a few moments and then move your awareness downward to a point two finger-widths below your navel and about three finger-widths inward toward your spine. After you become proficient in this practice, you'll be able to locate this area due to the heat generated there. This area—called the Real Lower Dantian—is the place for storing Etheric energy, and is classified as *Yang*. The Lower Dantian is the *Yang pole* and the Mud Pill Palace in the Upper Dantian is the *Yin pole*. They're in two different locations, but they function as one, much like the two poles of a battery.

Your attention must be 100% in the Lower Dantian for *Qi* to begin to accumulate there. Eventually, you'll come to feel that your whole body is breathing, condensing into your Lower Dantian with each inhalation. This process can also be reversed. That is, when exhaling, you expand Etheric force outward from the Lower Dantian. This is known as "Girdle Vessel Breathing." For now, though, we're interested only in storing *Qi* in the Lower Dantian. The sure sign of success is this:

As soon as you feel your physical breathing disappear and your Etheric energy starts breathing, this is true Embryonic Breathing.

Now that you've successfully condensed *Qi* to the three Dantians, there's one more important thing you must do. There's a point on the pelvic floor between the genitals and anus called the *Huiyin* cavity. We in the West know it as the *perineum* and it's where we find the PC (pubococcygeus), BC (bulbocavernosus), and IC (iliococcygeus) muscles used in sex, urination, and bowel movements. The *Huiyin* cavity is the meeting place of all four *Yin* vessels in your Etheric anatomy. The very word, *Huiyin,* means "meet *Yin*" in Chinese, and is the point of extreme *Yin* in your *Qi* network. In Embryonic Breathing practice, there are subtle movements of the *Huiyin* that assist in the storing, releasing, and circulating of bioelectricity. The movements must be done correctly; otherwise *Qi* will stagnate there or else be released and used up instead of stored and circulated. This is one of the reasons why the ancient Taoist documents refer to *Huiyin* as "the Tricky Gate." There are two methods for *Huiyin* and breathing coordination: the Taoist method and the Buddhist method. The method which I'm going to teach you is the Buddhist method.

First, you need to locate your *Huiyin* muscles and learn to move them properly. The traditional way to locate your *Huiyin* muscles and tense them properly is to stop the flow of urine in midstream. The goal is to use the *minimum* force required to do this. Once you've got the feeling for it, the next thing you'll need to do is carry that feeling over to your Embryonic Breathing practice and coordinate the movement of your *Huiyin* with your breathing.

The Buddhist method is more relaxed whereas the Taoist method is more aggressive. Because relaxation is so important when working with Etheric energy, it's best to begin with Buddhist breathing and then slowly advance to Taoist breathing methods.

In the Buddhist breathing method, your abdomen expands on inhalation and contracts on exhalation. At the same time, your lower back expands on inhalation and contracts on exhalation. The *Huiyin* cavity gently pushes down on inhalation and is gently held up on exhalation. The entire movement of the abdomen, lower back, and *Huiyin* is like that of a gently expanding and contracting balloon in coordination with your breathing. Breathe naturally and avoid strain or too much effort.

At this point, your attention should be completed absorbed in your Lower Dantian. Do not *concentrate* on your Lower Dantian, but rather, allow your awareness to come to rest there. Please note the distinction. A good analogy is that of a pool of muddy water (the mind). If you disturb the water (with too much effort) then it'll only get muddier. If, on the other hand, you allow the mud to settle on its own, then the water will eventually become clear and you can drink it.

At this point I'd like to bring something important to your attention, as it hold the key to Lucid and Pellucid Dreaming: the state of awareness accessed in Embryonic Breathing practice rooted in your Causal Body!

This means that the state of Trance is just deep dreamless sleep, but with one major exception: You're aware!

The Indian Sage, Ramana Maharshi, used to say of the search for the true Self that if *it's not present in deep dreamless sleep then it's not real*. Well, since literally nothing is present in deep dreamless sleep, what could Maharshi possibly be referring to?

He's referring to the Causal Body…

The ability to remain conscious in deep dreamless sleep literally represents a fourth state of awareness. Since the basic three states of consciousness are Awake, Dreaming, and Dreamless Sleep, then being aware during dreamless sleep is clearly a fourth state of consciousness. Not only that, it's the true key to achieving stable access to both Lucid and Pellucid Dreaming! Why? Because the Causal state is quite literally the root of your Self. If you can raise consciousness there, then you can raise consciousness in the Dream and Awake states as well. This is what the Zen classics mean when they say, "One simply sits quietly, doing nothing, and the grass grows by itself."

The "grass" is a reference to the Taoist concept of *Shen*. In Embryonic Breathing practice, you "raise your *Shen*," for only then can your mind truly direct Etheric energy. For many years I had no idea what *Shen* was or what it referred to. After many years of practice, I slowly began to understand. On the one hand, you can't do anything directly to raise your *Shen,* as we've seen. Any form of *doing* isn't the root of your being. How could it be? The root of your being is just that: *being*! However, raising and protecting your lifeforce can assist in *feeding* your *Shen,* as we've already discussed. However, your *Shen*—which, in this context, is just another way of saying Casual Body—can't be approached directly by your ego. You can't will yourself to a heightened awareness of the Causal Body, but you can, by way of Trance, drop down into the ever-present ground of your consciousness like a stone falling to the ocean floor.

As for how Embryonic Breathing practice "breathes"?

If you've ever remained conscious during the transition from Awake to Asleep you know that awareness of your breathing vanishes during the transition. When your breathing goes silent, and yet a tiny flame of awareness remains burning, then that is successful Embryonic Breathing. At that point *Qi* begins to accumulate. Then it can be circulated. This is the beginning of Microcosmic Orbit practice.

Lastly, if you can get used to the pungent taste, I recommend you purchase *Shilajit* resin and place a small amount of it under your tongue before beginning Embryonic Breathing and Microcosmic Orbit practice. The spot under the tongue where saliva accumulates is known in Taoism as "Heavenly Pond." When saliva accumulates there, swallow it and the *Shilajit.* It's not necessary, but it's a powerful stimulator of *Yang Qi* and assists in its circulation. Be sure to get authentic *Shilajit*! Avoid powdered forms and stick to the natural resin form. Also, a good organic *Ashwaganda* also works to relax the body, boost hormones, and enhance the effects of *Shilajit.* Pertaining to nootropics in general, please understand that some of them help *raise* your *Shen* while others merely *excite* it. It's important to understand this distinction because, depending upon your purpose, you may want to raise but not excite your *Shen,* or *vice versa.* For example, *Ashwaganda* and *Shilajit* raise *Shen.* This is ideal for Embryonic Breathing meditation as you wish to have a raised but calm *Shen* for this practice. On the other hand, having a raised and excited *Shen* is ideal for Lucid Dreaming. By "excited" I don't mean hyper. Rather, an excited *Shen* is a *stimulated* subconscious. Therefore, nootropics and entheogens such as Mugwort, Vinpocetine, Huperzine-A, Salvia Divinorum, etc., are appropriate nootropics for those endeavors.

Microcosmic Orbit Meditation

Do you recall our discussion on the Five Brainwaves? Remember the research being conducted on the **GAMMA** brainwave and its appearance on the EEG graphs of Lucid Dreamers? Well, the pathway in which this bioelectrical current travels is the same as that of the Microcosmic Orbit. In Taoist terms, the **GAMMA** wave follows the so-called "fire path," also called the *Governing Vessel*. As we've seen, *Qi* (bioelectricity) travels this route up the back of the spine, over the head, and ends at the nose-tip. What this means is that the Microcosmic Orbit is in complete alignment with the **GAMMA** brainwave! Personally, I don't think this is a coincidence. What I'm proposing is that this ancient practice has the power to initiate, cultivate, and strengthen, not only Lucid Dreaming, but all forms of OOBE.

Now that you're familiar with Embryonic Breathing, and have hopefully learned to store Etheric energy in the Real Lower Dantian, it's time to circulate that energy in the Governing and Conception Vessels. There are a few ways of doing this. The two methods which I'm going to share are known as the *Fire Path* and the *Wind Path*. The former method follows the path up the spine, around the head, and ends at the nose tip. The latter is simply a reversal of the Fire Path and moves upward from the Lower Dantian, up the front of the body and over the head, down the spine, and ends at the *Huiyin* cavity. The Fire Path is used to make the Etheric energy more *Yang* whereas the Wind Path is used to make it more *Yin.* Both methods, however, may be used to cleanse all twelve Meridians of the Etheric force.

The primary goal of Microcosmic Orbit is to strengthen the *Qi* Meridians. Quite literally, Microcosmic Orbit practice is a Subtle Body workout. A strong Etheric anatomy implies that your Gross (physical) Body is also strengthened by the practice, as the two are intimately related. This is also why Etheric medical practices, such as Acupuncture, work to heal the physical body even though they operate on the Meridians. For our purposes, we're using Microcosmic Orbit to cleanse, strengthen, and open the Meridians to fuel our behind-the-Veil activities. We're literally making our Subtle Body muscles stronger and more flexible.

There are a few different ways to begin Microcosmic Orbit. The way I was taught is to begin the circulation process at the location of stored energy: *The Lower Dantian.* It's important that your Lower Dantian feels warm before initiating the Microcosmic Orbit, as this signifies that *Qi* is abundant and ready to spill over into the Fire Path.

The Fire Path is the natural route of *Qi* circulation in the Governing and Conception Vessels of your Etheric system.

Before you begin the practice, you should be aware that there are three locations on the Fire Path where *Qi* tends to stagnate. These are the tailbone, the middle of the spine at level with the heart, and the back of the head directly above the neck. In Chinese, these are called *"San Guan,"* literally "Three Gates." Because of the narrow musculature of the tailbone area, *Qi* easily gets stuck there and can cause all sorts of trouble. The gate at the middle of the back is dangerous because of its proximity to the heart. If *Qi* deviates from its path, and goes to the heart instead, it can cause palpitations and even a heart attack. Finally, the gate at the back of the head is dangerous due to the narrowness of its location. Because it can be difficult to feel where *Qi* is moving here, it can deviate and go to the brain, causing vertigo and mental imbalance.

The key to avoiding the dangers of the Three Gates is to cultivate the skill of regulating the mind to be still, calm, and concentrated. Also, as you learn to circulate *Qi* in the Microcosmic Orbit, these gates will widen. The trick is to proceed gently, patiently, and above all, to *be relaxed.*

Mental and physical tension causes *Qi* to stagnate.

Here's a diagram showing the Microcosmic Orbit along with the locations of the myriad cavities found on the Governing and Conception Vessels. As you can see, the practice can be done while sitting in a chair. However, it's best to practice with legs crossed as this prevent *Qi* from escaping into the legs:

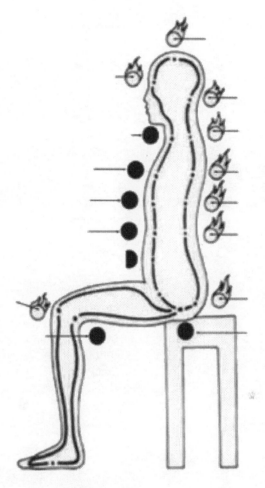

(In advanced levels of the practice, the "small circulation" of Microcosmic Orbit expands to become the "grand circulation" of the entire body. There are many versions of Grand Circulation, but they don't concern us here. For our purposes, we'll be following the Small Circulation paths of the upper body. Later, as your training advances, you may wish to include the Grand Circulation to the legs and arms. See the *Bibliography* for literature on this subject.)

The Practice

Before beginning Microcosmic Orbit circulation, you should first build up Etheric energy at your Lower Dantian by practicing Embryonic Breathing for at least ten minutes. As soon as you feel heat or trembling in your Lower Dantian, it's time to begin circulating this abundant *Qi* in the Fire Path. For this beginner-level method of the practice, it isn't necessary to feel all the *Qi* Cavities located on your Governing and Conception Vessels. Instead, your first goal is to learn to feel the Path itself. In other words, you must first feel the two *Qi* Vessels involved in the Microcosmic Orbit before you can learn to feel the Cavities. As your capacity for feeling develops, and the *Qi* Gates widen, you'll soon begin to feel the various Cavities of your Etheric system.

So, how do you use your inner feeling to locate the Governing and Conception Vessels?

As soon as you feel that *Qi* has reached an abundant level in your Lower Dantian, place your awareness in both your Lower and Upper Dantian at the same time. Remember, the best way to locate the *Yin* center of your Upper Dantian is to become aware of your "I Am," your very sense of consciousness devoid of all objects of perception. This will lead *Qi* to the *Yin* Center of the Upper Dantian, your Pineal Gland. Simply relax for a few moments and breathe in and out of these two Dantians. Don't forget to coordinate the movement of your *Huiyin* with your breathing! Also, keep the tip of your tongue to your upper palate for the duration of the session.

Next, while keeping your awareness situated in your Upper and Lower Dantians, inhale naturally and become aware of the front and back of your torso. The correct way to do this is through *feeling* rather than visualization. For some people this will be easy. For others it may take some time. At any rate, feel into the back and front of your torso and observe any sensations that arise. Pay special attention to the midline of your body: your spine, head, face, throat, chest, abdomen, groin, and perineum *(Huiyin)*. Feel especially for such things as temperature, tingling, movement, etc., as you'll be using these sensations to keep track of how and where *Qi* is moving in the Microcosmic Orbit. You want to be sure to keep your mind in this midline area for the duration of the practice. If your mind deviates from this Path, then *Qi* may be led to the wrong Path and cause trouble. At the very least, you'll waste the goal of your practice. Remember:

Where attention goes Qi flows!

Now, there should be three things included in your awareness at this point: your Upper and Lower Dantians, the coordination of your *Huiyin* and breathing, and the midline of the front and back of your torso. Because we're using the Buddhist breathing method for this practice, it should now feel as if your entire upper body is expanding with every inhalation, contracting upon exhalation.

Upon your next inhalation, try to feel outward into the space that surrounds your body. Feel into the space beneath you as well, as though the ground beneath you has disappeared. Do this while keeping your awareness rooted in your Upper and Lower Dantians. This simultaneity of awareness is very important to the cultivation of your Subtle Body. Personally, I find that using body temperature as a guide for feeling-attention works well to expand my awareness into my Etheric system. After a while, you'll begin to know the difference between your body heat and the feeling of your *Qi*. The latter feels like a sort of "nerve force" with parallels to an electrical current or field. Sometimes it creates body temperatures ranging from cool to warm to extremely hot.

Once you can feel into your Meridians to a workable degree, become aware of the heat in your Lower Dantian with a simultaneous awareness of your "I Am" in your Upper Dantian as well as the surrounding aura of your Etheric force. Even if all you can do is practice this simultaneity of awareness in a given session, then it's perfectly fine! I know that it seems like a lot of things to attend to at once, but I assure you that it gets easier with time and consistent practice. If you're ready to continue, let's move on to the next step.

Okay! Now that your attention is firmly rooted in your Etheric force, it's time to circulate the *Qi* you've gathered at your Lower Dantian. How to do this? Well, there are few ways to accomplish this. Through trial and error, I've discovered that the best way to do this is to first inhale and lead the sensation of heat in the Lower Dantian upward to just behind the navel and then outward from the stomach and downward to the *Huiyin*. This should be done on an inhalation of breath while gently pushing your *Huiyin* down. You want to time it in such a way that the sensation of heat reaches the *Huiyin* point at the end of your inhalation.

Next, as you exhale, sweep the sensation of heat past your tailbone, up your spine, and around the back of your head, ending at the point where the tip of your tongue touches your upper palate. Your awareness should reach this point at exactly the conclusion of your exhalation. It's important that you keep part of your feeling-awareness at least three inches away from your body while doing this. If you have 100% of your awareness inside your body while circulating Etheric force, then it's almost sure to stagnate. In fact, in the higher stages of practice, your Gross Body seems to vanish entirely, and your *Qi* is all you're aware of.

Finally, upon your next inhalation, sweep your feeling-awareness down the front of your body, starting at your throat, then your chest, your abdomen, and your groin, ending at your *Huiyin*. The timing is very important, and you must reach *Huiyin* at the end of inhalation and gently push it down and out. Remember to breathe naturally. Your awareness and timing should follow the natural flow of your breathing, not *vice versa*. In more advanced levels of practice, you'll deepen and slow your breathing down. For now, stay natural, start simple, and practice as much as possible. Your main goal at this stage is to become aware of your Etheric force and increase your capacity for inner feeling.

Continue circulating *Qi* in the Microcosmic Orbit until the entire process becomes seamless and smooth. Remember the following rules and you'll stay on the correct path of practice:

- There should be no pauses in the circulation of *Qi*.
- Your feeling-awareness should be about three inches away from the physical body, with an emphasis on the midline of your body.
- The simultaneity of attention must be trained until it becomes one unified and global awareness: rooted in your Upper and Lower Dantians, circulating in your Governing and Conception Vessels, with breathing and *Huiyin* coordination trained until you no longer need to be aware of them.

- Train your feeling-awareness until you can circulate very far away from your Gross Body. Eventually, you'll also include circulating *within* your Gross Body *and* your Etheric energy at the same time.
- Lastly, guard and maintain your Etheric force always. Avoid unhealthy foods, toxic environments, imbalanced emotions, and if male, too many ejaculations of semen. If female, avoid practicing during menses.

That's it! You've completed the Small Circulation of Microcosmic Orbit! Congratulations. If you've come this far you really do deserve to be proud of yourself. As far as Subtle Body cultivation is concerned, the two treasures of Embryonic Breathing and Microcosmic Orbit represent a real milestone and achievement. Later, when we begin our Dream and Astral work, you'll see exactly why I place so much importance on these two skills.

Lastly, remember that the circulation of Microcosmic Orbit can also be reversed and made to follow the Wind Path. Some people find it easier to circulate *Qi* in this Path than the Fire Path. Be that as it may, you should practice both methods to maintain the balance of *Yin* and *Yang* in your Etheric and Gross Bodies. The Fire Path follows the natural flow of *Qi* in the Governing and Conception Vessels. The Wind Path reverses this flow thereby calming the excess Fire *Qi* generated in the Fire Path circulation. Once you become proficient in Embryonic Breathing and Microcosmic Orbit, you've laid the foundation for serious Subtle Body work. I say "work" but really, you're going to have more fun than most people can imagine.

Literally…

THE 120-DAYS CURRICULUM

CHAPTER SEVEN

GET VIVID!

Now begins your first four weeks of the 120-Days Curriculum. The exercises in this section will not only increase your sensory experience behind the Veil, they'll also lay the foundation for the Lucid Dreaming exercises in the following section. Everything I'm about to teach you comes from firsthand experience working with these methods for over two decades. Still, not all practices are suitable for all people. After all, we're all unique in many important ways. The ideal way to approach the exercises is to proceed in the order in which they're listed. Of course, you can choose the practices that interest you and then, should you feel so inclined, return to the other practices later and give them a try. However, please understand that the exercises are given in a cumulative fashion. Therefore, each skill parlays over to subsequent exercises.

You should be made aware that, although the skills themselves are presented in a cumulative fashion, the process unfolds in more of a mandala-like fashion. It's perfectly acceptable to take one practice from each of the four weeks and practice them concurrently. We all have our own unique style by which learning is made fun and enjoyable. I only present the Curriculum in the present fashion to illustrate the reliance of each respective skill upon one another. However you choose to practice the following skills, you'll notice that the ladder to expertise is by no means a rigid step-by-step affair but proceeds in a spiral-like way with each newly acquired skill bolstering the others and gradually converging upon a center of mastery.

Many people make the unfortunate mistake of assuming that powerful *visualization* skills are all that it takes to have Vivid or Lucid Dreams. While in a certain sense this is true, the word "visualization" pertains to only one of the five senses: the sense of *sight*. However, the truth is that unless all five senses are involved in the dreaming process then you really can't call it Vivid or Lucid Dreaming. You may be able to call it *visual* dreaming, sure, but vivid? No. Lucid? Not really.

All five senses must be involved in the dream experience for it to be authentic Vivid and Lucid Dreaming!

So how does someone cultivate the skill of Vivid Dreaming?

Well, I once heard a great quote from the spiritual teacher, Ram Dass, in which he expressed shock at the number of individuals who are attempting to have out of body experiences. He suggested to such people, wisely, that they should first learn to have a complete *in the body* experience.

I couldn't agree more…

Many people reading this book are probably already well acquainted with Vivid Dreaming. Most people with an interest in Lucid Dreaming and Astral Projection already dream in full color, and are now trying to take their dreaming experience to the next level. Still, my suggestion to such people is that they not skip over this section, as there's more to the following exercises than meets the eye. For starters, many of the following techniques will enhance your current capacity for sensory experience in both the dream *and* awake states. Further, some of these methods are designed to sharpen your imagination, relaxation, and concentration to such an extent that you may even have a Lucid Dream while awake!

Yes, it's possible…

Finally, for those who have difficulty with visualization and imagination, the exercises in this section should suffice to build your inner vision. Dig in and have fun! If you sincerely and consistently practice these exercises you should see progress in your visualization abilities, your power of concentration, and the involvement of your five senses in your nightly dreams.

The exercises in this section range from simple to advanced. Using my own nomenclature, the Curriculum builds muscles in the Gross, Subtle, and Causal Bodies, with an emphasis on the *Veil of Dreams*, the *Veil of Ghosts*, and the *Veil of Bliss*. When you begin the Curriculum, you should start simply and slowly, building upon your practices with care and patience. If you expect quick results you'll only get frustrated, possibly even quit. The key to success in these practices is to do what you can, no matter how small, with each of the featured methods. I assure you that you'll eventually see results if you commit yourself to them.

Some of the following methods require a willingness and capacity to play with perception in an unorthodox way. If you're patient and persevering, I promise you'll be well rewarded. Many people reading this will have mini-breakthroughs because of these methods. These will serve to inspire you and let you know that you're on the right track.

I'd also like to point out that the exercises in this section not only increase your capacity for full sensory dreams, but they also flex your Astral muscles, so to speak. By learning to alter your perception and involve all five senses in the process, you're teaching your subconscious mind that it's okay to set aside your normal way of perceiving in favor of another possibility. The first thing you'll probably notice is that a doorway to spontaneous Lucid Dreaming is opened by the exercises I'm about to share with you. Since Lucid Dreaming is itself a form of OOBE, the Astral Projection experience is just right around the corner.

Now let's get started!

Week One: Channeling Intensity

Welcome to week one of the Curriculum! This first exercise is the foundation for all the other skills that you're going to learn in this book. You should continue practicing it until it becomes as natural as breathing. I first came across it in a Tantric document called the *Vigyan Bhairav Tantra.* I began practicing it in 2004 and was blown away by the results. When I first began the practice, I didn't realize what was in store and the level of commitment required, the doors that it would open, or the unpredictable effect that it would have on my Astral development. First, you must understand that the ways by which you can open, expand, and educate your Astral Body are legion. There truly is no "right" way to do it. However, regardless which method(s) you choose to adopt, you must proceed cautiously, patiently, and perseveringly. Remember this important point:

Your Astral Body is intimately connected with your emotions.

The technique that I'm about to share with you has the power to give you conscious and creative control over that connection, so you should practice it even while learning the other exercises in this book.

The essence of this technique lies in what's been called "channeling intensity." Certain Tantric and Tibetan schools have called it the "Mahamudra" or "Supreme Gesture." I'm referring here to the *One Taste* teaching of Mahamudra.

What? One taste? What's that?

Well, the Indian Sage, Gautama Siddhartha (Buddha), used to describe his experience of enlightenment with analogy to the salt water of the sea. Just as every inch of the ocean, no matter where you find it, has the same salty taste, so too does enlightenment have "one taste" no matter who's experiencing it.

What does this mean?

The following exercise will answer this question. Properly understood, the following technique has the power to:

- Get you in touch with your Astral Body.
- Enhance your overall Etheric energy.
- Deepen your emotional intelligence.
- Sharpen your senses.

Why do they call it the Supreme Gesture?

To answer this, you must understand that most of us live in a sort of waking dream. The average Joe or Jane truly believes that this little thing called "ego" is a concrete and living thing. It's understandable, too, since we need to develop a strong and healthy ego from an early age to survive in this world—which would be fine were it not for the fact that we mistakenly believe that our little self is all that there is to us.

The fragility of the ego is revealed in moments of exasperation, when we react in ways that contradict our self-image. We may be the very picture of poise and calm when things are going smoothly for us, but just a tiny bit of friction and immediately the mask falls off. Whenever we lose our temper, allow the environment to push us around, or respond in a knee-jerk fashion, we're showing our true colors, our "side B," the beast in the basement, as it were. To be sure, there's nothing wrong with these repressed urges and thoughts. In fact, once you strip them of their cultural taboo or remove the moralistic and judgmental weight that holds them down *you're left with raw energy!*

That's right. Any conceivable thought or emotion you possess is energy, first and foremost. Just think about how many uses electricity has, to give one example of energy. On the one hand, electricity is just natural energy. It's not trying to hurt anyone. Then someone like Nikola Tesla comes along and turns it into something productive and transforms human experience forever. Then a man like Alfred P. Southwick comes along and, using the same energy, creates a monstrous device called the electric chair! In much the same way your joy, sadness, excitement, sexuality, creativity, and so on, can be used creatively or crudely.

Another important point to understand is that an enormous amount of energy is wasted in this compartmentalizing of our emotions and thoughts. Each time we feel or think something which we deem or have been taught to believe is wrong, evil, or taboo, and we suppress it we're needlessly chasing our own tail and consuming vast quantities of energy in the process. We do this because we're employing *morality* to do a job that only *intelligence* can do properly. The fact is that most of our emotional reactions, and then our reactions to those reactions, are largely borrowed from the environment we're raised in. Truly, for many of us, we take for granted that we're not behind the wheel at all! Our parents, teachers, leaders, doctors, and priests, are speaking through us.

The practice of Channeling Intensity reconnects us with the greater portion of our energies so that we can claim them as our own.

So, let's begin!

The Practice

The fastest route to grasping the knack of Channeling Intensity is through your newfound skill of Trance. Recall the Zen practice of "just sitting" that we discussed earlier? Well, this is the same thing, only it can be done anywhere and anytime, not just while sitting on your meditation cushion.

Just as Zazen is the art of just sitting, Channeling Intensity could rightly be called the art of *just feeling*. It's one of the most difficult practices you'll ever commit too but also one of the most transformative experiences you'll have, I promise!

It starts with a firm resolution to surrender to the process and open yourself up to the full breadth of your emotions.

So, here's what to do:

You must start by being vigilant and alert to yourself, particularly to your *feeling* self. I don't just mean your emotions, but *all* your feeling. This includes the pain you feel when stubbing your toe, the sensation of an approaching sneeze, your emotional reactions to a movie, the sensations you feel while making love, or the anxiety you feel when giving a public speech.

I mean all of it!

Next, don't criticize, censor, or otherwise label what you're feeling. Just allow it to be fully present without any preconceived idea of what you should or shouldn't be feeling and how it should be dealt with. Also, notice your knee-jerk reactions to your feelings. Notice the almost instantaneous desire to repress, blame, express, hide, or excuse what you're feeling. Simply let all of those reactions flower and self-liberate in your inner space. Metaphorically speaking, this is how you take the base lead of raw emotion and turn it into the gold of refined awareness.

This is inner Alchemy!

Now, once you've got a feel for how to do this, notice an interesting paradox that arises here. In one sense, you removed the separative barrier between your persona and the greater portion of your being submerged beneath it, and yet now there's *more* space between you and this energy. On the one hand, there's this deep well of emotion and sensation churning inside of you, only now you're not present as a little voice in your head vainly dictating how these feelings should be dealt with. You've become raw awareness, like the bright summer Sun shining on the storm clouds. The more you shine your light on all that arises within you, the more sky you have available to you. Not only that, but you'll also notice over time that it enables you to shine even brighter! It's as if these freed emotions are a form of food for your very consciousness.

They are!

The keys to success practice are as follows:

1. Be very present and alert to your bodymind. This is like the relaxed alertness you'd have while fishing or waiting to spot a shooting star. When you experience powerful emotions or sensations, feel into them and follow their pathway through your body without personalizing it. Watch them as you would a passing storm.

2. Start small and gradually move on to more intense emotions. For example, begin by channeling your emotional reactions to a moving song or film. After some time, you may move on to more

emotionally challenging situations like a lover's quarrel or a feud with a coworker.

3. Always be sure to *breathe* through the entire process. Don't do anything with the breath! Simply include your breathing in your awareness. Eventually, you'll be able to regulate the effects that strong emotions have on your *Qi* Meridians with Embryonic Breathing and Microcosmic Orbit. For now, simply breathe while Channeling Intensity.

Continue with this practice until it becomes second nature. Remember, the real attainment is won when you achieve the stage of *regulating without regulating.* In Taoism, this process is known as regulating the *Xin,* or emotional mind. They refer to the *Xin* as "monkey mind" because of its wayward and impulsive nature. The Taoist term for that part of the mind used in Channeling Intensity is the *Yi,* or wisdom mind, which they liken to a horse because of its noble goals and perceptiveness. Once the *Xin* is regulated by the *Yi* through Channeling Intensity, then the *Shen* (union of subconscious/ conscious mind) can be raised, and *the grass grows by itself.* Once this becomes second nature, then practices like Embryonic Breathing and Microcosmic Orbit become something you're always doing in much the same way as your normal breathing goes on whether you're aware of it or not. At this stage, your Subtle Body development has reached an advanced level of cultivation. I can't tell you what happens at that stage because I'm still working on it myself! Rest assured, the possibilities are probably endless.

Week Two: Enhancing Sensory Experience

Now is where we begin our second descent down the proverbial Rabbit Hole. The skills I'm going to teach you here in the second week of the Curriculum are staples of being a Veiler. They hold the key to Vivid and Lucid Dreaming as well as the fully embodied Astral Projection experience. They're at the heart of the Western Hermetic Tradition and form the basis for self-hypnosis, neuroplasticity, and creative inspiration. As you're about to see, there's no conceivable limit to how far you can go with these practices.

I can only teach you what I know, but what I'm going to share will be more than enough to get you started on having intense sensory experiences behind the Veil—from crystal clear inner-vision in full color, auditory enhancement, tactile sensation, taste and smell. Imagine having intense sexual encounters that are more life-like than the real thing! Imagine flying to the moon with all five senses engaged. Well, the following practices will lay the groundwork for intensely Vivid Dreams with an eye to becoming Lucid as well.

In our discussion on getting Lucid, I'll expand on many of the following exercises. Then, when discussing Pellucid Dreaming, we'll explore the very root of sensory experience. Finally, when discussing Astral Projection, you'll learn to separate the root of your consciousness from your physical body. In my experience, *initial* attempts at Astral Projection are best performed from the Pellucid state (Causal Body). The reason for this is that there are minimal distractions from the five senses while in the Pellucid state. For this reason, one can truly distinguish between a Lucid Dream and an Astral Projection.

It all begins with enhanced sensory experience, both in the dream state *and* while awake.

When I first became aware of these practices I was ecstatic. What had formerly made me feel like a freak was suddenly transformed into a thing of immense beauty, for to be able to conjure and sustain sensory phenomena without the aid of any external stimulus is at the heart of many spiritual traditions. Through the power of willed and life-like inner sensory manipulation you can change your biochemistry, alter your state of consciousness, expedite the healing process, stimulate your subconscious mind, enhance your creative inspiration, provoke peak-experiences, and increase your chances of getting Lucid and going Astral.

Let's start with our senses of *sight* and *hearing*.

The Practice

You'll find in the *Appendix* a diagram which I've labeled *Diagram for Visualization Training.* I've included this as a visual aid for the following exercises. Place the image in front of you at eye level. Next, you'll have to do a test to gauge your level of mental agitation, as too much restlessness will interfere with the practice.

Close your eyes. Now place both of your palms over your eyes to create a black visual field. Next, stare gently into the darkness behind your eyes. Do you see a lot of colors or white spots? Are your eyelids twitching? If so, you're too restless for the following exercise and you'll have to calm your mind before proceeding. A great way to accomplish this is to practice Zazen for about ten to fifteen minutes until you enter the Trance state. Just sit in your meditation posture and focus on being still and attentive to your breathing until your mind settles. Then place your palms again over your eyes. If the field of vision behind your eyes is a relaxed, velvety black then you're ready to begin the exercise.

Open your eyes and gently stare into the diagram. Stare directly into its center without blinking. This fixed gazing is called *Trataka* in Yoga. Do this for about thirty seconds and then suddenly shut your eyes. Soon, the afterimage of the diagram will appear floating behind your eyes. It will be in contrasting colors to those of the actual diagram. What you're seeing is an exact replica of the diagram composed entirely of phosphene discharge. Later, you'll be able to willfully mold this substance into any shape, scene, or dream that you wish! For now, simply stare into the afterimage floating behind your eyes for as long as it remains. The more relaxed your mind, the longer the image will remain.

Once the image fades, recreate it with your imagination so that it reappears before your closed eyes. Be sure to include every detail. Do this for as long as you're able. Then repeat the entire process three more times before concluding the session. Practice this simple exercise every day for one week. Your goal should be to add ever more complex imagery to your practice. Eventually, you should be able to include entire vistas and scenes in your inner vision and actively sustain them with a relaxed but unwavering concentration.

You should expand this practice and perform the above steps on mountains, people, paintings, and so on, until you can dispense with the "afterimage" portion of the exercise and simply create an image behind your closed eyes at will. Begin with simple geometrical shapes and gradually expand to more complex images and scenes. With practice, you'll start to notice that you can manipulate and mold the phosphene discharge behind your eyes at will, without having to first do the fixed-gaze of *Trataka.* If you do this while falling asleep you can induce a **WILD** (Wake Induced Lucid Dream).

Mastery is attained when you can create an image in front of you with your eyes open. Go ahead and try it now! Begin by standing or sitting in front of a wall with a uniform color. It doesn't matter what the color is, only that it's uniform, like a blank canvas. Also, the room you're in must be a silent as possible for this exercise. If need be, purchase earplugs. Next, don't stare at the surface of the canvas, but rather, stare into it as if it were a window looking out onto a landscape. Sometimes the landscape will appear on its own and without any assistance. This is known in the Pagan community as *Skrying in the Spirit Vision.* Really, though, that's just a fancy way of saying that you're having a Lucid Dream while awake. What we're attempting to do here is the same thing, only we're going to control the process.

Conjure up the image of the *Diagram for Visualization Training* and allow it to float inside the "window" of the canvas. You should visualize it in full color, but now you're going to take it a step further. Without losing sight of the diagram, tune in to the ringing sounds in your ears. There must be total silence for you to hear these subtle sounds. In Yoga, meditation upon these sounds is known as *Suriya Shabda,* or *Listening to the Solar Currents.* For our purposes, I'm going to teach you how to use them to cultivate clairaudience and enhanced hearing in the dream state.

Maintain a relaxed focus on both the hovering image and the ringing in your ears. At this point, you'll probably notice that the tones become louder. This is exactly what you want! Don't focus overmuch on the tones; otherwise they'll decrease in volume. Simply include both the image and the sound in your awareness at this point. You may notice that you're beginning to hear voices, sounds, or perhaps even music within these inner tones. Don't worry, you're not going crazy! When this begins to happen you're ready to move on to the next step of manipulating the tones with your will.

Begin by willing the tones to go higher and lower in pitch. When you inhale make them go higher and when you exhale make them lower. Then try morphing the tones into simple vowel sounds. After you've gotten the hang of that, go ahead and add a consonant. You could use the infamous "OM" sound, but really any combination of vowel and consonant will do fine. Try them all! Experiment with "AAAH", "OOOSS", "FAAA", and so on. With time and practice you'll soon be able to form sentences within these tones! If cultivated properly, this technique holds the key to the psychic skill called "clairaudience."

If you find that you have difficulty doing this exercise, don't worry. If you can hear the tones and concentrate upon them you can use them for Conscious Dreaming. We'll be employing them again in our exploration of Lucid Dreaming. For now, it's important to note that voices will most often be heard coming from *within* the tones, and not as the tones themselves. Usually these are no more than projections of your own mind, which is what we're aiming for here, but sometimes they're something much more. That's a discussion for another time...

Enjoy this exercise for as long as you wish before bringing it to a close. It's recommended that you practice Embryonic Breathing to regulate the effects which these exercises have on your *Qi* network, and then circulate using Microcosmic Orbit.

Week Three: The Healing Hands

In week three of the Curriculum, we include inner *sight, sound*, and *feeling* in our practice. Feeling is truly the primary skill in all behind-the-Veil activity. Whether you're having a Vivid or Lucid Dream, going Astral, practicing Qigong, fantasizing, or going under hypnosis, you need a refined capacity for *feeling* to reach your goals as a Veiler.

This next practice is a technique for self-healing, but we're using it here to develop our behind-the-Veil senses of sight, sound, and feeling. They say that seeing is believing, and that's okay, but it's when you *feel* what you see that the true magic happens! At the end of week four of the Curriculum, I'll introduce you to a very challenging practice which brings all five senses to bear on the experience. Once you reach that stage you can expect some interesting transformations in your nightly dreams!

I call this technique "The Healing Hands." There are countless versions of this practice, but this is my favorite. Remember to practice in a quiet room where you won't be disturbed for the duration of the practice. Turn your phone off and remove any source of strong EMF such as a plugged-in laptop or cell phone (as always).

The Practice

Sit down in your meditation posture in a dark and quiet room. Close your eyes and slowly enter the Trance state. Enjoy this relaxation for a few moments. Now become aware of your Etheric energy by feeling into the space around your physical body. If you feel any physical sensations, such as tingling, skin-crawling, heat, cold, twitches, and so on, simply notice them dispassionately. Feel into your Gross, Subtle and Causal Bodies at the same time by relaxing, and enjoy this moment of conscious embodiment. If thoughts come, let them come and go without grasping or avoiding them.

Next, move your awareness to a few inches above the crown of your head. Using your body heat as a guide, try to feel for a point of energy there. When you feel tingling or heat on the top of your head you've found this point. In Taoism this spot is called *Baihui*. It's the Etheric counterpoint to the *Huiyin* point located at the perineum. Just as *Huiyin* is the most *Yin* spot in the body, *Baihui* is the most *Yang* spot.

Now, if you haven't already done so, become aware of your natural breathing rhythm, focusing more on the exhalation phase. At the same time, become aware of the ringing tones in your ears while vividly imagining two hands hovering over your head. The palms of the hands are open and emanating a warm, healing, golden light downward upon and into the top of your head. Feel the warmth of this light gently and lovingly penetrate your skull, bringing instant relaxation to your scalp, eyes, ears, and sinuses. As soon as this happens the tones should become lower in pitch.

Imagine now two more hands appearing from below your buttocks, about three inches below your *Huiyin*. The palms are facing up and emanating the same warm and healing light into your buttocks, coccyx, groin, and Lower Dantian. Wherever this light goes, instant relaxation and healing follows. At this same instant, the tones will become even lower in pitch. Remain aware of your natural breathing throughout this exercise.

Without losing sight, sound, and feeling of these two sets of healing hands and the tones, two more sets of hands appear on the left and right of you. They should be about three inches or so from your body and level with your shoulders. Their palms are open and facing you, sending warm and radiant heat into your shoulders, gently penetrating your lungs, and converging at the center of the inside of your chest where they form a bright golden ball of light. Feel these areas relax and smile from within.

Finally, two more sets of hands appear in front and behind you. They should be level with the center of your chest and back. These hands also send healing light toward and into your body. Without becoming tense, really try to visualize these hands as vividly as possible, including in your awareness your natural breathing rhythm, the inner tones, and the sensation of healing and relaxation wherever the golden light travels.

Next, imagine that the hands at your crown descend into your head, down your spine, and come to rest in your solar plexus. Then the hands below you do the same, ascending into your pelvis, up your spine, and settling in your solar plexus. These hands bring warmth, joy, and healing wherever they travel. There, at your solar plexus, these two sets of hands meet and clasp each other as if in greeting. A warm golden glow radiates from them. Enjoy this for a few moments.

Now imagine, and vividly feel, the two sets of hands before and behind you slowly rotating along the path of the Microcosmic Orbit. Really feel and see them moving along the Governing and Conception Vessels, bringing healing as they rotate. The other two sets of hands on either side of you remain where they are for now, and the two sets of hands united in your solar plexus also remain where they are. Try to make the inner tones rise and fall in pitch as the hands rotate in the Microcosmic Orbit. When you inhale, the tones rise in pitch; when you exhale, they lower in pitch. Breathe naturally, coordinating the rotating hands with the rise and fall of your breath. Rotate about twenty times, and then bring the two sets of hand to rest back at their original positions in front and back of you. Then, with an inhalation of breath, the hands enter the center of your chest and clasp each other in greeting. A warm glow radiates from them. Let the inner tones be as they are, but maintain awareness of them.

Now rest in this awareness of these two golden sets of healing hands, two clasped in your solar plexus and the other two clasped in the center of your chest, all the while breathing naturally and listening to the inner tones. They should sound as if they're surrounding you now. Feel for any tension or numb spots within and around your body. Send the other two sets of hands resting on either side of you to these blocked areas, bringing with them healing and relaxation. Sometimes it helps to picture them operating on these areas, stitching and repairing them. Do this for as long as you wish or until you feel joyful and warm.

This concludes the practice.

Week Four: Taste, Smell & the Touchless Orgasm

The fourth week of the Curriculum focuses on the senses of *taste* and *smell*. Because of how intimately related they are, these two senses are best trained together. Still, don't let that stop you from training them separately should you be so inclined. Remember, the exercises of the 120-Days Curriculum are meant to be introductory only. They're designed to get you started on the path to becoming a skilled Veiler and to build the foundation for Conscious Sleep and Astral Projection. Use them as springboards to further practice.

By now you should be regularly practicing Embryonic Breathing, Microcosmic Orbit, Channeling Intensity, Visualization, Dream Recall/Journaling, and the Healing Hands. Although you can be flexible with these practices, I really do advise that you work with them as often as possible. It's a shame that so many people are looking for a quick fix, wanting to master Astral Projection or Lucid Dreaming overnight. Not that there's anything wrong with searching for intelligent ways to access these skills as quickly as possible. I completely understand and honor that. However, there's so much more to be gained by taking an Integral and well-rounded approach to the subject, and that takes a little more time and patience. There are so many interesting gains to be had while taking the longer road home. It's much like hiking. Imagine how many sights you'd miss out on should you decide to helicopter your way to the summit of a high mountain! Or consider the difference between a virtuoso pianist and someone who just knows a few chords. In terms of depth of musical experience, they're literally worlds apart.

The essence of the following practices is simple. Pick a food or beverage with a strong scent and taste. Let's use coffee as an example. While the coffee is brewing, stand by and really hone in on your sense of smell. Allow the fragrance of the coffee to fill your nostrils. Turn it into a meditation! As you do so, try to conjure up the *taste* of coffee. Get your taste buds involved and really try to taste and feel the coffee on your tongue without drinking it. Once the coffee has finished brewing, drink and enjoy it as you would normally. Once you finish, wait a few minutes, and then try to recreate the scent and taste of coffee.

You can try this experiment on just about anything, but foods with both a strong scent and taste work best. Lemon is another favorite of mine. After performing the above steps on a slice of lemon, see if you can mentally recreate its smell and taste. If you can make your mouth water by mentally reproducing the sour smell and taste of lemon, then you've got it! Go ahead and spoil yourself a little and experiment on chocolate, ice cream, wine, or anything else that makes you smile. Personally, I use *Shilajit* resin, coffee, lemon, and any scent with memories attached to it. Smell is a powerful stimulator of memory, so bringing more awareness to it is a great way to stimulate Conscious Dreaming.

Remember, you can isolate any of the five senses and work on it individually. Mastery is attained when you can conjure and combine all five senses at once. At that point, you should notice a profound shift in how lifelike your dreams are becoming! I find that sensory objects which invoke primal responses are best to use. The next exercise I'm going to share with you isn't suitable for everyone. I decided to include the following technique because it operates directly on the intimate connection between the Upper and Lower energy centers. Succeeding with it will stand as irrefutable proof that you've attained something special.

I'm referring to something called *The Touchless Orgasm.*

Consider this: the ability to have an orgasm without the need for physical stimulation, using only the power of your imagination, is proof of a blossoming mastery over your inner world.

I discovered this method spontaneously, through my own experimentation. Because I regularly experienced Vivid and Lucid Dreams of a sexual nature that sometimes ended in very real orgasms, I found myself wondering if I could induce the same thing while awake. When I succeeded in doing so I was shocked. Then again, the only criteria for making it happen is the ability to feel, see, hear, smell, and taste oneself into believing that the sexual fantasy is real. Do that skillfully enough and the body responds accordingly.

For this to work you must give it your total attention. Get all of your senses and emotions involved in the process. Women will most likely approach this exercise differently than men, as each tend to experience sexuality in different ways. For example, men tend to be more visual than women. Consequently, most men may find that they can mentally *see* their way to sexual arousal, but they're unable to achieve orgasm past that point without physical stimulation. Women, on the other hand, may find that they can mentally *feel* their way to arousal but can't reach orgasm without direct stimulation.

I've modified the following technique with these important differences in mind.

One last thing! If you can't carry this experiment through to the end, don't take it as a failure. It's not. If you can be totally absorbed in the fantasy with all five senses involved, you've done well. Remember, the goal is to heighten your sensory experience *while awake* to such an extent that the ability spills over into our dreams. From there, you've laid the foundation for all other skills as a Veiler.

The Practice

Naturally, this practice requires a room with a locked door. Be sure that you won't be disturbed for at least half an hour. If it helps, create the mood by arranging the room accordingly. For some, this won't be necessary. Others may find that lighting candles, incense, dressing up in sexy clothes, and putting on romantic music, helps to stimulate sexual longing. Don't feel embarrassed or ashamed of autoeroticism. This is nothing but a celebration of your energies and of life itself. Enjoy it! Do whatever you need to do to get the most out of this celebration.

Mentally conjure up your favorite sexual fantasy. Everyone has his or her own fantasy which most arouses them. For some, this may be their romantic partner, wife, or husband. I personally feel that the presence of love is a powerful force to include in just about any practice, but this one benefits from it. That said, it's not necessary to succeed in this exercise.

Begin by physically stimulating yourself until you're very aroused. Try to include in your fantasy as much of your five senses as possible. If you're fantasizing about your lover, for example, try to smell her or his cologne, perfume, pheromones, etc. Really see her or him in your mind's eye as vividly as possible. Some people find that closed eyes are best for this, and others may find that they can do this with eyes open. Try both methods!

Continue until you feel orgasm approaching, and then *stop the physical stimulation.* Continue with the fantasy, but stop touching yourself completely.

At this point, many people feel nothing but frustration. If that's the case, alternate between physical stimulation and no stimulation at all. The main thing is to keep the fantasy going with all five senses engaged. In the example of fantasizing about one's lover, follow these five rules:

- See her/him
- Feel her/him
- Smell her/him
- Taste her/him
- Hear her/him

Alternate between short rounds of physical stimulation and prolonged periods of pure fantasy. The main objective is, of course, to reach orgasm by using mental stimulation alone. This takes a little practice, but if you can achieve it then you're probably already beginning to have Lucid Dreams as well as Vivid Dreams. Remember, this is an extreme example of a very common mechanism. It's no different than imagining a feast and then actually becoming hungry as a result. Or having a very sexual dream and waking up to a very real orgasm. The only difference is that, in this exercise, we're attempting to gain control of this mind/body interface. Why? Because this is just one of many ways you build and strengthen the conscious link between your Gross and Subtle Bodies.

If this exercise doesn't suit you, feel free to get creative. One great alternative to the Touchless Orgasm is the *Dustless Sneeze*. Try to conjure a sneeze without anything provoking it other than your intent. Or else try to conjure a yawn. Another favorite of mine is to change the size of my pupils according to my imagination of light or darkness. If you have access to a video recorder, go into a bright room and film a close-up of your eyes. Without closing them, imagine that you're in a pitch-dark room with no windows. Hold this visualization in mind for a few minutes and then watch the recording. If your pupils widen at the instant you began the visualization, then you've got it!

CHAPTER EIGHT

GET LUCID!

Until you make the unconscious conscious,
It will control your life and you will call it fate.

— Carl Jung

The topic of this chapter hardly requires an introduction. The "white whale" of many aspiring Veilers and sleep scientists, Lucid Dreaming has achieved a recent popularity second only to that of Astral Projection. Because it has now been scientifically validated, Lucid Dreamers are no longer reticent about coming out and sharing their experiences. As I said earlier, I've been having Lucid Dreams and other OOBE experiences since early childhood, only I didn't understand what was happening at the time. It took me many years to get past my fear of what was happening, evaluate it from a place beyond the narrow context of my upbringing, and finally explore this remarkably rich and textured landscape free of fear and confusion. Because of this struggle, I've pinpointed the mechanism by which all OOBE takes place and can now share it with you.

During this fifth week of the Curriculum, we'll explore the fascinating topic of Lucid Dreaming with an eye toward acquiring and refining the skill for your own enjoyment and evolution. We'll go a little further in-depth regarding the sleep cycle and how you can tap into it to access Lucidity. Remember, to become a skilled Veiler you must approach these skills both from the inside and the outside, as it were. Practices like Trance, Embryonic Breathing, Microcosmic Orbit, Sensory Enhancement, and so on are the inside part of training. Learning how to use the natural rhythms of the cosmos and your own bodymind are the outside part of training. In the former case, you're building the muscles necessary to perform these feats. In the latter case, you're approaching these realms at right angles, so to speak, and coming at them from the sides. It's much like building muscles by first using your own body weight *and then* going to the gym and using the equipment there. Or like training on the "inner wall" before rock-climbing on a real mountain. Both inner and outer approaches are required to access and maintain dream Lucidity in a full and balanced manner.

If you've followed the Curriculum up to this point, then you may have already begun to have Lucid Dreams. Because these skills are cumulative and transferrable, training one will typically give rise to the others. Still, you must approach each skill in a unique fashion, as each has its own unique architecture and mechanism. When you wake up inside of a dream, you know that what you're experiencing is unlike anything else that happens while you're sleeping or awake! In a Vivid Dream, you may have full-sensory experiences, but you're under a sort of hypnotic spell, whereas in a Lucid Dream you're in relative or full control of the experience. You're engaged in a conscious dance between the conscious and subconscious regions of your mind...and beyond.

It's important to understand that dream Lucidity isn't just a matter of waking up inside of a dream and manipulating the landscape or narrative. It's a matter of psychic projection being sustained by Etheric energy. Ask anyone with experience in Lucid Dreaming or Astral Projection if they've ever felt drained after a few adventurous nights. Most people with these skills have the first part of the formula, but lack the second. That is, they can do the psychic projection part, but lack the foundational Etheric economy to sustain prolonged periods of time spent behind the Veil.

Some people, especially those with so-called dissociative disorders, have natural access to these skills. As a result, they can effortlessly conjure a Lucid Dream or Astral adventure, but they have difficulty grounding their experiences or controlling them. It's not unlike a singer with natural vocal talent. Sure, they can sing, but without proper training they'll rarely reach their full potential and may even damage their voice. The same thing tends to happen to individuals who overuse psychedelics as a means of accessing rarified states of consciousness. Such persons often become moody, irritable, fatigued, or mentally ill. Without a stable and grounded approach—one that's fueled by abundant *Qi* and set in an Integral and holistic context—most subtle-realm experiences tend to leave the aspirant feeling drained and off center. Changed, yes, but not always for the better.

Dream Lucidity is a skill that requires the capacity for psychic dissociation fueled by a surplus of Etheric energy, is balanced by holistic evaluation, and grounded in an integral framework.

What do I mean by the term *Integral*?

To put it very generally, to be *Integral* means that you understand that all sentient beings, events, and aspirations, exist in a universe of other sentient beings, events, and aspirations. Not only that, but these things are also set within the context of a culture and political climate. As a conscious being, you have both a subjective and personal aspect as well as a physical and behavioral aspect, and you exist among other conscious beings who are in the same predicament. Furthermore, as a conscious being, you are *evolving*. You have strengths and weaknesses, and there are limits to what you can and can't do. As an evolving entity, your job is to use your strengths and challenge your weaknesses. You can't do that efficiently unless you take these basic facts of your existence into account. When it comes to the skills being taught in this book, you must continually check in with these aspects of yourself whenever you practice or experience something new.

So, what is the essence of the skill of Lucid Dreaming?

The ability to bring all of your senses to bear on creating something that isn't there, all the while knowing that it's an illusion, is the sole talent for Lucid Dreaming, and this applies whether you're asleep or awake.

That's right!

You don't have to be asleep to have a Lucid Dream!

For example, if my hands are cold and I can warm them by vividly imagining that I'm holding them over a fire, then I've just used Lucid Dreaming while awake. Literally, the only difference is that my Gross Body is awake while I'm dreaming. Personally, I believe this to be one half of the Tibetan skill of *Tummo,* a skill which allows monks to meditate naked in the snow and still break a sweat.

If I can play with my perception in this manner while asleep *and* awake, I've mastered Lucid Dreaming. The key is to have complete control over the illusion and, more importantly, to *know* that it's an illusion. Unless you try it, there's really no way to convey to you the feeling of creating a convincing illusion while simultaneously remaining aware that it's not real. The fun part is playing with the fine line that separates illusion from the rest of reality.

Developing your concentration and visualization abilities is the crucial key to success in Lucid Dreaming, and cultivating your spiritual center and psychological ground is the key to staying sane in the process. All too often I see books about Lucid Dreaming that completely ignore this very important point. You're learning how to play with your perception in very novel ways. Granted, you're doing this without the use of drugs or psychoactive substances, but it can still be just as dangerous if you're not careful. Furthermore, you need to know how to cleanse and balance the *Qi* Meridian system so that you don't end up with too much or too little *Qi* in any of your internal organs. This especially applies to the five *Yin* organs, as we've already seen.

We'll start by learning the rudimentary skill called the *dissociative reflex*.

I'm going to teach you several methods for acquiring and cultivating the film-projector reflex of the psyche. Please remember that Lucid Dreaming and Astral Projection are NOT the same thing. They both work along similar lines and utilize the dissociative talent, but Lucid Dreaming is almost 100% the conscious use of the dissociative reflex, whereas Astral Projection utilizes that reflex to get up and out, but then flies above and beyond the noise of one's own psyche. The two experiences often unavoidably merge and occupy the same session, hence the confusion, but they're not synonyms.

Then the question arises: if Astral Projection and Lucid Dreaming aren't the same, then how is it that Lucid and Vivid Dreams often reveal knowledge that couldn't have been known otherwise?

To answer this question you must understand that the subconscious part of your psyche is always picking up details which the conscious mind is totally unaware of. Advertisers know this all too well and employ it as an effective means of marketing: a subliminal message here, a flashing billboard sign there. The ever-open eye of the subconscious mind sees *everything*. Often our dreams reveal information of which we're consciously unaware, but subconsciously we know quite well. For example, I once lost my debit card and was shown in a dream where to find it. Sure enough, I checked the next morning and there it was. Even though my wife and I had searched for it there numerous times, my subconscious mind detected that the card was pressed up against an object of the same color and was therefore camouflaged by it.

That's not to say that this very same thing doesn't occur during Astral Projection. It does. The difference is that in Lucid Dreaming you're often seeing a memory of something that your conscious mind didn't register, whereas Astral Projection tends to reveal events in real-time, especially on the lower Planes. As always, time and testing will reveal for you the subtle but important differences between Lucid Dreaming, Astral Projection, and the many ways in which they merge. As you'll no doubt see for yourself, Lucid Dreaming and Astral Projection often merge into what we've been calling the *Astral Dream,* thereby combining elements of both. Personally, even though I use the term "bodies" to qualify the general levels of being (the Perennial Philosophy), I'm not wholly convinced that we leave the physical body during Astral Projection. Rather, I theorize that what's happening is that the brain is emitting and receiving electrical transmissions. These are then experienced by the nervous system and translated into sensory memories and experiences. Just as we can fuel electrical output by using water and wind, Astral Projection and Lucid Dreaming are fueled by *Qi* (Etheric force).

The exercises in this chapter have been culled from several different sources. I've also included my own discoveries and the exercises I've developed along the way. Before we begin, though, let's take a brief but closer look at the sleep cycle and what's occurring while your head's on the pillow. Remember, to understand the rhythm and pattern of your sleep cycle gives you an edge when trying to attain Lucidity in the dream state and beyond.

The Sleep Cycle Revisited

In *Chapter One* we explored the rudimentary aspects of the sleep cycle including the Five Basic Brainwaves and their corresponding states of awareness. In this section, we'll explore the sleep cycle more in-depth. Our goal is to become familiar with this cycle to spot opportunities for Lucid Dreaming. We'll learn the *when* and the *why* of Lucid Dreaming by examining the sleep cycle. After that, we'll learn the *how*. I'll teach you time-tested methods for achieving Lucidity and then introduce you to some of my own methods.

As we've already seen, a natural and healthy sleep cycle occurs roughly every ninety minutes and repeats about five times per night. Sleep starts out light and becomes heavier until deep sleep prevails. This soon gives way to short bouts of dreaming. Each time the sleep cycle repeats, the dreaming phase becomes longer. The technical name for this sleep pattern is *Ultradian Rhythm.* We've also seen that these sleep phases have bioelectrical correlates, with light sleep producing **ALPHA** waves, dreamless sleep producing **DELTA** waves, dreaming producing **THETA** waves, and Lucid Dreaming producing **GAMMA** waves.

Light sleep, and most periods of deep sleep, present themselves as something called **NREM** (non-rapid eye-movement). When profound dreaming begins, it presents as **REM** (rapid eye-movement). The greater portion of the sleep cycle occurs during **NREM**, with **REM**-like activity only appearing as short bursts of dreaming called "sleep spindles" (but not **REM** proper). Then, as the sleep cycle repeats, the **REM** phase becomes longer and dreaming more profound.

NREM dominates about three fourths of the sleep cycle. It's important to understand that Lucid Dreaming can and does occur during **NREM** and not just **REM** phases of sleep. Pellucid Dreaming can occur throughout the sleep cycle as well. However, the degree, strength, and type of Lucidity is very much influenced by what phase of sleep you're in. Other factors, such as training and practice, diet, and economy of Etheric force *(Qi),* also play a pivotal role in the strength and staying-power of Lucidity.

I've spotted and qualified three stages of Lucidity, which I'll list simply as:

- **LD-1**
- **LD-2**
- **LD-3**

In **LD-1,** we experience light Lucidity. Most people are familiar with this degree and type of Lucidity. As we fall from wakeful **BETA** to drowsy **ALPHA,** we begin to experience minor but noticeable dreamlike patterns called "hypnagogia." These typically present as swirling psychedelic colors, geometrical shapes, landscapes, and audio hallucinations. Sensations of falling are very common. With practice, one can learn how to enter and manipulate these minor dream manifestations using something I call the "hitchhiker" method (more on this later). At any rate, **LD-1** almost always lacks the strength to persist for more than a few minutes and is usually swallowed up by the deeper levels of **NREM**.

LD-2 is a stronger form of Lucidity, but still lacks the stamina required for sustained awareness through and into the deep phases of sleep. Oftentimes this stage of Lucidity finds the dreamer witnessing the dream scenario, but unable to control or fully participate in it. This mustn't be confused with Pellucid Dreaming, in which the dreamer has full Lucidity, but remains a passive witness of the dream scenario. **LD-2** is a huge step forward in the process of attaining Dream Control, but it's still not quite enough to fully withstand the spell of deep sleep.

LD-3, on the other hand, represents an unmistakable breakthrough in the consciousness of the individual who achieves it. Just one experience of full Lucidity will change your life forever. Unlike Vivid Dreaming, or even **LD-1** and **LD-2**, the attainment of **LD-3** is an authentic *out of body experience*. Here, we have finally achieved a consciousness which is capable of withstanding deep sleep and is present through the entire **REM** phase of sleep. When this happens, you've taken a momentous leap in the development of your spirit. To fully comprehend the power of this breakthrough, you must experience it for yourself. I'm going to do my best to help you do just that.

When training Conscious Sleep, it helps to know the difference between *sleep* and *rest* and, more importantly, which skills are best applied to each. When you're awake and the **BETA** brainwave predominates, you're technically asleep to the subtler aspects of your being and reality itself. By learning to bring more consciousness into the sleep, dream, and Astral aspects of your being, you're literally stimulating those realms and their respective energies to parlay into your wakeful life.

Says the poet: *"Not in entire forgetfulness, but trailing clouds of glory do we come!"*

Should you ever sit quietly and listen to the sound of the rain, not thinking or desiring to be elsewhere, you might fall into a sort of reverie in which the **ALPHA** brainwave predominates. However, you're still aware of your physical body, and so you're not truly asleep but merely at rest. This is the optimal state to be in for Etheric energy work such as Qigong, Reiki, Raja Yoga, and so on, to give just a few examples. Then, suddenly, your physical body vanishes from awareness. You might nod off for a moment and come back to **ALPHA**, but if you allow it, soon you're completely immersed in the dream realm and your physical body is totally asleep. Continue in this way for a while and dreams too will vanish, opening the door to the **DELTA** brainwave. Now you're totally asleep to the dream *and* the wakeful worlds. Should you manage to stay alert at this deep fathom of your being, **GAMMA** brainwaves predominate, and you're fully anchored in your Causal Body. Soon, this will give way to another sleep cycle and, if you can remain conscious, the Astral doors open!

Before we begin our Lucid Dreaming training I'd like to offer a few helpful tips. At this point, you may practice your Vivid Dreaming exercises as you wish. However, you must continue to regularly practice Embryonic Breathing and Microcosmic Orbit. You should also obtain an alarm clock, featuring a gradually increasing volume rather than one that jolts you from sleep with a sudden shriek. Alarms which can be set to go off at set intervals are ideal for learning Lucid Dreaming. Remember, we cycle through **REM** Dreaming roughly every ninety minutes, so setting your alarm to repeat at these intervals will train you to become aware at those times. The trick is to hover on the edge of wakefulness and sleep during these periods without fully waking up.

Also, start doing "reality checks" throughout the day. This is a popular method of engaging your conscious mind to make Lucid Dreaming both possible and desirable. It also triggers your subconscious to meet you halfway, and is one of the highly recommended practices in Tibetan Dream Yoga. Unfortunately, it tends to be very misunderstood. Periodically checking throughout the day to see whether you're awake or dreaming isn't the essence of this practice. Rather, it works by tapping into that magical mindset enjoyed by small children, and by questioning the realness of your perception itself. For example, hold an object in your hand. It can be anything from a pencil to a billiard ball. Now try to make it levitate. Really believe that you can make it happen and even go so far as to feel and see it lift off your palm and into the air. That's the first aspect of the reality-check exercise. You can experiment with other reality-check methods throughout the day, like trying to fly or move objects with your mind. Get creative! The whole point is to form a bridge between the wakeful and dreaming regions of your mind. The second aspect of the reality-check method is to see, not the objects of your awareness as a dream, but your very *consciousness* as a dream. If you can manage to sincerely question whether *you* are real, then you've understood the very essence of the reality-check method.

Finally, stay away from sedatives during these next four weeks. Avoid excess alcohol consumption, marijuana, and sleeping pills. Also to be avoided are excess physical and mental strain, overeating, excess ejaculation, and emotional conflicts. Anything that drains your energy and scatters your mind should be reduced or omitted for the time being. The skill of Lucid Dreaming requires discipline and a fierce commitment. You're not only forging a direct link to your subconscious mind, but you're also laying the foundation for Astral Projection, which is just Lucid Dreaming *plus*.

So let's begin!

Week Five: The Dissociative Reflex

All that's needed to learn Lucid Dreaming is a strong and consistent intention to do so. That, and a healthy abundance of bioenergy. In fact, the method of self-hypnosis called *Coueism* is just one example of how effective the cooperative use of Will and Imagination can be in cultivating Lucid Dreaming and other forms of OOBE. Regardless of what method you choose, if you make it a serious priority and attempt it every night before and during the sleep cycle, sooner or later you'll succeed in Lucid Dreaming. However, unless you're the type of person who has an inborn talent for Vivid Dreaming and the dissociative reflex, then you'll have to acquire them before you can simply demand Lucid Dreaming to become a regular *trait* of your consciousness and not merely a passing *state* that you sometimes glimpse.

Training the dissociative reflex, enhancing Vivid Dreams, performing reality-checks, and providing your consciousness with abundant Etheric energy are the only things you can do to consciously induce stable and recurrent **LD-3** stage Lucid Dreams. Other than that, there's really nothing you can do *directly* to access Lucid Dreaming. The reason for this is that the conscious part of you functions on a level and with a logic that stands on opposite ends to that of the dreaming mind. This is why something that can make total sense in a dream seems totally absurd to the conscious mind. Your goal as a Veiler is to bring more and more of your conscious mind into the dream state and more of the dream state into conscious awareness. Illustrated symbolically, the entire process is like a hexagram. The descending triangle represents your conscious mind, and the ascending triangle represents your subconscious mind.

That you can't access full Lucidity through a conscious *tour de force* is one reason why acquiring the skill of Trance is so important. The first thing you learn in Trance training is the art of non-doing, as we've seen. It's important to remember this as we approach these next four weeks. When it comes to Lucid Dreaming, it helps to remember this axiom:

Anything done by the conscious mind chains you to the conscious mind!

Oftentimes, simply by allowing this fundamental truth to operate while falling asleep or just waking up, Lucid Dreaming happens spontaneously. I've even seen it have a positive impact on mild insomnia. Why? Because acceptance of the fact that nothing can be done to willfully induce Lucid Dreaming, or even sleep for that matter, does two things. One, it conserves the energy needed to consciously step behind the Veil, and two, it moves you out of the way so that something else can break through. In weeks eleven through twelve of the Curriculum, I'll introduce you to a few methods that utilize your conscious mind in a creative and indirect way to induce Pellucid Dreaming.

Since we've already covered everything else needed to begin Lucid Dreaming, I'll now share with you some of my own methods for training the dissociative reflex. In a very literal sense, every one of us is to some extent *dissociative*. I don't mean that we're all mentally ill! Dissociative *disorder* is a pathological expression of the dissociative reflex. What I'm referring to is at the very root of the reflective mind itself. We've already discussed this elsewhere, but now we'll put it into practice. Without some degree of mastery over our psychic film-projector, you'll have difficulty acquiring the skill of Lucid Dreaming.

Here in week five, I'll introduce you to two methods for first-hand experience of the dissociative reflex. In week six, I'll teach you something that I call "The Hitchhiker" method. In week seven, we'll learn how to combine all the above while falling asleep. Finally, in week eight, we'll explore how to create the type of dreams you wish to have.

The Practice: The Trailing Method

Go into a dark room and sit down comfortably. Calm your mind so the field of vision behind your closed eyes is relatively black with minimal colors or white spots. Remember, the amount of phosphene discharge behind your closed eyes is a reliable way to gauge how tense your mind is. The greater the lightshow, the greater the tension. Once you've established a relatively black field of vision, go ahead and light a candle, any candle. Stare into the flame without blinking until you see a colored aura or afterimage appear around the candle's flame. Now blow the candle out.

Next, stand up and keep your eyes open while gazing gently at the afterimage of the candle flame. Eventually it'll begin to move. Follow it! Keep your eyes glued to it and simply follow it whenever it moves. There will come a point when the afterimage looks *completely* external. In fact, go ahead and let it sit in the palm of your hand. Just stare at it and watch its behavior. The more relaxed your mind, the longer the afterimage will remain.

I remember the first time I discovered this experiment. I was sixteen years old. Standing on my mother's porch, I stared into the porch light for a moment and looked away. The afterimage appeared, and I just decided to follow it (I'm weird like that). Eventually it came to rest in the palm of my hand and I watched it change into all kinds of different things! Geometric shapes, animals, and tiny scenes of mountains and lakes (dream scenarios). But the real surprise came when I discovered that I could decide what shape it took. Sound familiar? It should.

That's *dream control!*

Now you can do it, too. I'll even show you how to shape the phosphene discharge behind your eyes into anything you wish to see. Try it! Instead of staring *at* the afterimage of the candle flame, stare *into* it. If it moves, follow it but stare into its center. One of two things will begin to happen if you practice this for one week. Either the afterimage will morph into all manner of different things, or you'll begin to see scenes within the afterimage itself. You can also try this in bed at night before falling asleep or during sitting meditation. Simply stare gently into the colored blobs behind your eyes as you're drifting off to sleep and watch what happens! With practice, you can even decide what scenes should appear and what landscape you'd like to step into. If you guessed that this is how you can choose what to dream before falling asleep then you guessed right, but the important thing for you to take away from this little experiment is this:

The psyche projects itself.

When you experience the dissociative reflex while awake, the contents of your psyche are projected onto the screen of the physical environment. However, when you experience the dissociative reflex while your physical body is asleep, *you* are projected onto the screen of the psychic and Astral environment.

How so?

Well, while you're awake, your sense of "I" and "Me" is firmly rooted in your physical body and its five senses. On the other hand, as your physical body falls asleep, your awareness of bodily processes and sensations vanishes. I believe that this is because your presence gets in the way of the physical regeneration achieved through healthy sleep. To be aware of and mentally evaluating the events of daily life takes energy; therefore, nature has evolved dreams to keep you occupied while the body heals itself. Well, that's my theory anyway. More to the point, your awareness while in **REM** sleep is firmly rooted in what I've been calling the *Subtle Body*. If you can maintain awareness and keep alert while transitioning from awake to asleep, then you'll notice that the contents of your psyche, hitherto monitored and controlled by you, have now become externalized and appear to take on a life of their own! Inner self-talk becomes audible conversations. Mental imagery becomes lifelike scenarios. Biological and Etheric processes become elemental sensations. And you're placed in the midst of all of this.

So, how to transition from awake to asleep while fully alert? How to become immune to the intoxicating venom of the sleep serpent?

Sit down comfortably in a dark room. Follow the steps described above: gaze into a candle flame without blinking until you see an afterimage appear around the flame. Now blow out the flame and remain seated while continuing to gaze at the afterimage. This time, instead of merely following the afterimage until it becomes externalized, follow it until the dissociative reflex kicks in and then do this:

Feel your entire body moving in the direction of the afterimage.

In other words, if the afterimage moves downward and slightly to the left, then feel your entire bodymind somersault in that direction. At first, you'll probably feel dizzy or drunk. That's a good sign! If you have difficulty doing this, there's something else you can do:

Stand up in a well-lit room. Be sure to remove any sharp or blunt objects that you might fall on or may fall on you. It's also a good idea to practice this next to a bed or couch. Now spin rapidly in circles, moving in the direction of your dominant hand, until you get dizzy. At that point come to a sudden stop and sit down. Relax all your muscles and exhale all the air in your lungs naturally and without forcing it. Next, keep your eyes open and notice that the entire room appears to be spinning in the direction of your non-dominant hand. Finally, without moving your body and while keeping the air out of your lungs, feel as though your entire bodymind is moving in the same direction of the spinning room. The sensation will be much like letting go and surrendering to a strong current in a rushing river. The trick is to become quite dizzy and then allow yourself to become physically limp, sustain breathing, and allow your consciousness to drift in the direction of the spinning room. With time, and as you become accustomed to OOBE, you'll see that this is almost the same sensation that occurs during the Astral exit and the transition from **LD-2** to **LD-3** (more on this later).

I can still recall being a child of about ten and experimenting with these little tricks. It wasn't until quite recently that I learned that there's even a technical term for it. It's called *Phasing* in the neo-Astral Projection community (see the work of Michael Raduga). There are two broad definitions of Phasing. The first definition is exactly what we accomplished in our Vivid Dreaming practices. You bring all your senses to bear on an inner experience and really put yourself at the center of it. The second definition is the ability to manipulate your awareness in such a way that you can literally feel yourself in various spatial orientations different from where you're physically located. In my system of *Subliminal Cognition Training*, we utilize what's called *The Tetris Effect* to induce Phasing. Briefly, the Tetris Effect occurs when sensations associated with repeated activities are reproduced as you're falling asleep. For example, if you've been on a boat for most of the day, you might fall asleep feeling your body swaying as if you're still at sea. Or, if you've been jumping up and down on a trampoline, you'll feel as though you're still jumping up and down while drifting off to sleep.

In *Book Two* of this series, we'll be taking a closer look at the Tetris Effect and how you might use it to induce Phasing and **OOBE**.

One more thing before we move on to week six: just as Embryonic Breathing and Microcosmic Orbit practice strengthens and stretches your Etheric muscles, the practices in this section are designed to strengthen and stretch your Astral muscles. Soon, and with sincere and consistent practice, you'll see the gist of these methods and all will become clear.

Week Six: The Hitchhiker Method

The capacity to engage all five senses in imagination and to sustain a relaxed but unwavering focus on the experience are the two common features shared by almost every method taught in this book. If you adequately train these two abilities, then you'll have no problem succeeding in stepping behind the Veil. In fact, entirely new and exciting worlds open for you when you begin to see, hear, smell, taste, and feel into these secret spaces of your body, mind, soul, and the universe itself.

This next technique for the attainment of Lucid Dreaming makes use of these two indispensable skills. I call it *The Hitchhiker Method.* It's just one of many viable ways in which you can induce a **WILD** (Wake Induced Lucid Dream).

What's the difference between a **WILD** and a Lucid Dream which occurs spontaneously throughout the night?

A Lucid Dream which happens during **REM** sleep is often the result of long-term training in which the conscious and subconscious regions of the mind have agreed, as it were, to make Lucidity a part of the dreaming process. Whether through affirmation, reality-checks, or hypnosis, a non-**WILD** Lucid Dream usually happens without your intending for it to happen. On the other hand, a **WILD** is the conscious induction of a Lucid Dream. There are many ways of doing this. The following method provides the essence of just about every other **WILD** technique of which I'm aware. It can be practiced during sitting meditation, but it's designed especially for bedtime, just before waking up, or while taking an afternoon nap.

The Practice

This exercise is best practiced in a dark and quiet room while lying on your back. If possible, elevate your torso so that your upper body is on an incline of roughly forty-five degrees. Memory foam wedges serve this purpose well. This posture ensures that your body's relaxed enough to fall asleep, but your mind remains slightly alert. Also, it reduces the possibility of snoring, which robs your brain of much needed oxygen. A brain robbed of oxygen is a brain robbed of Lucidity.

Also, be sure to sleep in alignment with Earth's magnetic field. Your head should face magnetic North and your feet South. This may seem like a minor detail, but I assure you that it's extremely important. People who follow this principle enjoy better health, longer periods of **REM** sleep, and a host of other psychic enhancements. Readers interested in cutting-edge research in this field should consult the fascinating work of Michael Persinger.

As you lie there, feel yourself getting heavier and heavier. Cultivate the feeling of your body melting into the mattress with each exhalation of breath. Try to feel the mattress rise to meet your body as you surrender to gravity. Do this until your whole body feels relaxed and your mind is calm and content.

Soon you'll begin to feel drowsy. Be sure not to fall unconscious! As soon as you feel yourself drifting into sleep, gently stare into the darkness behind your closed eyes. Don't strain to do this, but rather, maintain a soft focus on the point about one inch above the tip of your nose. Cease all mental chatter and internal dialogue. If any remaining thoughts are lingering in your mind, simply ignore them and continue to focus on this point behind your closed eyes.

At a certain point, you'll begin to experience hypnagogia. The most common of these are bright lights, voices, psychedelic color patterns, buzzing and popping sounds, sensations of floating or falling, and so on, with visuals tending to be the most common. This is the beginning of **LD-1** and is the lightest form of Lucidity, most of which is spent in **NREM**. This is where you need to begin using the following technique.

As soon as you notice any hypnagogic hallucinations, gently focus on one of them and *stick to it*. That is, grab hold of it with your concentrated mind and don't let go. It's important to be relaxed about this as any tension will only serve to wake you up. If you turn it into a project, then you'll be right back at the **BETA** brainwave and wide awake. So simply relax and allow your awareness to rest on a dream object and come to a full stop. If you can do this for a few minutes, then you'll notice a profound shift in your conscious-ness, the most notable being that your breathing disappears, and your physical body goes numb or appears to morph into strange shapes.

This is the entry into **LD-2**.

If you've made it this far then you're one step away from full Lucidity! At first, it usually only lasts for a minute or two, but it will deepen with time and practice.

So, how to enter *full* Lucidity?

This is a little tricky to do because the sleep cycle does exactly that: it *cycles*. That's right. Even if you've managed to remain conscious up to this point you may still fall into the abyss of deep dreamless sleep **(DELTA).** This means that most of Lucid Dreaming is trained while entering the **NREM** phases of sleep, not the **REM** phase as most people think. Eventually, the subconscious mind gets the hint and begins to respond by triggering Lucidity while in the deep sleep phase of **REM**. One of the perks of mastering the Trance state is that you begin to learn the skill of Pellucidity, which allows you to remain aware even in deep dreamless sleep (more on this later). Consequently, your chances of remaining aware throughout the entire sleep cycle are greatly improved. That said, there's one more trick I can teach you to prolong the microbursts of **REM** that occur in **LD-1** and **LD-2**. To get the most out of it, though, you need to draw on your experience of the first four weeks of the Curriculum.

Here's what to do:

As soon as you've transitioned over into **LD-2** and hypnagogic hallucinations give way to dream scenarios, reach out and into the dream with one of your five senses. For example, if you're experiencing a particularly visual dream scenario, become even more involved with it by reaching out with your sense of hearing. Are there any sounds present? Listen for conversations or music and so forth. Or, perhaps, there are physical sensations you might feel within the dream. One example is the feeling of water or wind, maybe the warm sun on your face. And so on with smell and taste.

In week seven, I'll teach you how to utilize the Hitchhiker Method while in deep **REM** as well. At that point, you've achieved full **LD-3** Lucidity. When that happens, you've reached a milestone in your development as a Veiler. Why? Because, unlike **LD-1** and **LD-2,** in **LD-3** your emotions are fully involved in the experience. *You're* there, 100% in the dream world.

You're behind the Veil!

We'll delve into that in the next section. For now, in week six, I don't recommend that you try to get emotionally involved in the dream because we tend to lose vigilance when emotions are involved. For now, simply try to involve all of your senses in the dream process with the goal of rooting yourself within the dream for as long as possible before either falling totally asleep or waking up. Believe me, emotions will take center stage once you're able to maintain Lucidity throughout the **REM** phase of sleep, which is the focus of the seventh week of the Curriculum.

Practice the Hitchhiker Method for at least one week before moving on to the following exercise. Be sure to record the results in your Dream Journal! If you wish to build on this method, try combining the *inner tones* with the internal gazing at the beginning of the exercise. That is, while staring into the darkness behind your closed eyes, include in your awareness the subtle, high-pitched ringing sounds in your ears. This will have the effect of adding audio to the visual hypnagogia of **LD-1** and **LD-2**. Remember, the more you can involve all of your senses in the process of going behind the Veil the more chances you have of rooting yourself there.

Week Seven: LD-3 and Wake Induced Lucid Dreaming

While practicing these techniques bear in mind that not only are they powerful Lucid Dream *inducers,* they're also Astral Body *looseners.* That is, they train your awareness to "detach" and perceive from various perceptual angles without the need to relocate your physical body. At first this is merely mental gymnastics, so to speak. With time, however, it will blossom into full-fledged Astral Travel. In weeks thirteen through sixteen, we'll expand on these methods strictly for Astral Projection.

At this point you should begin practicing regular reality checks. If you've already been practicing them, now is the time to take them to the next level. How? Practice them more often. How often? As often as you can. Not only should you regularly question whether your daily life is a dream, but also, whenever you find yourself lost in thought and you've forgotten yourself, immediately realize that you've been dreaming. Of course, that flies in the face of what we like to think is common sense.

After all, how could I be dreaming if I'm wide awake?

Most people take for granted that there's not much difference between dreaming while the body's asleep and doing so while fully awake. In both cases you're lost in an internal narrative or fantasy. More specifically, *you* aren't there anymore. That is, you've stopped being self-aware and have been swept away by reverie and internal dialogue. So, it follows that you can train your mind to become spontaneously aware in dreams by making *self-remembrance* a regular habit. Unlike other reality-check methods, self-remembrance cuts to the very core of the dreaming mind itself. It undercuts our general ignorance of psychic processes that parlay into the typical non-Lucid Dreaming most people do.

The twofold essence of self-remembrance is this:

- The recognition that you're lost in thought, fantasy, or self-talk equals the spontaneous remembrance of your Self.
- In all activities you must be fully present without going on autopilot.

After a while, you'll notice that this newfound capacity for presence begins to penetrate your nightly dreams.

The next thing you need to begin practicing is waking up at roughly 4:00 am in the morning. **REM** sleep is particularly deep at this time, and dreaming lasts for a longer duration. Not only that, but the sleep hormone *melatonin* is diminishing at this time and your brain is beginning to flood your body with chemicals to awaken you. This twilight period is a powerful moment to trick your brain into Lucidity. In Taoism, this is the time when *Yin* is receding, and *Yang* is on the rise, both in Nature and in your bodymind. The Indians call this time the *Bramamuhurt* and consider it the best time for the human soul to communicate with the divine.

As for the burden of waking up so early, you'll only have to do this a couple of times with the aid of an alarm clock. Once your bodymind becomes accustomed to the new habit, you'll begin to wake up at that time spontaneously. In fact, many people find that they don't even need an alarm clock to make this happen. Oftentimes you can just make a firm affirmation to wake up at 4:00 am and you'll do so, and this is the best way to proceed if you can manage it. Indeed, this firm intention can also be used to induce Lucidity. Your subconscious mind is very responsive to sincere commands. It may take some time to work, but if you tell yourself to remain aware in dreams with enough sincerity and over a sufficient span of time, you'll succeed sooner or later.

Finally, provided your doctor gives you the okay, begin taking a nootropic if you haven't already been doing so. In these early stages of Lucid Dreaming training it helps to stack the deck in your favor by giving your brain a boost. Nootropic compounds assist in making dreams incredibly Vivid and sometimes Lucidity happens spontane-ously because of this. At any rate, turning the amplitude up on your nightly dreams increases your chances of grabbing hold of them and becoming Lucid, and nootropics are an excellent way to accomplish this. I suggest you try *Huperzine-A* with *Vinpocetine*. You'll see why if you do!

With all these considerations in mind, let's venture even further behind the Veil and access full scale **LD-3** Lucid Dreaming!

The Practice

First, arrange your bed so you're in alignment with Earth's magnetic field. It may take some time before you notice the effects of this magnetic harmony, but science has all but proven its effects. As an interesting side note, photos taken by satellites orbiting the Earth have captured images of cows over vast stretches of land all sleeping in a uniform arrangement aligned with Earth's magnetic field.

Make sure that your sleeping environment is completely dark, quiet, and free of distraction. Earplugs and eyeshades work well if you can't ensure a dark and quiet bedroom. Remove all sources of EMF, and if possible, WiFi as well. Unplug all nearby devices from the electrical outlets in your room. If you sleep with your body near a wall, be sure that any outlets on the other side of it aren't in use. I can't overstate the deleterious effects which "dirty electricity" has on your Etheric energy. If you've decided to use the nootropics that I recommended, take them at least thirty minutes before going to bed and beginning this exercise.

Now set your alarm for 4:00 am. Yes, I know that for many people this is quite early to be waking up and many people will resent this step, but if you've taken my advice regarding the Circadian rhythm and are going to sleep at sunset, you'll have very little problem waking up at 4:00 am. Besides, you'll only be awake for a moment.

Lie down on your back and rest your dominant hand on your navel and your non-dominant hand on the center of your chest. Feel the warmth from your hands permeating these two centers and gently focus on your breathing. Breathe naturally, and gradually move your breathing down from your chest to your abdomen. Now make a firm command to yourself that you wish to remain conscious throughout the sleep cycle.

Next, become aware of the inner tones ringing in your ears. At the same time, gently stare into the darkness behind your closed eyes. If there are any colors, spots, or flashes of light, simply watch them and stare into them as if watching television. All the while, remain simultaneously aware of your breathing, the inner tones, the feeling of warmth radiating from your hands into your lower abdomen and chest, the field of vision behind your closed eyes, and your affirmation to remain Lucid.

Depending upon a variety of factors, sooner or later you'll begin to drift off into the lightest phase of sleep with your awareness still intact. As soon as hypnagogia present themselves, gently but decisively concentrate on one of them and don't let go. Whether it's a dream image, a sound, or a physical sensation, latch on with your focus and hold steady.

At this point you reach a pivotal moment. You'll either continue to the second stage of the sleep cycle with full consciousness, or else you'll fall completely asleep, in which case you may have to wait another ninety minutes or so before another opportunity for Lucidity presents itself. If so, that's okay! You have until 4:00 or 5:00 am to practice Lucidity in this exercise, so keep at it.

A good way to sustain Lucidity from **LD-1** to **LD-2** is to do something proactive while in the Lucid state. You see, one of the primary things that lures consciousness out of Lucidity is this:

The logic of the dreaming mind is paradoxical, and the only way the conscious mind can deal with it is to get out of the way by going to sleep.

The best way to counter this habit is to actively participate in the dream scenario without getting lost in it. For example, if you see a purple elephant flying over a mountain top, don't get lost in the irrational narrative of the scene. Rather, make the purple elephant *do* something. You might will the elephant to come down and lie in front of you. Or you might will the elephant to become a dog. If you continue this way, you'll find that you can withstand the seductive pull of the dream to lull you into unconsciousness.

Lastly, there will come a point when **LD-2** fades into **LD-3**. Once this occurs, there will be a complete break with the physical world accompanied by total loss of Gross Body awareness. During this transition it's common to feel some strange sensations, sleep-paralysis being foremost among them. When this happens, you'll probably wake up immediately.

It usually takes some practice to sustain full-blown Lucidity. If you're unable to sustain Lucidity up to this point, don't worry. Most people can't. More commonly, people find that they can sustain awareness up to **LD-2,** at which point they invariably fall asleep until their alarm clock wakes them up at 4:00 am. At this time, **REM** is at its peak duration and strength, so it can be much easier to jump straight into **LD-3** at this point.

It's important to remember that your attempts at Lucidity as you first lay down to sleep serve as powerful affirmations to your sub-conscious mind that you're seeking opportunities for Lucid Dreaming. Consequently, you'll oftentimes find yourself in a spontaneous **LD-3** Lucid Dream at around 4:00 am. Remember, just as you can often command yourself to wake up at a certain time each day and your bodymind obeys your will, so too can you command your bodymind to become Lucid at specific points in the sleep cycle.

Once the alarm sounds at 4:00 am, shut it off and again lie down to sleep. As soon as a dream scenario presents itself, use the Hitch-hiker Method and grab hold of an aspect of the dream and don't let it go. Especially important here is that you get proactive and do something concrete within the dream, such as flying or manipulating the narrative, to avoid lapsing into unconscious dreaming. One of my favorite ways to do this is to recall the dream I was having immediately prior to the alarm going off and re-enter it with full control over the narrative. Many times I've awoken from a nightmare of, say, being chased by someone, only to re-enter the dream and fight off my attacker.

The possibilities are endless!

In closing, once you enter **LD-3**, you'll probably start to notice Astral elements blending in with the dream scenario (i.e., Astral Dream). Perhaps you'll even have a full-blown Astral Projection.

We'll be going more in-depth on this topic later. For now, just notice how stepping behind the one Veil immediately grants you glimpses of what lies behind another. Lastly, record your results in your Dream Journal.

Week Eight: Dream Control

One of the most remarkable perks of attaining Dream Control (besides enjoying endless adventures!), is that the confidence you gain from it begins to spill over into your everyday life. As a Veiler, you'll soon discover that by facing your demons (literally!), defying the laws of physics, and opening the lines of communication between the conscious and subconscious regions of your mind, you've been cultivating a more integrated self.

Although it's necessary to occasionally allow your dreams to be as they are, you're likely to find that dreams which contain valuable information will resist any attempt at manipulation anyway. As much as I hate giving clichéd analogies, it's not unlike what the Oracle tells Neo in the movie, *The Matrix*: nobody can see beyond the decisions they're not ready to make.

Dream Control works that way, too…

Recall that in our discussion on the Seven Categories of Dream, whenever you encounter a dream that resists manipulation you're having an *Educational Dream*. There's an important soul-lesson hiding behind it, and it's your job to find out what that lesson is. Sometimes the lesson is obvious; at other times it can be elusive. It often happens that the inscrutable meaning behind the dream suddenly dawns on you while you're going about your day. This is one of the more common reasons for the *déjà vu* phenomenon.

In this section, I'm going to introduce you to the skill of *Dream Control*. I realize that some seasoned Veilers will take umbrage at this, but I'd be remiss if I finished a discussion on Lucid Dreaming without at least introducing the best part! Of course, some will argue against it. Personally, I never understood why some Lucid Dreamers are so against the conscious control of dreams. Okay, so some folks get a little carried away with it. I get that. Still, should we all stop eating just because a few people have a problem with overeating?

As with all things, balance is key!

This next technique is designed to give you greater conscious control over your dreams. It's one of many methods of accomplishing this and you may have already experienced a degree of Dream Control if you've followed the Curriculum up to this point. After all, a degree of Dream Control is required to actively sustain **LD-3**. However, this skill can be cultivated to the point where you can literally dream about whatsoever and whomsoever you desire. You can defy the laws of physics, have superhuman strength, have mind-blowing sex, and even pre-program your mind for more inspiration and creativity.

There's no doubt that at least 90% of all Dream Control is an exercise of the ego. Still, that's precisely what many of us need! True confidence is hard to come by. Often, bravado is masquerading as confidence. As you become proficient in Lucid Dreaming, you'll eventually begin to gain greater control over how a given dream begins and ends. Typically, you'll wake up from a Vivid Dream only to fall back asleep, become Lucid and change the narrative, usually from a defeat to a victory. Maybe you've already had experiences like this. Well, soon you'll be quite adept at it.

The Practice: The Hangover and The Closure Methods

This technique has two parts. First, you'll utilize the "4:00 am Method" to jump straight into **LD-3** and change the outcome of the dream you were having just prior to waking up. In the second part, you'll learn how to create the dream you want to have before you fall asleep. With practice, you can enjoy any type of dream you wish to have. I've even finished, reworked, and continued dreams up to two days after having them!

The first part is easy:

Simply perform the same steps from the exercise in week seven all the way to the 4:00 am mark. Next, stay in close mental contact with the dream you were having before you woke up. It's more important to recall the general theme than the details of the dream. For example, if you were having a Hedonistic Dream, simply stay in contact with that energy and mood when you awaken. If you do recall the details that's even better.

Now re-enter the dream and take control! That is, do something concrete and dramatic to change the overall trajectory of the dream. If you were previously having a dream about being chased, for example, re-enter that dream, turn around and face your pursuer. You can even use super powers in your dream to fend him off.

Believe me, this can get pretty fun!

Another popular way to access Dream Control is to go back to whatever dream you were having before waking up and then *FLY*. This is a universal method of Dream Control as it can be used in just about any dream scenario. You simply reach for the sky and soar! It's not uncommon that Astral Projection also occurs because of this flying method.

The second part of Dream Control is, well, a little bit trickier:

First, you must decide what type of dream you wish to have. Scan through the Seven Categories of Dream and select one. Pick a category and affirm it throughout the day and before you fall asleep. For example, if I'd like to relive some event of my previous day and change its outcome, then what I wish to have is a Biographical Dream. Then I'd go about my day contemplating the event in vivid detail exactly as it occurred. Then, as I fall asleep that night, I'd make a firm affirmation to dream about that event. As soon as I become Lucid I can then begin to take control of the outcome. As you might guess, this is a fantastic way to find closure to certain unhappy moments.

The same can be done with any other category of dream. Take, for example, the Hedonistic type of dream. Let's imagine that you desire to dream about being famous. A great technique is to watch a film or documentary about, say, a famous actor. After you've watched the film, replay in your imagination some of your favorite scenes, only put yourself in the place of the celebrity. Do this throughout the day and as you're falling asleep, and you'll eventually have a dream about being famous. At first these dreams may not be Lucid, but with practice you'll be able to remain conscious throughout the dream.

As an interesting side note, sleep scientists have recently discovered that people who play video games are more likely to have Dream Control than non-gamers. The theory is that because gamers are accustomed to manipulating a virtual reality, that skill carries over into their dream life. Personally, I'm not a gamer so I can't verify this theory, but why not give it a try?

Another secret to accessing Dream Control is something which I call *The Closure Method.* In this technique, you begin a vivid mental fantasy about what or whom you'd like to dream about. You go deep into it, with as much detail as possible, only you stop short of full satisfaction. In other words, you visualize your desired scenario fully but leave the *gestalt* out of the fantasy. For example, let's imagine that you wish to have a Lucid Dream about being a superhero. First, you'd watch a good film featuring your favorite superhero. Then, as you're falling asleep, you'd imagine one of your favorite scenes from the film, with you in the place of the actor playing the super-hero. Lastly, you'd stop short of rescuing that damsel in distress or defeating your arch-nemesis. This withholding of closure and satis-faction will then reemerge in the form of a dream. Now combine this with any of the methods for attaining dream Lucidity and you've achieved Dream Control!

At more advanced levels of Dream Control, you begin the work of manipulating dream content in such a way that gives you full control over the five primordial Elements of *Earth, Water, Fire, Air,* and *Spirit.* For example, you might blend Water and Air by breathing under water in a Lucid Dream, or blend Fire and Earth (physical body) by walking through fire in a Lucid Dream, and so on in vari-ous other combinations. The primordial Element of Spirit represents not Lucid but *Pellucid* Dreaming and the eventual attainment of Astral Projection. Other forms of Dream Control manifest somewhat spontaneously as the ability to transcend the egoic limitations spawned by the daily constraints of the Laws of Physics. The most common of these is unquestionably Lucid Dreams of flying, but other forms of expression are the ability to become tall or short or change the size, color, and shape of dream objects and landscapes. In this introductory course, however, it's only necessary that you become capable of choosing both *what* to dream and *how* the dream narrative plays out.

These two methods are to be used in combination for the entirety of this week. Finally, be sure to record all results in your Dream Journal.

CHAPTER NINE

GET PELLUCID!

If it's not present in deep dreamless sleep then it's not real.
— Ramana Maharshi

Pellucid Dreaming is probably the most neglected aspect of Conscious Sleep. Just about any book you read on the subject focuses solely on Lucid Dreaming and Astral Projection. In my opinion, this is like teaching someone how to exercise while neglecting the importance of a healthy diet. At their core, Lucid Dreaming and Astral Projection are just two spokes in the wheel of which Pellucid Dreaming is the central hub. Furthermore, true Astral Projection will be nigh impossible to achieve without profound Causal Body development.

Pellucid Dreaming is a Causal Body skill.

It's called the *Causal* Body because, when you're centered in it, it feels as if it's the cause or witness of all passing states and experiences. All phenomena experienced in the awake and asleep states appear as so many passing clouds in a vast immovable sky, and *you are that sky*. There's no intention or desire to move outside of yourself or escape the Now. You're just a flame of awareness burning in, and as, the pure and simple silence of being.

Sound familiar? It should!

If you've been regularly practicing Embryonic Breathing and Microcosmic Orbit, then you've already got an intermediate understanding of Pellucid Sleep.

As we've discussed, the secret key to enhancing Causal Body awareness is what the Taoists refer to as "raising *Shen.*" We've also discussed some methods for accomplishing this, such as proper diet, regulating the sex drive, the practice of Trance, Mindfulness and Self-Remembering, Nootropics, and so on. In this section, we'll take this raised *Shen* deep into the sleep cycle to accomplish Pellucid Dreaming and lay the groundwork for Astral Projection.

Unlike Vivid and Lucid Dreaming, which are best accessed in the **REM** stage of sleep, Pellucid Dreaming is best learned during **NREM** stages of sleep, at least initially. This is great news since **NREM** sleep makes up roughly 75% of the sleep cycle! That means that there are more opportunities for Pellucid Dreaming than there are for Vivid and Lucid Dreaming. Indeed, some people learn Lucid Dreaming spontaneously because of learning Pellucid Dreaming first (more on this later). In fact, I believe that's how Tibetan Dream Yoga was developed. Skilled meditators, capable of carrying their meditation through the entire sleep cycle, eventually discovered that they can choose to either engage or passively witness their dreams. After all, Lucid Dreaming is impossible without at least some degree of Causal Body (Pellucid) development.

The goal of learning Pellucid Sleep is the ability to sustain it into and past **REM** sleep. I should point out that it's notoriously difficult to maintain stable Pellucidity during the transition from **NREM** to **REM**. It's not unlike being given a powerful psychedelic while attempting to meditate. Imagine trying to remain psychologically centered and calm after taking LSD or DMT! Naturally, this requires patience, regular practice, and time.

Pellucidity has four broad phases of depth and stability. I refer to these levels of skill as:

- **PS-1**
- **PS-2**
- **PD-3**
- **PD-4**

Phases one and two are more properly named Pellucid *Sleep* rather than Pellucid *Dreaming*, as you're not really dreaming during **NREM**. You were introduced to **PS-1** and **PS-2** in Embryonic Breathing meditation. In sitting meditation, **PS-1** presents itself as total cessation of abstract thinking and mental chatter, deep relaxation of the physical body and subjective warming of the hands and feet. **PS-2** presents itself in sitting meditation as total loss of bodily awareness, "nodding off," occasional snoring, and sensory withdrawal. This is the most regenerative stage of sleep, when the **DELTA** brainwave predominates, and it's for this reason that the practice of Embryonic Breathing targets this stage of Pellucidity. Remember, the main purpose of Embryonic Breathing is to store abundant *Qi* in the Lower Dantian to fuel the regeneration process.

The third and fourth stages of Pellucid Sleep represent Pellucid Dreaming proper:

PD-3 is achieved the moment you can sustain awareness through hypnagogia, microbursts of dreaming, and the sedative brainwaves called K-Complexes, without getting lost in them or falling asleep. This is harder than it sounds. Unlike the Pellucidity achieved during sitting meditation, the capacity to remain alert during this phase of sleep *while lying down* is exceptionally difficult, which is one reason why most meditation methods are practiced in a sitting posture. The habit of falling asleep while lying down is very deeply ingrained, and it's a habit that must be kicked with both feet while learning Conscious Sleep.

PD-4 is the most profound level of Pellucid Dreaming. It's been achieved the moment you can sustain awareness into **REM** sleep without getting lost in Vivid or Lucid dreams. It's difficult to describe what this feels like. The most that can be said is that it's like being in the womb of the universe itself, silent and peaceful, but very much aware of the distant parade called *life*. Dreams come and go. Feelings come and go. Indeed, most things that arise are happily disregarded in favor of the profound bliss of pure being. The only thing that tends to jolt most people out of the immovable calm of **PD-4** is the shock of Astral Projection exit-symptoms.

In this section you'll learn four powerful methods of achieving Pellucidity. In weeks nine and ten, I'll teach you how to deepen the Pellucid Sleep of Embryonic Breathing and sustain it while lying down rather than sitting up. In weeks eleven and twelve, I'll introduce you to **PD-3** and **PD-4** through two beautiful methods that utilize but transcend the other techniques for Pellucidity.

Week Nine: Progressive Relaxation

One of the best ways to induce Pellucid Sleep is through progressive relaxation of the body. Due to the combined use of profound physical relaxation and what I call *Mobile Mental Focus* **(MMF)**, you're gradually and seamlessly guided past the Veil and into the sleep cycle while still fully conscious. The physical relaxation puts your body to sleep while the **MMF** keeps your mind awake. Furthermore, because your mind is mobile during the process, it tends to steer clear of dreaming. Why? Because dreaming is, if nothing else, an internal psychic movement. In a sense, dreaming is a nightly surrogate for the daily activities of your bodymind. Thus, by keeping the mind moving during the transition from awake to asleep, you fulfill that need and negate dreams as a result—at least temporarily. As an important side note, if you've deepened your Microcosmic Orbit practice to the point where you can sustain it into **NREM**, you've already seen this mechanism at work! Here, we're going to take that skill a step further.

During these next four weeks, it's important that you cease all other practices for Vivid and Lucid Dreaming. Just allow them to happen naturally. Also, if you've been taking nootropics, discontinue them for the time being. Eventually, you'll reach a point where your being will decide whether to have a Vivid or Lucid Dream, or just relax into a night of Pellucid Sleep. Remember, the goal of a Veiler is to achieve continuity of consciousness and make that consciousness *mobile*. This is a very relaxed affair once it's achieved and stabilized. Other than Dream Control, which is a willful decision to participate in and manipulate a dream, the continuity of consciousness is a movement, not of your ego, but of your very soul. Once this is stabilized, you can dispense with these methods because the Veil no longer exists for you.

The practices that should be continued throughout the Curriculum are Embryonic Breathing, Microcosmic Orbit, Channeling Intensity, the Healing Hands, and Dream Journaling/Recall.

The Practice

As always, be sure that your sleeping space is dark, quiet, and without distractions. Use earplugs and eyeshades if necessary. Remember to align your body with Earth's magnetic field. Don't eat anything for at least an hour before beginning any of these exercises, as the digestive process steals energy from your *Shen* and therefore weakens your vigilance.

This technique is divided into two parts. Here, in week nine, you'll learn the first part, which is meant to get you into stable **PS-1.** In week ten, you'll deepen your practice to access stable **PS-2.** Please read the instructions carefully, a few times if necessary, before attempting the exercise:

To begin, simply close your eyes and relax into your sleeping posture. You should lie on your back, preferably on a Memory Foam wedge, so your upper body is on a forty-five degree incline. If not, the traditional supine posture is fine. Practitioners of Hatha Yoga will immediately recognize the following posture as the Savasana posture which typically concludes a yoga routine. Indeed, I learned the present exercise in 1999 from a Yogi named Dr. John Mumford (Swami Anandakapila Saraswati), and I learned Pellucid Sleep as a byproduct of the practice.

Savasana Posture:

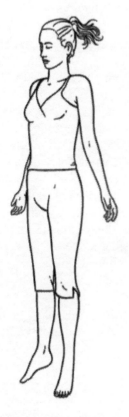

Notice that the palms are facing up and the legs are at least twelve inches apart. This is important in that it aids in the sensory withdrawal required for the following technique. Also, the surface upon which you practice this posture is extremely important to your health first and foremost, and to your level of comfort. In this exercise, you'll be learning how to completely surrender your body to gravity, and therefore your mattress should be customized to fit the needs of your physical structure so you can fully and comfortably let go of physical tension. I originally learned this practice on a carpeted floor, but through years of wear-and-tear from my job and martial arts, my body responds best when I practice on a good mattress. However, a firmer surface is better for this exercise because it assists in the melting sensation you'll be cultivating in this exercise. Lastly, be sure to adjust the climate of the room so there's good ventilation and it's not too cold or hot. Remember that your body temperature drops as you fall asleep, so having a blanket covering your midriff is a good idea.

With these requirements met, lie there for a few moments and simply relax. Feel the temperature of your mattress becoming warmer as it absorbs your body heat and feel the weight of your body against the bed and pillow. Notice especially which areas feel heavier, lighter, warmer, and cooler than others. Enjoy this moment of tactile awareness, and wholeheartedly embrace the Now and all that it contains.

Now become aware of your natural breathing rhythm, and with each exhalation feel your body becoming extremely heavy and sinking into the bed. As always, breathe through your nose. Imagine that the bed is almost rising to meet your body as it melts downward and into the mattress. The melting sensation should begin at your extremities and end at your core. Repeat four or five times before moving to the next step.

Don't fall asleep!

Now we're going to take it a step further and remove any lingering restless energy in your muscles. To this end we'll employ a popular biofeedback technique which utilizes a *tense-hold-release* mechanism. As you'll soon see, this is a powerful method for deepening the true relaxation of the muscles.

Start by becoming aware of your right arm. Gently feel into its structure—the skin, blood, temperature, muscle, bone—and then, on your next natural inhalation of breath, gently extend your arm downward as if reaching for your foot, make a tight fist and extend the contraction up the forearm, ending at the shoulder. At the same time, raise your arm a few inches off the bed. Hold this contraction for roughly five seconds. Then, upon exhalation, let your arm go completely limp and flop back down onto the mattress. It's important that you allow your arm to go completely limp, as if it's dead. Don't make any adjustments, no matter how subtle or minute. Just let it lie there as though lifeless. Now repeat the same sequence with your left arm. Note any sensations you feel in your arms. Is there heat? Cold? Tingling? Etc.

Now follow the same procedure with your legs. Starting with your right leg, inhale slowly while gently extending your leg downward, flexing your foot backward so that your toes are pointing toward your head, and extend this contraction upward to your knee and finally to your hip. Once the contraction reaches your hip, raise your leg a few inches off of the mattress, hold the contraction for a few seconds, and then exhale naturally while allowing your leg to flop back onto the bed as if lifeless.

Repeat the same procedure with your left leg. Note any sensations that you feel in your legs.

Next, upon inhalation, gently press the back of your head into the mattress (or pillow), hold for a few seconds, exhale and release. Note any sensations in your head, neck, and upper back, and allow these areas to remain motionless and relaxed.

Now bring your attention to your core. Inhale while pressing your lower back into the mattress by gently contracting the muscles of your abdomen, much like doing a subtle "crunch" sit-up. Then, upon exhalation, allow these muscles to go limp and remain relaxed and motionless.

Lastly, mentally scan your entire body for any trace of tension or pain. With each exhalation, feel these areas open and relax downward into the mattress. Feel your whole body surrender to gravity *completely*. You're aiming for a slight extension of your extremities coupled with extreme relaxation of your muscles, ligaments, and joints.

At a certain point during this exercise, you'll notice a few things. Foremost among them is the growing tension between your conscious control and the approaching sleep cycle. This tension is important. It's literally the *Yang* and *Yin* of Conscious Sleep! It's important because this *Yang* (awake)/*Yin* (asleep) dynamic creates *energy*. This coming together of two opposing forces creates a third force. I refer to this force—this *Yin/Yang* lovechild of Awake and Asleep—as *Etheric Dissonance,* and its skillful application can result in many different experiences and psychic skills, such as Lucid Dreaming, Remote Viewing, and Astral Projection, to name a few.

Practice this for one week before moving onto the second part of the exercise.

Week Ten: The Sixteen Marmasthanani/Mobile Mental Focus

At this point you should be proficient at accessing **PS-1**. In this second part of the exercise, I'm going to teach you how to deepen your Pellucidity to **PS-2**. Our goal is to put the Gross/physical body completely to sleep while, at the same time, remaining alert and fully conscious. As we've already discussed, we're going to accomplish this alertness by way of *Mobile Mental Focus*, which is a method of engaging awareness in such a way that precludes and curbs unconscious dreaming.

As an added perk, this practice is an excellent method for opening the *Qi* channels in the body, and would be classified as a form of *Wei Dan* "Grand Circulation" by Chinese Taoists. If you've gathered and stored enough Etheric energy through Embryonic Breathing and Microcosmic Orbit (small circulation), then the following practice will spread this abundant *Qi* to the rest of the body in a powerful way to remove blockages and sluggish *Qi* flow.

The Yogic tradition of India divides the major zones of the body into Sixteen *Marmasthanani*. Beginning at the feet and ending at the top of the head, we're going to mentally feel into and progressively open and relax these sixteen zones until stable **PS-2** is achieved. Not only that, but by performing this mental sweep of the body, we're also keeping our awareness engaged so that we don't fall asleep and get lost in dreaming.

The Practice

First, perform the first part of this technique until you feel sufficiently relaxed. Then, proceed through the Sixteen Marmasthanani as follows:

FEET: Inhale naturally while squeezing your toes together as if making a fist with your feet. Hold this contraction for a few seconds, and then exhale and release, feeling with each successive exhalation that your feet, ankles, and Achilles tendons, are melting into the mattress. Spend at least three minutes doing this before moving on to the next zone.

SHINS: Become aware of your shins and, upon inhalation, flex your toes back toward your knees, hold the contraction for a moment, exhale and release. Feel your shins melt downward with each exhalation. Relax this area fully before continuing.

CALVES: Bring your awareness now to your calves. Inhale naturally and flex your calves by pointing your toes forward. Hold for a moment, exhale and release, while cultivating a heavy melting sensation in both of your calves and Achilles tendons.

KNEES: Now bring your awareness to your knees. Inhale while pressing the backs of your knees into the mattress, hold, exhale and release, allowing your knees to completely surrender to gravity. Feel into the kneecap as well as the joint itself to open and relax these areas.

THIGHS: Feel into your inner thighs all the way to the groin area. Inhale and tense this zone by pointing the toes of both feet at each other while simultaneously imagining that you're squeezing a large beach ball between your thighs. Hold, exhale, and release downward.

SOLAR PLEXUS: Although this zone centers primarily on the Solar Plexus, you're going to include the lower abdomen, buttocks, groin, and hips. First, bring your awareness to your Solar Plexus (three finger-widths above your belly button). Upon exhalation, withdraw your abdomen as if trying to touch your navel to the back of your lower spine, then allow the inhalation to happen naturally while squeezing the muscles of your buttocks together. Hold, exhale, release and relax. Try to feel all these areas open and relax downward with each exhalation.

CHEST: Moving now to the chest, inhale completely while fully expanding your chest like a balloon. Hold, exhale, release and relax. Feel into your lungs and diaphragm and surrender them to gravity. Avoid being overly conscious of your heart as this may lead too much *Qi* to it and cause palpitations.

SPINE: Now become aware of your spine, including the musculature, vertebrae, and the spinal cord itself. Inhale from your abdomen, and feel the lumbar region of your spine gently press down into the mattress. Hold, release and relax. Extend this relaxed heaviness to include your spine and entire back as you cultivate a melting sensation with each exhalation.

HANDS: Move your attention to your hands. Inhale while clenching your hands into fists. Hold, exhale, release and relax your hands and wrists, surrendering them to gravity with each exhalation.

FOREARMS: Bring your attention to your forearms (wrist to elbow). Inhale while opening your hands and extending your fingers as much as possible. Hold, exhale, release and relax.

UPPER ARMS: Now move to your upper arms (elbow to shoulder). Inhale while pressing your elbows into the mattress. Hold for a moment, exhale, release and relax.

THROAT: Move now to your throat. Inhale while pressing your chin downward toward your throat. Hold, exhale, release and relax. Feel your neck, throat, larynx, and vocal chords melt downward with gravity.

JAW: Now bring your attention to your jaw, including your teeth, tongue, gums, and jaw muscles. Inhale while pressing your tongue firmly against the roof of your mouth. Hold, exhale, release and relax.

EYES: Move on to the eyes. Inhale while firmly squeezing your eyes shut and scrunching your face muscles. Hold, exhale, release and relax. Feel your eye and face muscles melt downward with gravity. The sensation in this zone is typically very pleasant, as we hold much tension in this area throughout the day.

BACK OF HEAD: Now bring your attention to the back of your head. Inhale while pressing the back of your head against the mattress or pillow. Hold, exhale, release and relax.

SCALP: Bring your attention to your scalp. Inhale while raising your eyebrows. If you can also draw your ears back slightly, do that too. Hold, exhale, release and relax.

At this point you may already be in **PS-2**. If not, continue with Mobile Mental Focus by once again going through the sixteen Marmasthanani, only this time don't employ the *tense, hold, and release* mechanism. Simply feel into each zone and note any sensations you feel while cultivating a profound sense of heaviness in each area. Also, move through the sixteen zones faster this time. Continue in this way until your body is quite asleep while you remain uninterruptedly aware. The Yogic tradition refers to **PS-1** and **PS-2** as *Yoga Nidra,* or *psychic sleep*, and this is just one of many methods of inducing it. Practiced with enough sincerity and perseverance, it has the potential to not only refine your Lucid Dreaming and Pellucid skills, but also to open the door to conscious Astral Projection.

As always, practice this for one week before moving on to the next exercise.

Week Eleven: PD-3 and the Internal Dialogue Method

Have you ever had a dream in which you were observing yourself as the main character? If so, you've already got an inkling of how this next technique works. Some people *only* dream in this way, with the projected image of themselves as the key player in a dream while their real self simply observes from afar. Unfortunately, most of these dreams tend to be totally unconscious with little or no Lucidity/ Pellucidity. Also, the difference between this type of dream and true **PD-3** is that the former is still an involvement in the dream process. That is, you can still get lost in a dream scenario whether you embody or project yourself as a character within it, whereas true Pellucid Dreaming is marked by an awareness of dreaming but a total disinterest in getting lost or identified with it.

If you've ventured this far into the Curriculum, and if you've had any success with Dream Control, you'll notice at this point that the process of becoming a skilled Veiler isn't at all a ladder-like affair. Eventually, you'll begin to experience these capacities as so many hallways, as it were, which you can choose to walk down at leisure. Sometimes you'll find yourself wanting to go Astral. At other times you'll want to have a Lucid Dream. Or perhaps you're very tired and just want to bathe in the silent depths of Pellucid Sleep.

The choice is yours!

Another thing you'll notice as your skill increases is that you no longer have unconscious dreams as often as you used to. It gradually becomes impossible to not recall your dreams, or to have a full night's sleep where nothing interesting happens. Sometimes this can be exhausting, which is why it's so important to keep your spirit of vitality high and your energies fresh, clean, and abundant. Even though being a Veiler doesn't make you a genius, your brain most certainly is functioning at a higher level than it was before, and this requires fuel, as we've already discussed.

This next practice is something I call the "Internal Dialogue Method." Its primary purpose is to open the door to **PD-3**, but it can also be used to create a *Wake Induced Lucid Dream* **(WILD),** though that's not how we'll be employing it here. Just as we kept the mind from slipping into dreaming by way of Mobile Mental Focus, so too can we prevent ourselves from getting identified with the dreaming mind by way of internal commentary. This is like working on a creative project, and then stepping back for a moment to contemplate it before resuming the work. Or else it's much like listening passively to a piece of music rather than getting lost in the lyrics.

The Practice

For this exercise, you'll only be venturing into the light phase of sleep. Your goal is to allow for microbursts of dreaming and hypnagogia, all the while remaining a detached witness of the entire show. The practice is very easy, but incredibly potent. In fact, it was the method by which I learned Dream Control and the deeper levels of Pellucid Dreaming.

Perform the progressive relaxation exercise of week nine. Repeat this a few times until you begin to feel drowsy, and then allow yourself to drift off into light **NREM** sleep, staring gently into the darkness behind your closed eyes and relaxing deeper and deeper with each exhalation. Then, the moment hypnagogia begin to present themselves, silently begin to describe whatsoever you perceive as if you were talking to someone else. Imagine, for example, that someone else is with you and perceiving the same dream scenarios that you are. If you catch yourself drifting in and out of identification with the dreaming process, include that observation in your internal dialogue. For example, you might say, "I drifted off there for a minute! I'm back now. What did I miss?"

The conversation can take on any form you like. You might approach it in a jovial spirit, for instance, like watching a movie with a good friend. Or you might opt for a more objective, journalistic conversation-style, cataloging everything that arises in a detached and scientific manner. The tone is totally arbitrary. What matters is that you remain objective and detached without sacrificing the relaxation required for **PD-3,** and that you avoid getting identified with the dreaming mind.

Finally, become aware of the feeling of your body against the bed and internally comment on what you feel. At the same time, become aware of your breathing and any sounds or smells you perceive in the room you're in, and comment on those. Continue in this way until you're completely awake.

There! You just had a Pellucid Dream.

Continue with this practice for a week, all the while trying to extend your internal dialogue deeper and deeper into the sleep cycle. In week twelve, I'll introduce you to **PD-4** and how you can use your newfound skills of Trance and Microcosmic Orbit to access it. Remember, **PD-4** is the threshold to true Astral Projection. To be clear, all you need to access stable and sustained Astral Projection is an abundant *Qi* supply, courage, and mastery of **PD-4.**

Week Twelve: PD-4: Gateway to Astral Projection

You may be wondering why I've chosen to present Lucid Dreaming and not Pellucid Dreaming first in the Curriculum. After all, if Pellucidity equals Causal Body awareness, and if Causal Body awareness is at the root of waking, dreaming, and dreamless states of awareness, wouldn't it make more sense to learn Pellucid Dreaming first?

It's true that many people gain proficiency in Lucid Dreaming via Pellucid Sleep rather than the other way around, but there's a lot of sense in learning Vivid, Lucid, Pellucid, and Astral skills first and in that order. Why? Well, imagine that Pellucid Dreaming is a paint-brush and your consciousness is a canvas. You first need a palette full of colorful paints before you can put your paint brush to use and create a work of art. That is, without first developing the ability to dream in vivid color, how can you expect to have a Lucid Dream worth remembering? Furthermore, how can you expect yourself to rest in pure Pellucidity without first becoming familiar with Lucid Dreaming to the point where you can easily put it aside and avoid the temptation to dream? Regardless, having at least a rudimentary understanding and experience of Pellucidity is indispensable when trying to learn Lucid Dreaming, which is why I introduced you to Embryonic Breathing and Microcosmic Orbit practice before Lucid Dreaming. Still, Lucid Dreaming is *not* dependent on first acquiring advanced Pellucidity.

By now you know that dreams follow their own logic, and it can be easy for the mind to get lost in that world. When this happens, you lose all sense that you're dreaming and you fall into non-Lucid dreaming. Learning Lucid Dreaming before delving into Pellucid Dreaming acclimates you to the intoxicating lure of the realm of dreams. Unlike most people, who are taken in by the absurdity of dream-logic, a skilled Veiler becomes *more* conscious when confronted by it. The absurdity of, say, a flying kangaroo, immediately alerts a skilled Lucid Dreamer to the fact that she's dreaming. Most unskilled dreamers would simply embrace the flying kangaroo as a matter of fact and fall into unconscious sleep. In my experience, if you approach Lucid Dreaming by way of Pellucid Sleep, you'll hardwire your neuronet to see Pellucid Sleep primarily as a means toward Lucid Dreaming. There's nothing necessarily wrong with that, if that's what you're looking for, but for our purposes it's crucial that you hardwire your neuronet to equate Pellucidity with a doorway to Astral Projection rather than to Lucid Dreaming. My main reason for this is that this route tends to bypass the Astral/Lucid confusion, whereas approaching Astral Projection through Lucid Dreaming and Lucid Dreaming through Pellucid Sleep only serves to confuse the issue, at least in my experience.

That said, this next practice is for the cultivation **PD-4.** As you've no doubt guessed, the technique builds upon the last three methods.

The Practice: PD-4 and Grand Circulation

First perform the exercises of weeks nine through eleven so they combine and become one exercise. This takes about one hour to complete. Be sure to use earplugs and eyeshades to ensure complete sensory withdrawal. It's very important that you remain completely undisturbed and undistracted for the duration of this exercise.

The important thing is to put your body totally asleep while your mind remains awake. As by now you should know, this *awakeness* isn't the same alertness you have while you're awake, though it's in some ways similar. Once you reach **PS-1,** you should immediately employ the Internal Dialogue and Mobile Mental Focus techniques as much as necessary to avoid falling into unconscious sleep. A good way to combine them is to mentally scan through the sixteen Marmasthanani while engaging Internal Dialogue about the sensations you feel in each zone. For example, if you feel heaviness and coldness, you can internally say, "That area feels very heavy and cold right now. Let me see if I can send some warmth there."

And so on with the other fifteen Marmasthanani. The important thing is to stay mentally engaged without waking up. Quite possibly this may simply be a matter of keeping a light **BETA** brainwave while heavy **THETA** and **DELTA** are taking center stage.

Once you reach **PD-3,** continue with Internal Dialogue but cease Mobile Mental Focus. As this state deepens, slowly begin Microcosmic Orbit and jettison the Internal Dialogue. Begin the circulation the same way you would while sitting, starting at the Lower Dantian and sweeping down past the groin and the tailbone, up the spine and around the head, and back down the front of the body to complete one rotation. Try your best to synchronize the Etheric circulation with the natural rhythm of your breathing, inhaling down the front of your body and exhaling up your spine, around the back of your head, and ending at the point where the tip of your tongue touches the upper palate of your mouth.

Once you've circulated in the Microcosmic Orbit a few times, you're then going to expand the circulation to include your lower body as well. Beginning at the tip of your tongue, inhale Etheric energy down the entire length of the front of your body, sweeping down your torso, past your groin, down the front of your legs, and ending at the soles of your feet. From there, begin your exhale and sweep the energy up the back of your legs, past your tailbone and up your spine, around the back of your head and over the top, down your face, ending at the tip of your tongue to complete another rotation. Continue circulating in this way, feeling the energy circulating close to your body at first but then expanding further and further away from your physical form with each rotation.

If performed properly, eventually this Grand Circulation will carry you across the threshold to **PD-4.** Like **LD-3,** the transition to full-blown **PD-4** is heralded by some very specific (and at first uncomfortable) sensations, so be prepared. The most common of these is the total loss of awareness of breathing. At this point, because of your Lucid Dreaming training, you may already be familiar with this alarming sensation. If not, don't become frustrated if this or any of the other disturbing sensations of stepping behind the Veil jolts you back to full consciousness. With practice, you'll soon become used to the peculiar symptoms of Conscious Sleep.

Another common symptom is the appearance of a bright light. For me, this light is almost always gold or bright yellow in color, and can take the form of a steady and bright spotlight shining directly into my eyes, or the sun, or a rotating light like those found in light-houses, or a bright and sudden flash of lightning. Go ahead and stare into it! Usually this is nothing more than the initial drawing back of the curtain leading to **LD-3** and Astral sight. At that point, you can usually decide whether to engage or rest in **PD-4.** Obviously, our present goal is the latter.

Lastly, just as in **LD-3,** in **PD-4** you're in a position where Astral Projection is imminent. There are many ways to induce Astral Projection, but quite often it happens naturally and with no effort on the part of the person experiencing it. In the last four weeks of the Curriculum, we'll explore four powerful methods for inducing Astral Projection. For now, practice this method for training deep Pellucid Dreaming and get a good feel for it. You'll notice that every category of dream is available to you in **PD-4,** only the psychedelic nature of dreaming is more pronounced than it is in Lucid Dreaming. The reason for this shift is that Lucid Dreaming is an experience that you're *in* whereas Pellucid Dreaming is an experience that you're *having*. The real fun is in dancing on the thin line between them.

Chapter Ten

Get Astral!

If Lucid Dreaming is the crown jewel for most Veilers, then Astral Projection is the Holy Grail. As we've discussed, there's a fine line that separates Lucid Dreaming and Astral Projection, so the confusion is quite understandable. I've been practicing these two arts for over twenty years, and I'm still in the process of teasing them apart. Indeed, a great number of Veilers live their entire lives with these two abilities in a state of consistent overlap. Regardless, once you experience your consciousness separate from your physical body, your life is forever changed. This is especially true once the experience is validated by events in real-time.

My first encounter with Astral Projection occurred when I was ten or eleven years old. Next to my bed, level with my head, was an unused telephone jack. I was awoken one night to the sound of buzzing that at first seemed to be coming from somewhere inside my head. When I came to full consciousness, I realized that the sound couldn't possibly be coming from inside my head. I had an intense phobia of bees as a child. I'd been stung a few times and had acquired an irrational fear of the honey-makers, so that was my next thought: There were bees in my room!

As soon as the terrifying thought of bees took hold I discovered that I was unable to move. Also, the sound of my breathing seemed be coming from somewhere below me. I would later learn that this is just one of the myriad unpleasant symptoms of sleep paralysis, but at the time I was dumbfounded. Then the buzzing abruptly stopped and the paralysis lifted. I lay there in a cold sweat, wondering what the hell just happened to me. In my childlike reasoning, I drew the conclusion that a bees' nest must be inside the telephone jack, and my unusual paralysis was merely the result of my innate fear of being stung. So, I took some toilet paper, stuffed a small chunk of it into the outlet, grabbed some Scotch Tape and taped it shut.

Despite my attempts to find a solution to the odd buzzing noises and sleep paralysis, the same scene would repeat again and again over the course of the next few nights, only it quickly evolved from an irritating buzzing sound and paralysis into full-fledged Astral exit-symptoms. One night the peculiar buzzing sound intensified and eventually gave way to a horrifying feeling of imminent atomic explosion. Images of being crushed under a mountain of rock flooded my brain as I struggled to snap out of it and come to my senses. I tried to cry out for my mother, but to no avail. Just then, and totally against my will, I felt my consciousness separating from my body!

This was something that I was determined to prevent...

Somehow, with a herculean act of will, I managed to get up and move my physical body. The feeling was very uncomfortable. Reality seemed to be moving at the speed of light all around me, but my body felt as if it weighed a ton! Movement came only with great effort and there was a tangible presence in the room. In fact, it felt like a crowd of people were in my bedroom watching me struggle to my feet, trying desperately to reach the door leading from my room out into the hallway. My mother soon woke up and snapped me out of it, but with extreme difficulty. The sensation of being slammed back into my physical form left me shaking and covered in cold sweat for the next hour or so before I finally fell asleep.

As time elapsed, my Astral Projection experiences ceased, largely due to the primal fear induced by my then lack of understanding of the process. By age sixteen the psychic moat was fully constructed and it took a few years to regain access to Astral Projection. Through this process I learned the basic mechanism by which Astral Projection works, and it's my pleasure to be able to share it with you. You see, once you eliminate the fears and uncertainties associated with Astral Projection, the experience undergoes a radical transformation. What once seemed terrifying or impossible suddenly becomes exhilarating and real.

In last four weeks of the Curriculum, I'll show you how you too can gain access to this marvelous ability. Indeed, if you've followed the Curriculum thus far, you may have already had a spontaneous Astral Projection or two. If so, congratulations! This is a huge milestone in your development as a Veiler. If not, then the following four techniques will certainly jump-start your Astral battery. In the meantime, I encourage you to explore the work of other seasoned projectors while working on the following exercises. It never hurts to get as many perspectives as possible while simultaneously working on these core techniques.

Let's get started!

Week Thirteen: The Art of Phasing

The multi-platinum recording artist, Peter Gabriel, once advised an auditorium full of fans to lie down in some grass and look up at the sky until it appeared to be no longer above but below them. That's solid advice! In fact, what Mr. Gabriel is suggesting is one of the fundamental secrets to a time-tested technique for inducing OOBE called *Phasing*. We've already discussed Phasing, but here we'll learn how to employ it specifically for Astral Projection.

There are three broad components of successful Phasing. They are:

- The Dissociative Reflex.
- Bi-Locationality.
- Malleable Proprioception.

Let's discuss them in the order listed above.

We've already discussed the Dissociative Reflex. Without this ability, natural or cultivated, you'll have minimal success in Lucid Dreaming and Astral Projection. Vivid and Pellucid Dreaming don't require this skill, but it's indispensable to OOBE. Throughout this book I've tried my best to stress this point and offer methods by which the dissociative reflex can be trained. Do experiment with them and give this skill the attention it deserves.

Now, what do I mean by *Bi-Locationality*? Quite simply, this is the capacity to occupy in imagination positions in space not occupied by your physical body. For example, if you're lying on your bed, can you convincingly imagine and feel yourself standing at the foot of your bed staring at your body? Or can you imagine and feel yourself on the ceiling staring down at your body on the bed?

That's Bi-Locationality ...

But, you might say, isn't that the same as Astral Projection? Well, not quite. When true Astral Projection happens, you'll know it! Bi-

Locationality is just a practice that assures your mind that Astral Projection is possible and desirable. By cultivating the ability to mentally occupy spaces other than where you physically are, you're wiring your neuronet in a manner capable of experiencing the real thing.

So that's that...

Now what in the name of all things hard to pronounce is *Malleable Proprioception*? Unlike Bi-Locationality, this skill focuses on the *separation* phase of Phasing. That is, just as Bi-Locationality teaches your mind to allow conscious Astral Projection away from your physical body, the cultivation of malleable proprioception acclimates your mind to the most difficult but crucial step in OOBE: *the separation from your physical body.*

In week thirteen of this training, I'll teach you how to successfully train Bi-Locationality while fully awake. In week fourteen, I'll show you how to combine Bi-Locationality with Malleable Proprioception training while awake. In week fifteen, you'll learn how to take these skills into the **NREM** stages of the sleep cycle. Finally, in week sixteen, you'll learn how to properly deal with exit-symptoms and gradually travel further and further away from your physical body.

The Practice: Bi-Locationality Training

As I've said, these next eight weeks of the Curriculum feature exercises that are trained while fully awake. That's really the proper place to start because, after all, that's where *you* are! Remember, the entire process of effectively rewiring the bodymind to house these new capacities is symbolically much like a hexagram. Training your mind while awake is the downward pointing triangle while training them while asleep is the upward pointing triangle of the hexagram. That's the shape of the key that unlocks the Veil.

We begin the process of Bi-Locationality training in the good ole' outdoors. It doesn't matter where you go to practice this exercise if you'll be relaxed and undisturbed for the duration of the practice, which takes a minimum of thirty minutes to complete. It's best practiced on a warm day with a partly cloudy sky and slices of blue. Training at dusk, dawn, or night time, is ideal. For starters, these are potent times for this type of work. Also, as you'll soon see, you want to avoid blinding sunlight. A local park, beach, your own backyard, or a mountain top, are all great examples of suitable practice areas.

Do *not* wear sunglasses. Also, I suggest bringing some music along with you to listen to while you practice. Instrumental music is better than music with lyrics as the latter tends to stimulate the analytical part of the brain, which you want to avoid for this practice. You can analyze later! Be sure to select pieces that evoke emotions of wonder, love, joy, and peace. This adds to the power of emotional reward to the training.

Once you've established where you'll train, lie down comfortably on your back and stare up at the sky. Allow yourself to relax more and more with each exhalation of breath while you take in all at once the vast and arching dome of heaven. It's important that you not focus on any one detail of the sky, but rather take in the entire panorama in one global stare. Allow yourself to blink whenever needed and simply lose yourself in this moment of sky-gazing.

After you've become sufficiently relaxed, your next step is to flip your perspective upside down, or rather, *downside up*. Instead of seeing the sky as being a vast ceiling high above the earth upon which you lay, imagine that the sky is *below* you. This requires a nifty little maneuvering of your awareness. It isn't merely imagination, remember. It's not simply a visualization either. It's a full-bodied sensation of feeling yourself on the bottom portion of the planet Earth, in which case the sky truly is below you! It doesn't matter if you're geographically occupying such a place while doing this exercise. All that matters is whether you can achieve and sustain this sensation for at least half an hour. Once you succeed in doing so, you may only be able to sustain this sensation for a few minutes at a time. That's fine! Just keep trying until thirty minutes have elapsed. If you find that you really enjoy the practice, continue for an hour before finishing up.

Some people experience dizziness and nausea while practicing this technique. If this happens, discontinue the practice for a few minutes and relax before resuming. After you've become accustomed to this novel sensation, the dizziness should diminish. Not to mention that, despite the discomfort, these symptoms are signs of progress! If your body responds to the imagined change of perspective, then you're doing it right.

I should mention that this exercise can even be practiced while walking down street, going for a jog, and even while driving on the highway (although I don't recommend it). Once you get the gist of the technique, you can practice just about anywhere. As you'll soon see, the best place to practice is in the room you regularly sleep in.

Practice this method for one week before moving on to week fourteen of Curriculum.

Week Fourteen: Bi-Locationality and Malleable Proprioception Training

Now that you've got some idea of what Bi-Locationality is and how to wire your brain to experience it, you must now train your Astral Body to be willing to separate from the Gross physical body with minimal resistance. How to do this effectively is the purpose of Malleable Proprioception training. Without this training, you might still succeed in Astral Projection, but probably with considerable difficulty. I wish I had access to this training secret when I was a child suffering from the discomforts of sleep paralysis and exit-symptoms. Anyway, better late than never!

To begin, revisit the second part of the Trailing Method of week five of the Curriculum. The Skill cultivated in that section is applied and deepened in the following exercise, only this time you won't be using a candle flame to induce it. Properly understood, this next technique is the culmination of the entire 120-Days Curriculum. It holds the key to successful Lucid Dreaming and Astral Projection and to where and how they overlap.

Malleable Proprioception is the most ignored aspect of Astral Projection training, for whatever reason. Most methods focus almost solely on Bi-Locationality. This may work for some people, but it's my opinion that most failed attempts at Projection can be narrowed down to an omission of this crucial step.

I hope to presently satisfy this lack with the following technique.

The Practice

Take a trip back to your established outdoors training area. Don't forget your music! Lie down comfortably on your back and relax as much as possible without falling asleep. Once you've relaxed your body to the point where it doesn't intrude on your awareness, close your eyes and feel inside of your bodymind. That is, get into your *feeling* body, your Subtle Body, and occupy it fully.

Breathe naturally and allow yourself to enjoy this moment before moving on to the next step.

Next, keeping your eyes closed, feel your body rotate in a backwards somersault upward towards a hypothetical ceiling. The sensation should be the same as if you we doing a reverse somersault on the floor, only here the feeling of the floor is absent, and the somersault is in a vertical line *upward*. Picture a professional gymnast performing a high leap into a back flip and you'll have a general idea of the feeling we're trying to cultivate here. The only differences are we're lying down and performing the back flip slowly, as if floating in an upward and backwards somersault toward an imaginary ceiling. This follows the Wind Path of Microcosmic Orbit, only this time it isn't just *Qi* moving in this path, but your very awareness itself.

The key to making this practice work is to conjure up how it would really feel were your physical body performing this feat. Try to imagine the effects that gravity would have on the various parts of your body were you to float upwards in a slow back flip toward a ceiling. For example, while upside down, you'd feel blood rushing to your head and your bones, tendons, and muscles relaxing downward. As you transition from upside down to right side up, you'd feel a similar effect exerted on your lower body. Feel the ground beneath your body disappear as you revolve upward. This takes a great deal of concentration to achieve.

Roll upwards in this fashion for two rotations and come to rest with the back of your body against an imaginary ceiling. Really feel this ceiling as the back of your buoyant body presses against it. Cultivate the sensation of weightlessness and enjoy it for a moment.

Now slowly open your eyes and once again look at the sky as if it were beneath you. Stay in this feeling for a few minutes, and then imagine that you're slowly losing buoyancy and are being gently pulled downward towards the floor of sky beneath you. Close your eyes and feel this downward fall first in your legs and then in your upper body until you're in a rapid free fall. Strongly cultivate the sensation of a descending broad backward somersault utilizing all the same sensations felt on your ascent. Rotate at least two times, slowing down on your second rotation, before gently coming to rest on the ground of the sky. Slowly come to a sitting position. Then open your eyes.

Practice this for one week before moving on to next week's practice.

Week Fifteen: The Astral Projection Experience

If by following the Curriculum up to this point you haven't yet had a spontaneous Astral Projection experience, you most certainly will now! The following technique represents the culmination of everything you've learned thus far. Not only that, these methods are time-tested and have worked for innumerable Veilers.

At this point it's crucial that you store and circulate a plethora of Etheric force. As I've already stressed elsewhere, the most efficient way to do this is to avoid excess ejaculation, maintain a temperament that's cool and calm, avoid overwork and physical exhaustion, eat organic and non-GMO foods while drinking only pure water (never from the tap!), and regularly practice Embryonic Breathing and Microcosmic Orbit meditation. There's another powerful way to gather *Qi* from Nature and other people (willing partners), but this discussion must be reserved for a future publication.

Here, in week fifteen of the Curriculum, I'm going to show you how you can combine your Lucid Dreaming and Pellucidity skills to consciously induce Astral Projection. I can't overemphasize the impact this experience is going to have on your life. It's important to remain level-headed and humble, especially during your initial success in this magickal art. Above all else you must be courageous and not allow fear to become a habit; otherwise the door will close and may never open again. I promise you that so long as your intentions remain pure, your heart filled with love, and your behavior is one of integrity and resolve, that you'll be successful and have nothing to fear. Once you've had a taste of true Astral Projection, we'll deepen this experience in week sixteen by taking Astral *Projection* into Astral *Travel*. As you'll soon discover for yourself, the ability to leave your body is one thing, but the ability to travel further away from it is an entirely different issue. Why?

Because the Gross physical body has *gravity*, that's why!

My own Dream Journal is filled with frustrating accounts of what I eventually came to call "the Anchor Effect." This is experienced by most Veilers in the early stages of Astral training. What causes the Anchor Effect? Well, a few things are at work here. For starters, awareness is very intimately bound to the physical body. Even the most cerebral of us have a tenuous identification with our physical form. Most people have trouble imagining themselves as separate from their bodies, and this strong affinity for physical embodiment carries its own energetic magnetism.

Another reason for the Anchor Effect is lack of Etheric fuel. The storing, purifying, and circulation of Etheric energy is unfortunately ignored by many practitioners. Like a balloon filled with an insufficient amount of helium, they can get up and out, but not up and away. Hopefully you've taken this matter seriously and have decided to make Embryonic Breathing and Microcosmic Orbit meditation a regular part of your life.

The Anchor Effect does tend to lessen as you gain experience with Astral Projection. It's much like learning to swim. Sure, you might start out with the doggie-paddle and dead man's float, but with enough practice you'll eventually be able to swim laps, swim under the water, and move from the shallow to the deep end of the pool.

The Practice

When attempting Astral Projection, it's very important that you're undisturbed for the duration of the session. If by chance you're startled by something, it could seriously damage your nervous system. Not only that, but it will cause your *Qi* to deviate and go down a wrong path in your Etheric circuitry. This can cause serious harm to your health so please take it to heart and make the necessary arrangements.

The following technique draws upon your newfound skills of Lucidity, Pellucidity, and Astral and Etheric malleability. All of these serve to make Astral Projection more accessible to you.

First, lie down comfortably on your back in a dark and quiet room. Be sure that the temperature in the room is suitable and that your head is facing magnetic North and your feet South. Also, make sure that your clothing and bed sheets are made of natural fibers such as cotton or silk. Synthetic fibers disrupt the natural circulation of your *Qi.* Disconnect all EMF producing devices for the same reason.

With these prerequisites taken care of, perform all the exercises of weeks nine through twelve of the Curriculum. Once you've reached the Microcosmic Orbit phase of the exercise (week twelve), circulate for a few moments, expanding the circles of Etheric force further and further away from your physical body. Keep doing this until you feel the onset of **PD-3**. Why not **PD-4**, you ask? Well, you can begin the next step at **PD-4**, but you've probably already noticed that once you're deeply embedded in the Causal Body you don't want to *will* anything! On the other hand, if you begin the following step at **PD-3**, you'll notice that your awareness can remain mobile, which is an unavoidable requirement for conscious Astral Projection.

This is the pivotal moment! Here's the trick:

Feel yourself rolling in a somersault along the same axis as the Microcosmic Orbit!

Normally, when practicing Microcosmic Orbit, you circulate *Qi* while your awareness stays rooted in your upper and lower Dantians. In this exercise, it isn't just your energy that circulates, it's *you* that circulates. Do this several times and then come to a sudden stop, but not where you started. Rather, do this:

Suspend the rotation at the point when you're upside down, as if you're doing a headstand.

It's important to *really* embody the perspective of feeling perpendicular to your sleeping physical body, with your head facing downward. This little maneuver of your proprioception will trigger your Astral Body to stay up and out after you've successfully loosened it by rolling your awareness in Microcosmic Orbit. If you've ever had the common experience of being jolted from sleep because you felt like you're falling, then you've inadvertently used this method.

Now, once you've consciously entered **REM** sleep, the exit-symptoms which herald an impending OOBE will begin. The best advice I can give you at this point is:

Don't panic!

As I've said before, if you panic then you'll abort the Astral exit. Worse, you'll build a psychic wall (the psychic moat) that makes achieving Astral Projection more difficult in future attempts. Believe me, I know all too well how difficult it can be to remain calm during this phase of separation from the Gross Body. Be that as it may, I can also tell you with absolute certainty that you've got nothing to be afraid of. If you're left undisturbed while it's occurring, Astral Projection is completely natural and safe. Are there frightening things on the Astral Plane?

Absolutely!

Just as there are beautiful and pleasurable experiences on the Astral Plane, so too are there ugly and disquieting ones. The beings dwelling there are just as varied in temperament as human beings and animals, but in my experience you needn't be worried about them. To be honest, the entity you need to be most concerned about while going Astral is *yourself!* After all, the first thing that you'll probably encounter on the Astral Planes are reflection of your own intentions, fears, hopes, traumas, passions, and so forth, and this especially applies to exit-symptoms.

So how to best deal with exit-symptoms?

The loud buzzing, popping, arcade bleeps and bloops, voices, physical sensations, flashing lights, vibrations, adrenaline surges, and presences associated with an imminent Astral exit are undeniably distracting. It may take some getting used to before you can successfully ignore them. Once you're in the clear, they'll vanish, and you'll be free to focus on phase two of Astral Projection, which is to travel further away from your physical body. We'll tackle that in the next section.

For now, please note that there are dozens of ways to induce the separation phase of the Astral exit. The "flip and roll" method above is by far one of the more potent ones. I encourage you to experiment with variations of that method before trying other techniques: your training thus far has led you to a point where Astral Projection is best induced in this manner. What are the variations? Well, to give one example, remember the Trailing Method offered in week five? Instead of using the Somersault Method to induce Astral separation, why not try rolling to the side toward your non-dominant hand? You've already become accustomed to the sensation, so you can simply recreate it in your feeling-awareness and roll out of your body. This is one of my own favorite methods for going Astral. Try it and see!

Another well-known technique for inducing an Astral exit is the so-called Rope Technique. In this method, as soon as the exit-symptoms begin, you visualize a long rope or ladder suspended from high above your sleeping body. Then, using Malleable Proprioception, you feel yourself climbing up until you're completely Astral. Still other methods skip the separation phase entirely and utilize a Bi-Locationality technique. In these methods, you simply wait until you're approaching the **PD-4** phase of Pellucidity, and from there imagine yourself standing at the foot of your bed looking at your sleeping physical body. That approach has innumerable variations. To be honest, though, Bi-Locationality methods tend to induce Lucid Dreams that resemble genuine Astral Projection but aren't the real deal. In my opinion, methods which skip over the separation phase of Astral Projection are incomplete and lead, at the most, to Astral Dreams. That said, give them a try and see if you have any luck!

In closing, always be sure to practice Embryonic Breathing and Microcosmic Orbit within twenty-four hours after attempting Astral Projection and Lucid Dreaming. This ensures a proper rebalancing of *Qi* in the Etheric energy, particularly the Five *Yin* meridians.

Week Sixteen: Astral Projection to Astral Travel

Astral Projection and Astral Travel are often used as synonyms. The truth, however, is that the latter isn't nearly as common as the former. Astral Projection technically occurs every time we enter **PD-4** or **LD-3**, only we're usually not conscious of it. As we've seen, this is primarily due to lack of awareness during the transition phase between wakefulness and various phases of the sleep cycle.

In this section, I'll teach you how to travel further and further away from your physical body. I'll discuss the Anchor Effect and how you can get past it. I'll also discuss some of the things you can expect to find as you separate from your body and travel further away from it. This is a rather complex topic which I'll elaborate on in a future publication Readers interested in learning more about the various phenomena associated with Astral Projection are encouraged to consult my website and blog and join the discussion at:

http://behindtheveil.simdif.com

Tips, Tactics, and Trade Secrets

The sensations associated with Astral Projection will be familiar to anyone who has ever consciously entered **LD-3** or **PD-4**, especially the transition period. They're the same. In fact, Lucid Dreams are just one more exit-symptom which needs to be ignored for true Astral Projection to occur! If you haven't already had a taste of Astral exit-symptoms, and you're wondering what happens once they cease, here's what I can tell you:

First, when you begin to leave your physical body, you'll know it! There'll be no mistaking it, believe me. At first, you'll either feel as though you're falling off your bed or from some high place. Some Veilers feel the opposite. That is, they feel as though they're rising through the air, usually at a rapid pace. Sometimes dream scenarios reflect the approaching Projection, and Lucid Dreams of flying or falling or swimming beneath water will arise. Sensations that can only be described as a sudden rush of adrenaline may appear, threatening to crush you or explode from somewhere deep inside you. Oftentimes this sensation is accompanied by powerful vibrations pulsing through your body, especially in the heart area. Internal tones resembling the electric hum of high voltage wires will sometimes be heard. These are usually accompanied by bright flashes of light, usually yellow, blue, or white. Regarding this light, a little trick I learned is to try to sustain this light by staring directly into it for as long as you can. Eventually, if you can sustain concentration for a few seconds, this light will give way to *Astral Sight.* You'll either begin to see the room you're in through your closed eyes, or else you'll see on the Astral Planes. Either way, if you continue with your exit technique at this juncture you'll have a very quick route to full Projection. The key is to focus on the separation and ignore the flood of imagery, sensations, and sounds you're almost certain to experience.

At any rate, once you're up and out, you'll probably only get so far before you either slip into a Lucid Dream, remain anchored near your physical body, or wake up completely. Don't get frustrated! This isn't a failure. Quite the contrary! If you've gotten this far, you've already succeeded in Astral Projection, and that's a big deal. With practice, Astral Travel will become easier to do. I've been doing this my whole life and I still get tripped up on the basics. Twenty years into being a Veiler and I still sometimes get confused between the Astral Planes and Lucid Dreams, exit-symptoms and genuine entities, and so on.

There are a few things you can do to avoid the Astral Anchor Effect. First, as we've already discussed, don't eat a heavy meal before bedtime or before attempting Astral Projection. The same rule applies to alcohol. You may still be able to Project if you break these rules, but getting past the Projection phase and into the Travel phase will be nigh impossible. I find that breaking these rules leaves me stuck in the lower Astral Plane, which has something of a nightmarish quality to it. In fact, I've often wondered if my early experiences of Astral Projection as a child were nightmarish due to the asthma medication I was forced to take in those days.

Another thing which has a deleterious effect on Astral Travel is depression and anxiety. Sadness, self-pity, sexual obsessions, fear, and envy are just a few of the heavy emotions you'll want to transmute while learning Astral Travel. There may be a few people who can Project and Travel successfully even while intoxicated by these emotions, but for the most part they just weigh you down, weaken your lifeforce, and keep you tethered to your physical body. This is probably due to the fact that these emotions are centered on self-preservation. Just think about it for a minute. When you're feeling anxious, what happens to your body? Your breathing becomes shallow, your skin becomes cold and clammy, and your body language suggests a sort of shrinking away and inward. The opposite of *open up and out!* This is important to understand because this inward shrinking is the very root cause of most failed attempts at Astral Travel. You can get up but you can't get out.

So those are just some of the things to avoid when learning Astral Travel.

Some of the things you can be proactive about to bypass the Anchor Effect involve the opposite of the above prohibitions. Notice how I said that you need to *transmute* the aforementioned "heavy" emotions? I didn't say that you should *avoid* them! What do I mean by "transmute"? Transmuting negative emotions means that you encounter them without suppressing, repressing, projecting, or expressing them. If you've been following the Curriculum thus far, then you've already learned the secret to transmuting negative emotions and thoughts.

We've been calling it *Channeling Intensity*.

It helps to remember that every thought and emotion is, before it's anything else we make it into, pure and raw *energy*. Ideally, you want your energy to be of high quality and flowing freely and smoothly. Whenever you get hung up on an emotion, even some positive ones, your energy loses its *Yin/Yang* balance. This inevitably happens to all of us, but it helps to know how to ameliorate this situation as best one can. We've been doing it every time we practice Channeling Intensity in combination with Embryonic Breathing, Microcosmic Orbit, Healing Hands, Mobile Mental Focus and Progressive Relaxation. Many Veilers refer to this process of transmuting emotions as *raising your vibration.*

Regardless what you choose to call it, the basic mechanism involves keeping your energies clear, abundant, unobstructed, and balanced. To the religious Taoists, Astral Projection is regarded as the highest attainment and is synonymous with spiritual enlightenment. Such a person is referred to as a "Heavenly Fairy." When he or she dies, it's said that such a one has "left his shoes" (left the physical body). The practitioner who fails to accomplish this is said to have not accumulated enough *De. De* is a Chinese word which means "Virtue," but not in the sense of moral fortitude or ethical refinement. Rather, the Virtue being referred to suggests the evolved version of one's essential nature. For instance, when we speak of the medicinal virtues of a certain plant, we're referring to the plant's *De.* When it comes to human beings, our "virtue" is found in the harmonious flowering of our Gross, Etheric, Mental, Astral, and Causal energies. When this occurs, only the best of what we have to offer flows out of us in the same way in which a flower gives off its perfume without any conscious intention to do so. This is probably why many so-called "saints" have had spontaneous experiences of Astral Projection, Lucid Dreaming, and so on, without any training whatsoever.

So, the four-fold secret to getting past the Astral Anchor Effect is:

- Transmuting *heavy* emotions.
- Keeping your energies abundant and flowing freely and smoothly.
- Avoiding heavy meals or excess alcohol before bed.
- Willing yourself to a destination beyond the pull of your physical body.

That last one takes center stage here in this last week of the Curriculum.

If Astral *Projection* is largely an exercise of abundant *Qi* and Malleable Proprioception, then Astral *Travel* is largely an act of Bi-Locationality and *Will*. In fact, it's very common for Projectors to spontaneously find themselves in locations or with people that hold special significance to them. For example, some people Project and—seemingly without intention—find themselves visiting their children or close friends. That center of authentic emotional charge is the root of the *Will*. That's the difference between Will and Desire. Desire is fleeting and doesn't tend to stick around long enough to effect any real change, whereas Will is focused intention in alignment with genuine affinity. In other words, what you want may not necessarily be what you need. Astral Travel is best learned by Projecting to destinations that are in alignment with one's Will.

During this last week of the Curriculum, focus specifically on getting up and out. Focus on getting accustomed to Astral exit-symptoms and on sustaining the out-of-body state. Usually this means hovering close enough to your physical body that your breathing sounds like you're under water and breathing through a snorkel! Once you've gotten used to this stage of Astral Projection and the realization sets in that this is happening, do the following:

Throughout the day of your next Projection attempt, make the mental affirmation to check the time on, say, the kitchen stove, when you Project that night. Do this throughout the day and be very specific about which clock you'll check while out of body. Then, later that night once you've successfully Projected, will yourself into the area where the clock is. Be sure to choose a clock in an area that isn't too far away from your physical body, otherwise you'll have difficulty reaching or seeing it while out of body. It's not uncommon to have difficulty seeing or moving during your initial trips away from your body. I still have difficulty in this department!

Once you're successful, check the time on the clock, return to your body, wake up and then *go check the time.* Depending on how long it took you to wake up and check the clock, the time should be roughly a few minutes past what it was while you were Astral! This will be your first validation of success. It isn't easy, I assure you, but with time and consistent training it'll become easier.

Once you've become proficient at the time-checking exercise, take it a step further and try to visit someone you know and love— someone with whom you can discuss these matters and consents to being visited. If you know such a person, try visiting her or him while out-of-body. The best way to make this happen is to through-out the day affirm your desire to do so. Then, that night, before attempting Astral Projection, reaffirm your intention and go!

I've only succeeded at this a handful of times, admittedly with most of them being spontaneous and unplanned. The important thing is that each success was validated by the person I traveled to. The interesting thing about Projecting to people and places in what expert Projector, Robert Bruce, calls the "real-time zone," is that it truly does seem to be in alignment with chronological time. This isn't the case with Projections to the Astral Planes. In these events, time seems to behave in the same way it does when the mind is under the influence of a powerful psychedelic. You may have an Astral experi-ence that seems to last several hours only to come back to find that only a few minutes have elapsed! The converse is also very com-mon, and you may think that you were Astral for only a few minutes when you were gone for several hours!

Traveling to the Astral Planes is a very riveting experience. To discuss it thoroughly would require a separate volume. That said, you're almost certain to encounter the Astral Planes at some point, so let me issue a word of caution:

Always remain impartial, calm, objective, and grounded when assessing anything you encounter on the Astral Planes.

Record everything and everyone you encounter in your dream journal and be as descriptive and thorough as possible. Some of the more common things you may encounter are Astral Landscapes, Shadow People, Archetypal Beings, Deceased Loved Ones, Voices and Visions (often prophetic), Voids, Astral Dreams, and much more. You might also notice that your dormant psychic abilities are waking up. You might start seeing auras around people, trees, animals, and inanimate objects. At one point, roughly between the years 2006–2010, these energetic patterns became so pronounced that I had difficulty engaging people in conversation! These auras initially appeared as something akin to heat waves emanating off asphalt. I saw colorless waves of heat emanating from people's bodies, darting to and fro, and I eventually noticed patterns within these waves. For example, if someone were about to cough or sneeze, I'd see it in their aura first. I'd see these waves reach out from a person's hand toward a cup of coffee just seconds before they reached for it. Soon I became accustomed to these phenomena, the waves eventually began to evolve into colors, and it became a source of excitement for me. To this day, if I see red flashes in my wife's aura, I know it's going to be a romantic evening!

Another common psychic ability which tends to be galvanized by repeated excursions to the Astral Planes is *intuition*. You might notice that you can feel energies more strongly, such as high EMF zones from power lines, WiFi, and "dirty electricity." You might also notice that you become sensitive to areas where these toxic energies are absent, such as high mountain elevations, forests, and near the sea. You may even begin to feel the effects of the moon and solar activity! The intentions and overall "vibe" of people around you might become more pronounced. And synchronicities will increase in frequency and meaningfulness.

All of these experiences are perfectly normal and are even to be expected. The main thing is to stay objective, search for meaningful patterns, and record everything in your journal.

AFTERWORD
SUBLIMINAL COGNITION TRAINING
AND THE INTEGRAL PHILOSOPHY

That's it! You've completed the 120-Days Curriculum. The exercises you've just learned have literally changed the *shape* of your bodymind. If a neuroscientist with the proper equipment took a photo of your neuronet before you began the Curriculum, and then held it up next to a photo taken of your neuronet now, you'd see that you don't look quite the same as you did one-hundred-and-twenty days ago. The same would happen if a Clairvoyant saw you before and after your training.

That's a big deal...

I strongly believe that the current explosion of interest in these psychic capacities represents a milestone in our evolution as a species. Skills which used to be reserved for a few eccentric members of a tribe are now emerging within the lives of people all over the world at an astonishing rate. Everyday people are noticing a palpable shift within the very core of their psyches, and as the rarified experiences that come along with this massive shift give rise to questions, it's my hope that books like this one will serve as guiding lights for the Veilers of tomorrow.

The Curriculum represents the practical core of my own system. I call this system *"Subliminal Cognition Training"* or **SCT**. It's the kind of system I would have wanted when I was wandering in the desert of confusion and social alienation. The core tenant of this system is that everybody has access to the three broad states of *Wakefulness, Dreaming*, and *Dreamless Sleep*, and what **SCT** aims to do is bring more skillful awareness into these three states of consciousness. Of course, this is nothing new, and there exists countless variations on this theme. The Perennial Philosophy being the ubiquitous map that it is, has spawned innumerable methods and systems for accessing the clandestine powers of the human bodymind.

The original contribution which my system offers is threefold:

First, **SCT** is *Integral*. When I first discovered the Integral Philosophy, I felt overwhelmed by it. Because it attempts to demonstrate how everything and everyone fits together, the maps used to explain this can at first appear rather daunting. So, I gave up! Not for long, though, because I soon stumbled upon the work of a brilliant American Integral thinker by the name of Ken Wilber. I rejoiced that I'd finally found someone who could make sense out of a system that called to me, but confused me at the same time.

Briefly, Wilber successfully demonstrated that every conceivable person, place, or thing in this universe has at least four basic aspects to its existence. These aspects give rise to, and are predicated on, one another. Take away one of them and the others either cease to exist or, at the very least, become pathological.

What are these four fundamental aspects to the universe?

According to Integral Theory, the universe has four qualities (called Quadrants):

- Personal (subjective)
- Behavioral (objective)
- Cultural (race, creed, shared values/traditions)
- Social (political climate, economic system)

Without going into the finer details of this system, the Personal makes up the upper left Quadrant, the Behavioral is the upper right Quadrant, the Cultural is the lower left Quadrant, and the Social is the lower right Quadrant. Every thought, feeling, impulse, idea, conversation, skill, or personal philosophy you have is anchored in the realities represented by these four Quadrants. How they all interact and function together is a rather messy affair, but the main point for you to remember is that these aren't static and unchanging concepts or realities.

I, It, and *We* evolve! It's a unified meshwork of depth, height, and dynamic interplay.

My system of training is anchored in this Integral framework, with an obvious emphasis on the Subjective aspect. That, in my opinion, is the first thing which makes **SCT** unique in the field of Conscious Sleep. After all, most authors focus either on Lucid Dreaming or Astral Projection, sometimes a cavalier blend of both.

That's the second thing offered by **SCT**: it offers a seamless training of the three broad states of Wakefulness, Dreaming, and Dreamless Sleep.

This is very important. Training just one or another would be the equivalent of lifting weights to build muscle in only one arm. On the other hand, if you train Astral Projection alongside Vivid and Lucid Dreaming, Pellucid Sleep/Dreaming, Meditation, Diet, Geomancy, Qigong, etc., and you root this training in a community of fellow Veilers, then you have at your fingertips a system aimed at incorporating all levels of your being. More importantly, this training aims at cultivating these skills until your Gross, Subtle, and Causal bodies are experienced as one unified and seamless whole.

Lastly, **SCT** aims at turning the students of today into the teachers of tomorrow. With its emphasis on establishing a community of like-minded individuals, the fruitful exchange of information on all levels of skill is built into the very fabric of the system. The motto is ever and always, "If it works, I'll use it!" One of the unfortunate tragedies of an Integrally uninformed system is that it tends to leave out so much of what makes you *You.* We are each faced with our own unique set of circumstances, have our own strengths and weaknesses, and our own natural proclivities. Sadly, many systems seem primarily concerned with teaching according to the *system* and not according to the *individual* approaching that system.

All too often I've opened the pages of a book about Lucid Dreaming only to discover that the author has written the book under the assumption that the reader has dreams in the first place! I don't mean dreams *per se*. You probably remember your dreams if you're reading a *How-To* book about Lucid Dreaming. Rather, the author will just assume that the reader's dreams are as colorful and vivid as his own. Without first cultivating a colorful and vivid dream life, your Lucidity will be shallow, yes?

The same holds true for many books on Astral Projection. You're rarely going to open the pages of a book on Astral Projection and see a detailed explanation of the differences among the various types of OOBE, a presentation devoid of metaphysical assertions or cultural presumptions, or any possible medical explanations or neurological aspects of the Astral Projection experience. In my opinion, **SCT** satisfies this lack.

I hope this book has helped you in your quest. Whether you're a beginner or an advanced Veiler, someone seeking an explanation for psychic phenomena being written off as "sleep disturbances," or just an evolving human being seeking to expand your horizons, it's my sincere hope that I've satisfied that craving in your heart for clarity, understanding, and passionate spirituality.

But let's not satisfy it completely, aye? After all, lighting the fire is only half the job. Keeping the fire burning is where the real work begins.

Your Fellow Traveler,

Daniel Allen Kelley
30 July 2017, 9:44 am
Hyde Park, NY

ABOUT THE AUTHOR

Daniel Kelley is an author, poet, musician, and Integral Life Practitioner with over two decades of experience in the esoteric arts. He is the creator of Subliminal Cognition Training. Daniel was born in 1979 to Baptist parents in Waterloo Canada. His father was a Baptist preacher. After a profound and prolonged transpersonal crisis in early childhood, he broke away from his strict Christian upbringing to study the wisdom traditions of the world. At age sixteen he suffered a breakdown that culminated at age twenty-one in a transpersonal breakthrough. After joining various Hermetic societies and practicing their methods, he found his spiritual home in Chinese Taoist Alchemy, Integral Life Practice, and the Yogas of India and Tibet. He practices and teaches Internal Chinese Martial Arts, Qigong, *Taijiquan* and *Xingyiquan*. He lives with his wife and daughter in upstate New York.

http://behindtheveil.simdif.com

Appendix
Diagram for Visualization Training

BIBLIOGRAPHY

Exploring the World of Lucid Dreaming: Stephen LaBerge/Howard Rheingold.

Journeys Out of the Body: Robert Monroe.

The Two Week Lucid Dreamer: Derek Ralston.

Dreaming Wide Awake: David Jay Brown.

The Art of Dreaming: Carlos Castaneda.

One Taste: Ken Wilber.

Qigong Meditation/Embryonic Breathing: Dr. Yang Jwing Ming.

Microcosmic Orbit: Dr. Yang Jwing Ming.

Astral Dynamics: Robert Bruce.

Reflections On Life After Life: Raymond Moody.

Consciousness Beyond Life: Pim Van Lommel.

Sex, Ecology, Spirituality: Ken Wilber.

The Multi-Orgasmic Man: Mantak Chia.

Journey to Dylan: Carlos Castaneda.

Astral Projection in 90 Days: Robert Bruce.

The Book of Secrets: Osho.

Dream Therapy: Clare Johnson, Ph.D.

Tibetan Dream Yoga: Stephen LaBerge

Skygates of the Mind: Ivan Kos.

Integral Dreaming: A Holistic Approach to Dreaming: Fariba Bogzaran/Daniel Deslauriers.

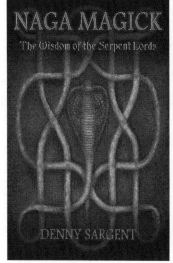

FROM ANTERO ALLI

ANGEL TECH
A Modern Shaman's Guide to Reality Selection

Angel Tech is a comprehensive compendium of insights and techniques for the direct application of Dr. Timothy Leary's Eight-Circuit Brain model for Intelligence Increase. What Dr. Leary posited as theory and Dr. Robert Anton Wilson brilliantly demonstrated in sociopolitical, mathematical and intellectual proofs, Antero Alli has extended into tangible tasks, exercises, rituals and meditations.

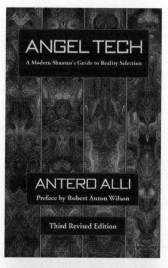

THE EIGHT-CIRCUIT BRAIN
Navigational Strategies for the Energetic Body

The Eight-Circuit Brain advances and expands the material presented in *Angel Tech,* a compendium of techniques and practical applications based on Dr. Timothy Leary's 8-Circuit Brain model. After more than twenty years of research and experimentation, Antero's earlier findings are significantly updated and enriched.

THE *Original* FALCON PRESS

Invites You to Visit Our Website:
http://originalfalcon.com

At our website you can:

- Browse the online catalog of all of our great titles
- Find out what's available and what's out of stock
- Get special discounts
- Order our titles through our secure online server
- Find products not available anywhere else including:
    – One of a kind and limited availability products
    – Special packages
    – Special pricing
- Get free gifts
- Join our email list for advance notice of New Releases and Special Offers
- Find out about book signings and author events
- Send email to our authors
- Read excerpts of many of our titles
- Find links to our authors' websites
- Discover links to other weird and wonderful sites
- And much, much more

Get online today at http://originalfalcon.com

99170696R00143

Made in the USA
Columbia, SC
05 July 2018